Latin
American
Liberation
Theology

Latin American Liberation Theology

The Next Generation

Ivan Petrella, editor

ORBIS BOOKS

Maryknoll, New York 10545

Founded in 1970, Orbis Books endeavors to publish works that enlighten the mind, nourish the spirit, and challenge the conscience. The publishing arm of the Maryknoll Fathers and Brothers, Orbis seeks to explore the global dimensions of the Christian faith and mission, to invite dialogue with diverse cultures and religious traditions, and to serve the cause of reconciliation and peace. The books published reflect the views of their authors and do not represent the official position of the Maryknoll Society. To learn more about Maryknoll and Orbis Books, please visit our website at www.maryknoll.org.

Manufactured in the United States of America
Typesetting by Joan Weber Laflamme

Library of Congress Cataloging-in-Publication Data

Latin American liberation theology : the next generation / edited by Ivan Petrella.
    p. cm.
 Includes bibliographical references and index.
 ISBN 1–57075–595–7 (pbk.)
 1. Liberation theology—Latin America—History—20th century. 2. Latin America—Church history—20th century. I. Petrella, Ivan, 1969–
  BT83.57L37 2005
  230'.046'098—dc22

                           2004026507

Lo que hace falta es empacar mucha moneda,
vender el alma, rifar el corazón.
Tirar la poca decencia que te queda,
plata, plata . . . y plata otra vez. . . .
Así es posible que morfés todos los días,
Tengas amigos, casa, nombre y lo que quieras vos.
El verdadero amor se ahogó en la sopa,
la panza es reina y el dinero es Dios.

—ENRIQUE SANTOS DISCÉPOLO

Se acabaron los robustos,
si hasta yo que daba gusto,
cuatro kilos he bajao. . . .
Hoy no hay guita ni de asalto
y el puchero está tan alto
que hay que usar un trampolín. . . .
Si habrá, crisis, bronca y hambre
que el compra diez de fiambre
hoy se morfa hasta el piolín.

—ENRIQUE CADÍCAMO

Contents

Contributors

Marcella Althaus-Reid is senior lecturer in Christian ethics, practical theology, and systematic theology at the University of Edinburgh, as well as a Freirean educator among the working poor. Her work ranks among the most innovative and controversial in contemporary theology. Her "indecent theology" emerges from a rereading and revision of liberation theology from the perspective of queer theory and is the first attempt to link these two currents of thought. She is the author of *Indecent Theology: Theological Perversions in Sex, Gender and Politics* and *The Queer God*, as well as myriad articles and book chapters.

Nancy E. Bedford is the Georgia Harkness Chair at Garrett-Evangelical Theological Seminary. Previously she was Professor of Systematic Theology at ISEDET in Buenos Aires, Argentina. A member of the Argentine Baptist Church, Bedford is a deacon in her local church, where she founded several outreach programs for women. Her work combines liberation theology, feminist theory, and theology within a Baptist framework. She is the author of *Jesus Christus und das gekreuzigte Volk*, a forthcoming volume *Nuestra Fe*, as well as articles and chapters in several books.

German Gutiérrez is a researcher at the Departamento Ecuménico de Investigaciones (DEI), the premier interdisciplinary think tank based on a liberationist perspective. In addition to his own research, he coordinates and leads DEI's annual three-month-long seminar, which exposes social activists, educators, grass-roots organizers, and indigenous leaders to the writings of liberation theologians (and often to the many liberation theologians who participate in the seminar and present their own work) and to contemporary social theory, practically free of cost. His work deals with ethics, economics, and liberation theology from a global perspective. His two most recent books are *Globalización: Caos y Sujeto en América Latina* and *Etica y Economía en Adam Smith y Hayek*.

Nelson Maldonado-Torres is an assistant professor in the Department of Ethnic Studies at the University of California, Berkeley. He is the most able young exponent of the theological/philosophical tradition personified by Enrique Dussel. His work encompasses reflections on religion, philosophical anthropology, social and cultural formations in the Americas, and the role of critical intellectual activity in the context of global coloniality. He has published in *Intersticios*, *Listening: Journal of Religion and Culture*, and *Review: A Journal of the Ferdinand Braudel Center for the Study of Economies, Historical Systems and Civilizations*.

Manuel J. Mejido is an associate researcher at the Center for Advanced Studies at the University of Santiago, Chile. His work is one of the few attempts to reread Latin American liberation theology and U.S. Hispanic theology in unison. He has published articles in the *Journal of Hispanic/Latino Theology*, *Social Compass*, and *Koinonia*, as well as chapters in several edited books.

Ivan Petrella is an assistant professor of religious studies at the University of Miami, Coral Gables. A citizen of Argentina, he spends almost half the year in Buenos Aires, where he participates in political and social debates about the country's future. He is the author of *The Future of Liberation Theology: An Argument and Manifesto* as well as articles in the *Journal of Hispanic/Latino Theology* and the *Journal of the Caribbean Philosophical Association*. In his spare time he roams Buenos Aires and Miami Beach in search of pickup soccer games.

Silvia Regina de Lima Silva is the leading Afro-Brazilian liberation theologian. She is dean of the Universidad Bíblica Latinoamericana in San José, Costa Rica, and coordinator of the women's commission of the Association of Theologians of the Third World. She is the author of *En Territorio de Fronteras: una lectura de Marcos 7:24–30*, as well as numerous articles and book chapters.

Jung Mo Sung is a professor of religion and education at Catholic University in São Paulo, Brazil, as well as a social activist and consultant to social movements and base communities. He is the most original voice within the mainstream of contemporary Latin American liberation theology and the author of numerous books that seek to critique and revise liberation theology for its new context after the fall of the Berlin Wall in 1989. Most important among these works are *Economía: Tema Ausente en la Teología de la Liberación; Deseo Mercado y Religion*; and *La Idolatria del Capital y la Muerte de los Pobres*.

Introduction

Latin American Liberation Theology

Past, Present, and Future

Ivan Petrella

LATIN AMERICAN LIBERATION THEOLOGY—the most important theological movement of the twentieth century—is now being reinvented for the twenty-first century. A new generation of Latin American theologians has taken the reins of liberation theology, developing its themes and hopes in new directions. Most people interested in theology in the North Atlantic academy—by which I mean the Western European and U.S. academy—know that there is a second generation of black theologians as well as womanist theologians, and that Latino/a theology today goes beyond Virgilio Elizondo to also include a younger generation. Yet few are aware that a new generation of Latin American liberation theologians exists. Here they are.

LATIN AMERICAN LIBERATION THEOLOGY: THE PAST

At night I listen to their phantoms
shouting in my ear
shaking me out of lethargy
issuing me commands.
I think of their tattered lives
of their feverish hands

> reaching to seize ours.
> It's not that they're begging
> they're demanding
> they've earned the right to order us
> to break up our sleep
> to come awake
> to shake off once and for all
> this lassitude.
>
> —CLARIBEL ALEGRIA, "NOCTURNAL VISITS"[1]

As if echoing Claribel Alegria's "Nocturnal Visits," Latin American liberation theology was born at a time when phantoms shouting in hunger shook a continent out of its lethargy. In particular, liberation theology emerged at the crossroads of a changing Latin American church, the rise of dependency theory, and the revolutionary political and economic hopes of the late 1960s and early 1970s.[2] The Second Vatican Council made possible a fundamental rethinking of the relation between Christian faith and the world by asserting the value of secular historical progress as an integral part of God's work. Encyclicals such as *Mater et magistra*, *Pacem in terris*, and *Populorum progressio* focused on workers' socioeconomic rights as well as the rights of poor nations in relation to rich nations, while Vatican II gave national episcopates greater freedom to adapt and apply church teaching to their particular contexts. In addition, radical Protestantism grew throughout South America.[3]

Dependency theory provided the framework within which Latin America's political and economic structures were analyzed and understood.[4] As José Míguez Bonino states: "The major historical shift was the rise of dependency theory. It was a dividing of the waters. When people influenced by the Catholic renewal were confronted with the dependency crisis, there was a parting of the ways. Some remained in the modern European renewal and others left to pursue liberation."[5] Within this framework the economic development of the rich countries is the flip side of Latin American underdevelopment. Merely copying the North Atlantic—Western European and U.S.— path of development cannot solve the problem of massive exclusion plaguing Latin America.[6] Quite the contrary, capitalism necessarily produces underdevelopment in the Third or 2/3 World.[7] Latin America thus needs to decide between two poles—capitalist underdevelopment or socialist revolution. There are no other options.

Finally, the Cuban revolution, the failure of the decade of development and Kennedy's Alliance for Progress, and the exhaustion of import substitution models of development also led to the rejection of reformist measures to deal with the massive poverty that plagued Latin America. Political and economic views radicalized as priests, workers, and students organized in militant revolutionary groups espousing socialism. At the same time, a succession of military coups imposed national security states.[8] These religious and political trends came together at the Second General Conference of Latin American Bishops (CELAM) at Medellín, Colombia, in 1968. Here the Latin American church sought to preach and practice the gospel from the standpoint of the suffering poor. Its documents analyzed Latin America's social situation and argued that the continent suffered from structures of institutionalized violence caused by foreign exploitation that created a situation of internal and external colonialism.[9] Mere development, the documents asserted, could never overcome this condition of dependency and remedy the poor's plight. The notion of liberation emerged as an alternative.

Liberation theology's foundational texts—works such as Gustavo Gutiérrez's *Teología de la liberación,* Hugo Assmann's *Teología desde la praxis de la liberación,* and José Míguez Bonino's *Doing Theology in a Revolutionary Situation,* among others—were thus written from within a world view with the following presuppositions: first, a sharp dichotomy between revolution and reformist action, the former deemed essential, the latter seen as ineffective or even as an ideological smoke screen to uphold the status quo; second, a view of the poor as the primary and at times exclusive agents of social change; third, a sharp dichotomy between capitalism and socialism, the latter seen as the social system that could overcome the injustice of the former; and fourth, emphasis on politics as the struggle over state power, paying little attention to issues of gender, race, ecology, and popular culture.

LATIN AMERICAN LIBERATION THEOLOGY: THE PRESENT

> The more there are suffering, then, the more natural
> their sufferings appear. Who wants to prevent
> the fishes in the sea from getting wet?
> —BERTOLT BRECHT, "THE WORLD'S ONE HOPE"

Today liberation theology's historical context—that is, the sociopolitical and religious context within which liberation theologians work—has undergone dramatic changes. At the level of the church the main changes lie in the rise of Pentecostal groups and the Vatican's attempts to clamp down on liberation theology by silencing theologians and replacing progressive bishops with conservative ones.[10] On the political and economic fronts, the first change lies in the collapse of socialism. For liberation theology, the fall of the Berlin Wall represents the loss of a practical alternative to capitalism.[11] In fact, the prospect of an alternative seems to have disappeared from view. A second change lies in the perceived decline of the nation-state's ability to control economic activity within its own boundaries. The third change lies in the upsurge of culture as a politically contested site and the subsequent downgrading of the traditional political sphere, the struggle for state power.[12]

This massive shift in context has led some to suggest that liberation theology is in decline.[13] According to Christopher Rowland: "If book sales offered an accurate guide to its continuing influence, the situation would seem rather hopeless. Whereas books on the subject might have expected to sell a decade ago, there is little market for them now."[14] In this specific case a string of recent books by liberation theologians and about liberation theology suggests the opposite.[15] Liberation theology, however, was never about publications. Instead, as Juan Luis Segundo once wrote, "The most progressive theology in Latin America is more interested in *being liberative* than in *talking about liberation.*"[16] According to Cardinal Joseph Ratzinger, "The fall of the European governmental systems based on Marxism turned out to be a kind of twilight of the gods for that theology."[17] This statement, however, is more a statement of desire than a statement of fact. Such a critique misunderstands and/or misrepresents the role Marxism played within liberation theology. Marxism was a tool used to better understand the reality of oppression—nothing more. The use or non-use of Marxism as a social-scientific mediation, the rise or fall of the Soviet Bloc, in no way affects the continued relevance of liberation theology. Indeed, what the shift in context hides is the reality of a Latin American and global misery that remains the same no matter what else changes. Liberation theologians, in fact, have responded to the challenge by revising aspects of their theology. Even before the fall of the Berlin Wall figures such as Gustavo Gutiérrez, Leonardo Boff, and Jon Sobrino, to name just a few, had begun to nuance their class analysis with insights from race, gender, cultural, and ecological studies.[18] In addition, female theologians such as Ivonne Gebara and Elsa Tamez have claimed a voice of their own. All these theologians stress that the foundational liberationist ideas—the preferential option for the poor, liberation, the reign of God—remain relevant in the current historical context. Yet they now refuse to accept a strict dichotomy between reform and revolution, they reject the simple belief in the poor as a unified and homogenous revolutionary subject, and they embrace popular culture as well as civil society as valid arenas of liberation. Liberation theology was never really in decline. Liberation theology was being rethought to best address the needs of the poor in a new context while the North Atlantic academy, blind to its own blindness, turned its attention to other issues.

LATIN AMERICAN LIBERATION THEOLOGY: THE FUTURE

> History says, Don't hope
> On this side of the grave,
> But then, once in a lifetime
> The longed-for tidal wave
> Of justice can rise up
> And hope and history rhyme.
> —SEAMUS HEANEY, "VOICES FROM LEMNOS"

These essays are the future of liberation theology. Here you will find the emerging theological and political paths that will define the shape of liberation theology in the next decades. Here you will find new assessments of its past as well as new visions for its future. These essays build upon, but at times also define themselves against, the accomplishments of liberation theology's foundational figures. They tackle new issues such as liberation theology's heterosexual matrix, the theological import of Latin Americans globalized as migrants, and the relationship between liberation theology and U.S. Hispanic theology, and they rethink issues such as the ethics of neoliberalism, the partnership between theology and the social sciences and the role of historical projects in pursuing liberation, to name just a few. In the process the tools available to liberation theology are expanded to include, among others, comparative political economy and legal theory, queer theory and border thinking, psychoanalysis and poststructuralist social theory. These liberationists, moreover, do not come from the clergy and so are immune to the potential wrath of the Vatican. Despite differences between them and early liberation theology, in every essay the original liberationist goal is at the forefront. As Leonardo and Clodovis Boff once wrote, "There is only one goal—the liberation of the oppressed."[19]

The volume opens with Jung Mo Sung, the most prolific next-generation voice within mainstream contemporary Latin American liberation theology. In his contribution Sung rethinks the categories of liberation and historical subject. He suggests that first-generation liberation theology overestimated the capacity to enact liberation in history. For Sung, liberation theology understood Jesus Christ from the perspective of the Exodus paradigm, in which God liberates the enslaved Israelites within history, rather than from the perspective of the crucifixion and resurrection. Unlike the Exodus, the latter paradigm recognizes that God does not undo the boundaries of history and the human condition—a condition in which liberation is always frail, partial, and incomplete. This recognition has important consequences. First, it reminds us that liberation theology's originating practice was the experience of finding God in the face of the oppressed rather than in the pursuit of any political action. Second, it provides a basis to criticize today's dominant global ideology, the belief that the free market is a global panacea to all of society's problems. Within history no such panacea is possible. Finally, it provides an alternative understanding of liberation in which liberation is not just the struggle for a more just society but also the recovery of the human being as subject. In a global order that defines people according to their capacity to consume, the poor are necessarily excluded. Yet when the individual is revealed as a subject resisting oppressive relations, that person recognizes his or her ultimate value irrespective of any social role. The historical subject, therefore, is not the poor as a special class that drives history forward. Instead, every individual struggling or aiding the struggle for a dignified life is revealed as a subject in grace (a recognition of pure gratuity beyond all social conventions) and faith (seeing what is invisible to the eyes of the world).

Marcella Althaus-Reid ranks among the most innovative and controversial theologians working within the liberationist tradition. Her own project, "indecent theology," rethinks liberation theology from the perspective of queer theory and is the most daring attempt to link these two currents of thought. Her contribution places her work in relation to liberation theology's founding figures and then moves beyond them. She notes that liberation theology was an indecent theology, that is, a theology that transgressed what was defined as "normal" for theology. Liberation theology was indecent when it questioned the alliance between church and authoritarian governments, when it challenged the unjust economic structure of society, and when its exponents were persecuted and murdered for struggling on behalf of the dispossessed. However, liberation theology operated with a "straight" category of the poor that failed to question rigid identities between poor men and women based on prejudiced sexual assumptions. Here liberation theology's proposed focus on the experience of the poor was blind to the various sexualities at play in the lives and spiritualities of the poor. An indecent liberation theology thus needs to liberate praxis from forms of oppression normalized by patriarchal heterosexuality. In the process, the arena of liberation is widened and transformed—both the poor and God are freed from the prison of heterosexual ideologies.

Nelson Maldonado-Torres carries forth the theological/philosophical tradition personified by Enrique Dussel. He begins his essay with the provocative claim that liberation theology's partnership with the social sciences, one traditionally claimed by liberationists as a distinguishing mark of their theology, is a problem that needs to be faced. According to Maldonado-Torres, this partnership, born of the need to realize liberation concretely in society, may not be liberating enough for the new challenges ahead. After examining radical orthodoxy and Slavoj Žižek's Lacanian-Hegelian Marxism as failed critiques of liberation theology's partnership with the social sciences, Maldonado-Torres argues that liberation theology failed to grasp fully the situation of colonial heterogeneity lying underneath the "poor" it sought to address. The dependency theory that was so central to liberation theology, for example, emerged from one specific sector of that heterogeneity (usually male and formally educated), while the struggles of women, blacks, and indigenous peoples remained peripheral. Dependency theory's blindness contributed to liberation theology's blindness. Today, for Maldonado-Torres, liberation theology needs to renew itself with contributions from border thinking—the epistemological formations that emerge in physical, emotional, and epistemological frontiers. Border thinking addresses the fact that colonialism was cultural and epistemic, not just material. To best challenge the colonial legacy, liberation theology thus must move away from its monolingual and monological understanding of liberation and move toward a radical "diversality" that incorporates the contributions of all excluded groups. Ultimately, real material liberation can only emerge together with epistemic and cultural liberation.

Silvia Regina de Lima Silva is liberation theology's leading Afro-Brazilian theologian. She notes that Latin American feminist black theology emerges in relation to a dual challenge. On the one hand, like feminist theology, it seeks to challenge the white, male, and elitist theology that has dominated Latin America. On the other hand, it seeks to reflect upon the lived faith experience of black women. In the process, Latin American feminist black theology recovers the black female body as part of God's revelation. To reclaim the black female body is to recover a sense of dignity as a child of God. In addition, Latin American feminist black theology seeks to recover the history and memory of blacks in Latin America. To reclaim past history is the first step in asserting a place as subjects making history in the present. Finally, Latin American feminist black theology seeks a dialogue with ancestral religious experience. Here Christianity is enriched by the encounter with other understandings of God—a God with a female face, or a God closer to nature who at times might even blend in with the land and rivers of ancestral experience. This theology thus seeks to construct individual, social, and imaginative emancipatory spaces where God can be revealed. As such, it is a theological and political undertaking that sets itself against theologies that attempt to kidnap and reduce God to one expression and social order.

German Gutiérrez, a leading researcher at the Departamento Ecuménico de Investigaciones (DEI), Latin America's most important liberationist think tank, claims that there are three main ethical systems in conflict today: (1) a functional market ethics, (2) the ethics of thieves, and (3) an ethics of life. In the first case the functional market ethics is based on the right to property and the enforcement of contracts as the background upon which moral behavior takes place. Here the most efficient mechanism for coordination among individuals is the market that ensures that individuals can realize their aims within the context of a harmonious competition. Gutiérrez argues, however, that this ethic applied in Latin America has led to the polarization of society into a small rich elite and a large disenfranchised class. The upshot is that increased state repression is required to stem society's discontent. In the second case, Gutiérrez shows that positivist legal thought draws an equivalence between this market ethics and an ethics of thieves (as in Adam Smith's famous example of an ethics of thieves to show the need for a normative order to society). The future of the global majority excluded from the possibility of sustaining their lives (that is, it is not a question of whether to be exploited or not—exploited is a good option, the other option is death) hinges on the outcome of the struggle between these two ethics and an ethics of life. In this ethic every institution must first be judged by whether it sustains human life. Life is not a value that can exchanged on the market; life is prior to value, the condition that makes values possible in the first place.

Nancy Bedford's essay reflects on the theological contribution of an unexamined component of globalization in Latin America—Latin

Americans globalized as migrants. Since the United States today has the world's fourth largest Spanish-speaking population, as well as many immigrants from Brazil and the Caribbean, liberation theology finds itself needing to step beyond the borders of Latin America as traditionally understood. What does it mean for theology when, as a result of transnational migration, we begin to speak of God from more than one place? Bedford reflects on this question by examining the metaphor of *locus theologicus*, a metaphor that has played an important role in theology in general as well as in liberation theology in particular. This metaphor of "place," however, is too static for the migrant's *locus* which, as a result of globalization and migration, has become unstable and not easily recognizable as a social and physical location. Instead, she suggests that within liberation theology itself there is the possibility of speaking of God as a *via* or "way" rather than a locus or place. The metaphor of way makes room for the migrant's experience of a homelessness rooted in economic causes. Indeed, as Bedford notes, the figure of the migrant falls within liberation theology's focus on the poor, because migrants come from the most economically disadvantaged groups. The migrants' "way," in turn, enables the discovery of a new reservoir of meanings in the biblical text and stresses that the best God-talk requires epistemological ruptures—just like the migrants' experience of constantly being exposed to others in new ways.

Manuel Mejido has emerged as one of the most original voices reflecting on Latin American liberation theology and U.S. Hispanic theology in unison. His essay suggests that liberation theology's break from North Atlantic theologies stems from the fact that, with the former, theology is for the first time understood as a critically oriented science rather than a historical-hermeneutic science. While historical-hermeneutic theology seeks to interpret transcendence, liberation theology as a critically oriented science operates with an emancipatory cognitive interest that seeks to "make" transcendence. Mejido, however, also argues that currently liberation theology is being eclipsed by the postmodern turn to language, alterity, and the plurality of particulars in two ways: first, liberation theology is being reduced to a historical-hermeneutic science; second, liberation theology's emancipatory project is being liberalized through the naturalization of global liberal-democratic capitalism. The end effect is that today liberation theology is no longer explicitly critiqued by other theologies; instead, liberation theology is assimilated as a dialogue partner within a community of "particular" theologies. Within this conversation, understanding is the goal, not liberation. Surprisingly, due to its links with liberation theology, Mejido points to U.S. Hispanic theology as a key culprit in this reduction of the liberationist project. Indeed, for him, U.S. Hispanic theology's misunderstanding of the liberationist project has the effect of undermining its own attempts to speak from (and to) the lived reality of U.S. Hispanics. For Mejido, allowing both theologies to reclaim their status as critically oriented sciences requires passing through the postmodern linguistic turn without, however, reducing it to the hermeneutic conception of language. He concludes by showing how psychoanalysis, understood as a critically oriented science that examines the discourses upon which social orders are constructed, can be the basis for this recovery.

Finally, my essay reconstructs liberation theology around the notion of a historical project. I suggest that in early liberation theology the development of historical projects—that is, alternative models of political and economic organization—served two functions. First, they were the primary means by which a social and material liberation was pursued. Second, they were the way liberation theology gave specific content to its terminology and thus differentiated itself from other groups that used the same vocabulary while in reality holding very different socioeconomic positions. The development of historical projects, in fact, was central to liberation theology's understanding of itself as a theology different from those produced in the affluent North Atlantic nations. The shift in context I described at the outset of this Introduction, however, deprived liberation theology of its preferred historical project—socialism. I argue that despite this fact the development of such projects can and must be recovered as an integral part of liberation theology. In particular, I suggest that liberation theology's current inability to think in terms of historical projects stems mostly from internal deficiencies rather than the shift in context. Here, therefore, there is cause for hope. I show that rethinking the role of the social sciences within its methodology and revising its understanding of capitalism will allow liberation theology to once again be able to develop historical projects. Only then can the promise of a theology that pursues liberation where it matters most to most people—in the political and economic structure of society—be kept.

Jorge Luis Borges once wrote, "Nothing is built on stone, everything is built on sand, yet our duty is to build on the sand as if it were stone."[20] Today, perhaps more than ever, Borges seems to be in the right. Liberation theology is caught in a world where misery is rampant and the "end of history" as the end of institutional experiments to address that misery is jubilantly proclaimed. In such a context, liberation theology may seem more sand than stone, as its project—a theology built around and geared toward the liberation of the poor—seems hopelessly out-dated. For there to be sand, however, there must first be stone. And since liberation theologians are not lacking duty or heroism, in the face of persecution and martyrdom, they will find stone underneath the sand. I hope the essays in this volume may aid that task.

NOTES

[1] The poems that introduce each section of this Introduction are taken from Paul Farmer, *Pathologies of Power: Health, Human Rights, and the New War on the Poor* (Berkeley and Los Angeles: University of California Press, 2003), 49, 251, and 248. Farmer's book is an excellent example of the continued relevance of insights from Latin American liberation theology, this time applied to medical anthropology.

[2] For a quick but good overview of liberation theology's development up to the early 1980s, see the first chapter of Arthur McGovern, *Liberation Theology and Its Critics: Toward an Assessment* (Maryknoll, NY: Orbis Books, 1989). For a longer overview, see Christian Smith, *The Emergence of Liberation Theology: Radical Religion and Social Movement Theory* (Chicago: The University of Chicago Press, 1991). For a good overview in Spanish, see Enrique Dussel, *Teología de la Liberación: Un Panorama de su Desarrollo* (Mexico City: Potrerillos Editores, 1995). For an examination of liberation theology since the mid-1990s, see John Burdick, *Legacies of Liberation: The Progressive Catholic Church in Brazil* (Aldershot, England: Ashgate, 2004), and Ivan Petrella, *The Future of Liberation Theology: An Argument and Manifesto* (Aldershot, England: Ashgate, 2004). Parts of this introduction are taken from the first chapter of this last work; I thank Ashgate for letting me reuse those sections.

[3] On this often forgotten fact, see José Míguez Bonino, *Rostros del Protestantismo Latinoamericano* (Grand Rapids, MI: William B. Eerdmans, 1995).

[4] For an excellent analysis of liberation theology and dependency theory, see Jung Mo Sung, *Economía: Tema Ausente en la Teología de la Liberación* (San José, Costa Rica: DEI, 1994). For more on liberation theology and dependency theory, see Chapter 4 of Petrella, *The Future of Liberation Theology*. For dependency theory generally, see Cristobal Kay, *Latin American Theories of Development and Underdevelopment* (New York: Routledge, 1989).

[5] José Míguez Bonino, cited in Smith, *The Emergence of Liberation Theology*, 258 (from an interview with Míguez Bonino in 1987).

[6] The belief that all countries face the same problems and need to follow the same path toward prosperity finds its intellectual home in modernization theory. For a classic encapsulation of this position, see Walter Rostow, *The Stages of Economic Growth: A Non-Communist Manifesto* (Cambridge: Cambridge University Press, 1960).

[7] While the term *Third World* has fallen out of style, it does capture the disparity of power between the First World and the Third World—they are,

in fact, worlds apart. The term *2/3 World*, in turn, captures the fact that the Third World is the majority of humankind.

[8] For the classic liberationist analysis of national security states see José Comblin, *The Church and the National Security State* (Maryknoll, NY: Orbis Books, 1979).

[9] For the documents, see Joseph Gremillion, ed., *The Gospel of Peace and Justice: Catholic Social Teaching since Pope John* (Maryknoll, NY: Orbis Books, 1976).

[10] Michael Löwy, for example, argues that "the main challenge to liberationist Christianity is Rome's neo-conservative offensive in Latin America" (Michael Löwy, *The War of Gods: Religion and Politics in Latin America* [New York: Verso, 1996], 131).

[11] For early attempts to deal with this fact see José Gomez Caffarena, "Dialogos y Debates," in *Cambio Social y Pensamiento Cristiano en América Latina*, ed. José Comblin, José I. Gonzalez Faus, and Jon Sobrino (Madrid: Editorial Trotta, 1993), 330; Frei Betto, "A Teología da Libertação: Ruiu com o Muro de Berlim?" *Revista Eclesiastica Brasileira* 50, no. 200 (December 1990): 922–29; and Leonardo Boff, "A Implosão da Socialismo Autoritario e a Teología da Libertação," *Revista Eclesiastica Brasileira* 50, no. 197 (March 1990): 76–92.

[12] For a more detailed exposition of each one of these points, see José Comblin, *Called for Freedom: The Changing Context of Liberation Theology*, trans. Phillip Berryman (Maryknoll, NY: Orbis Books, 1998), xv–xix.

[13] For an examination of how liberation theology has responded to the change in historical context, see Petrella, *The Future of Liberation Theology*.

[14] Christopher Rowland, ed., *The Cambridge Companion to Liberation Theology* (Cambridge: Cambridge University Press, 1999), 249.

[15] See, for example, Petrella, *The Future of Liberation Theology*; Burdick, *Legacies of Liberation*; Marcella Althaus-Reid, *The Queer God* (New York: Routledge, 2003); Marcella Althaus-Reid, *Indecent Theology: Theological Perversions in Sex, Gender and Politics* (New York: Routledge, 2000); Joerg Rieger, ed., *Opting for the Margins: Postmodernity and Liberation in Christian Theology* (Oxford: Oxford University Press, 2003); Daniel M. Bell Jr., *Liberation Theology after the End of History: The Refusal to Cease Suffering* (London: Routledge, 2001).

[16] Juan Luis Segundo, *The Liberation of Theology* (Maryknoll, NY: Orbis Books, 1985), 9.

[17] Joseph Ratzinger, "Relación Sobre la Situación Actual de la Fe y la Teología," in *Fe y Teología en América Latina* (Santa Fe de Bogota, Colombia: CELAM, 1997), 14.

[18] For an analysis of liberation theology's responses to its shift in historical context, see Petrella, *The Future of Liberation Theology*, chap. 1. For a focus on the Brazilian case, see Burdick, *Legacies of Liberation*.

[19] Clodovis Boff and Leonardo Boff, *Salvation and Liberation: In Search of a Balance between Faith and Politics* (Maryknoll, NY: Orbis Books, 1984), 24.

[20] Jorge Luis Borges, *Obras Completas 1923–1972* (Buenos Aires: Emece Editores, 1974), 1012.

1.

The Human Being as Subject

Defending the Victims

Jung Mo Sung

Any kind of Christian theology today, even in rich and dominant coun-tries, which does not have as its starting point the historic situation of dependence and domination of two thirds of humankind, with its 30 million dead of hunger and malnutrition, will not be able to position and concretize historically its fundamental themes. Its questions will not be the real questions. It will not touch the real person. As observed by a participant in the Buenos Aires gathering, "theology must be res-cued from its cynicism." Certainly, in the face of the problems of today's world, many theological writings are reduced to cynicism.[1]

—HUGO ASSMANN

THEOLOGY AND ETHICAL INDIGNATION

IN THE BEGINNING OF THE 1970s a group of Latin Ameri-can theologians introduced to the world and to the Christian churches a theology with two new epistemological novelties: a new methodol-ogy and the perspective of the poor. This theology received, as we know, the name of liberation theology. As I consider the current and deep crisis of this theology, I realize that its essential proposition was neither its name nor the historical objective implicit in the name: the *liberation* of the poor. It was rather those two epistemological novelties. From the beginnings its theologians have made it clear that liberation

1

theology was and is a second moment. The first moment is the praxis of liberation, born out of the ethical indignation in view of the situations in which human beings are reduced to subhuman conditions. Such indignation is strong enough to make people assume one another's risks and pains. This was perceived as a spiritual experience—the experience of finding the person of Jesus Christ in the face of the oppressed and crushed ones.

This intrinsic relationship between liberation theology and praxis was seen as one of the fundamental differences between liberation theology and other theologies. Certainly it was taken for granted that "traditional" theologies were also somewhat related to Christian practice. However, as stated by Assmann, "the fundamental structures of the traditional theological language are not historical. Its determinant categories aim at establishing the truth in itself, without the intrinsic connection with a praxis. That praxis is seen as something which happens later, as a derivative, as an 'application' of the 'preexisting' and real truth."[2]

I think that it is fundamentally important to rescue and recover this basic and original intuition of liberation theology, considering that we are frequently tempted to search not only in books (including the "Holy Scriptures") but also in theories that happen to be in fashion for some previous truth, unrelated to the real problems of praxis, that might enlighten us and help us cope with the crisis in which the Latin American theology finds itself immersed. In other words, liberation theology cannot wish to solve its impasse by means of analysis and/or deductions of the concept of God or any other concept but by starting with experiences of God in the center of history and with critical analysis of the concepts we use to interpret such experiences.

To propose building a theology intrinsically linked to praxis does not mean to abandon the rigor of thinking. It means precisely the opposite. For Gustavo Gutiérrez, for instance, such theology must be "a serious discourse, aware of itself, in full possession of its conceptual elements" with "a clear and critical attitude regarding the economic and socio-cultural issues in the life and reflection of the Christian community" so as necessarily to be "a criticism of society and the Church in so far as they are called and addressed by the Word of God."[3] Thus understood, he used to say that theology carries out its liberating function regarding human beings and the Christian community to the extent that it avoids "every fetishism and idolatry."[4]

To talk about this intrinsic relationship between the praxis of liberation and liberation theology may sound passé, since only a few people still use the expression *praxis of liberation* or even *liberation of the poor*. The collapse of the socialist bloc, the crisis of the popular movements in Latin America, the aggressiveness of the media with its daily message from which there is no escape, and to which there is no alternative, the capitalist market system, and the desire to imitate the success of the "religious shows" appear to have forever buried such expressions. Certainly we must recognize that there was an exaggerated expectancy regarding the liberation of the poor, a point we will consider later. However, the first moment of liberation theology never was such expectancy. It certainly was not what the theologians were talking about. The first moment was always the practice of what, at the time, was known as the liberation that results from the spiritual experience of finding Jesus Christ in the face of oppressed persons. In other words, the first moment was, and is, service in defense of the life and dignity of the victimized poor. In the 1970s and 1980s this service was seen as the praxis of liberation. However, this usage does not exhaust the wealth of possibilities that can emerge from such experience. There are other ways to interpret this expression. To quote Gutiérrez: "The Christian community professes a 'faith which works through charity.' It is—at least ought to be—real charity, action and commitment to the service of others. Theology is reflection, a critical attitude. Theology *follows*; it is the second step."[5] This strangeness related to the "languages of liberation" indicates that we live in a time quite different from the 1970s and 1980s. It further reflects the limitations of the "traditional" language of liberation theology in interpreting and expressing the faith experience of those who are feeling ethical indignation regarding today's massive social exclusion as well as other forms of oppression of human beings and their environment. At the end of the 1960s, the gestation period of liberation theology, Rubem Alves wrote that

> man's language is a mirror of his historicity. It does not emerge only from the metabolism that takes place between man and his world, but rather expresses itself as an answer to concrete situations that surrounds him. . . . It conveys the *human interpretation* of the message and challenge that he sends to the world, stating what he believes to be his vocation, his place, his responsibilities, his direction and his function in the world. . . . Therefore the emergence of a new language announces the birth of a distinctly new experience, a distinctly new self understanding, a distinctly new vocation, and consequently a distinctly new man.[6]

Liberation theology was this new language of a new self-understanding on the part of the Christian community in Latin America and the world. However, today we experience a certain fatigue in this language of the 1970s.

I myself believe that this language can be rescued, provided that some structural problems are solved.[7] On the other hand, I also think that what matters most is not the "survival" of liberation theology, but the continuity of the theological production reflecting a critical reflection about the charity/service born out of ethical indignation in view of the situations and rationale that reduce human beings to sub-human conditions. The perspective of the victims must be prominent in such a theological endeavor. In other words, we must pursue the formulation of religious and theological languages that enhance a better expression as well as a critical understanding of the experience of faith, of ethical indignation, and of commitment, in defense of the lives of the victims.

To that end we need to accept the permanent challenge to reflect critically about our presuppositions and concepts. In this chapter I want to contribute to this task with some considerations regarding the concept of historical subject, which has always been associated with the concept of liberation of the poor.

ETHICAL INDIGNATION AND THE SUBJECT

The founding experience, called by liberation theology the first moment, is, as stated before, the experience of ethical indignation. Not everybody feels such indignation, no matter how grave the social problems are. There are those who do not feel it because they do not see the victims, or because they have excluded the victims from their vision field, or even because they no longer consider the victims as persons. There are also those who feel uncomfortable with the unveiling of the victims' suffering, but since the discomfort does not result in ethical indignation, they forget about it as time goes by.

What happens when one feels ethical indignation? It is clear that this question cannot be fully answered. Each experience is different and presupposes worlds and histories of the involved persons. But I would like to point out for our reflection two aspects related to the concern.

For a person to be indignant in view of a situation in which someone is being mistreated or reduced to a subhuman condition, such a person must recognize the humanity of that individual. Without this recognition no ethical indignation is possible, for nobody feels indignant regarding a situation in which a subhuman being is being treated as subhuman. This is so because, in this case, the humanity of such a mistreated person is not recognized.

This difficulty in recognizing the victim's humanity in such situations is due to the difficulty in differentiating the social place and role from the dignity of persons as human beings. More and more human dignity is confused with social status. In a consumer culture the pattern of consumption is the determinant factor in defining both the identity and the dignity of individuals. Non-consumers are seen as non-persons; the lower their place in the sociocultural hierarchy, the less human they are.

In ethical indignation the humanity of persons is recognized irrespective of their social place or role. Persons are recognized in gratuity, that is, independently from their consumption capacity, as well as their social, sexual, religious placement in society. For instance, just to mention an extreme possibility, if we find an individual who is a poor, black, lesbian, AIDS-infected, disabled, ugly, and old prostitute, and still see this individual as a human being in her fundamental dignity, we will be undergoing a spiritual experience of grace (recognition of pure gratuity, beyond all our social conventions) and faith (seeing what is invisible to the eyes of the world).

In our society, characterized by the irrepressible pursuit of success as a way to "justify" human existence, this gratuitous recognition among subjects, in the face-to-face subject-subject relationship, is a true spiritual experience of grace and justification by faith. It is an experience that justifies the existence of not only the oppressed person but also of the person who feels the indignation. That is why this experience is perceived as liberating for the one who feels the indignation, as well as for the victim, then recognized as person. That is also why the experience of ethical indignation, which leads to social commitment, has been and must be interpreted as a true spiritual experience.

A second important aspect, presupposed in ethical indignation, is its horizon of utopian desire, that is, the utopian horizon of an environment where persons are recognized and respected, irrespectively of their social condition. Such a vision leads one to see the prevailing situation as ethically unacceptable, that is, as a situation that must be transformed. Without this yearning for a different world we could not feel indignation. In its turn, indignation is what makes us "see" this utopian horizon.

In a first moment this horizon looks to us as a product of a utopian imagination, that is, as the dream of a free world, a world liberated from all kinds of oppression and objectification of human beings. In due time this image is further developed and appears to us as a *project* for a new society (sometimes, in Christian circles, as *God's project*).

To the extent that this (imaginative or utopian) project is what permits us to understand the prevailing reality as unacceptable, while being, at same time, an object of desire, we begin to believe—because we so desire—that this project is fully doable in the interior of history. From the desire of its possibility we come to the belief in its possibility. And sometimes such desire leads us to believe that the project is not only possible, but unavoidable.

Believing it doable, we must then face the need of a subject that will make it real, or "build" this project/horizon in the interior of history. At this point the utilization of concepts such as *historical subject, history's subjects,* and *history's protagonists* enters the scenario.

These two aspects of ethical indignation, which are complementary and intrinsically related, carry two notions or features of the subject: (1) the subject is recognized and recognizable irrespective of roles and social status; and (2) the subject is a doer or builder in the fullness of either the utopian horizon or the project of a wholly new society, the one of the new earth and the new human being. At this juncture we want to submit some reflections about this concept of a subject.

HISTORICAL SUBJECT AND HUMAN CONDITION

The concept of a historical subject was so deeply identified with liberation theology and Christian communities committed to the lives of the poor that, when it was confronted with a crisis, beginning with the fall of the socialist bloc, there were several attempts to rescue it. Probably the most recurring one was the use of the expression *new historical subjects* or *new emerging subjects.* Acknowledging the crisis of the concept, then applied to the working class or to the poor, many submitted other social groups (such as women, blacks, indigenous people, and others) as new subjects. Thus they kept the concept alive and simply changed the concrete definition of who the subject would be.

Another attempt to preserve the concept came up from the theological dialogue with the new theories of physics. Frei Betto, one of the most influential people in the Latin American Christian left, is one of the exponents of this line. For instance, in his article "Indeterminação e complementaridade," he proposes a dialogue with quantum physics in an attempt to supersede the crisis of the utopias. In the last page of the article, which has the meaningful subtitle "Resgate quâtico do sujeito histórico" (Quantum rescue of the historical subject), he implies that this subject would have the mission of "confronting the great challenge of ensuring that the capital—in the form of money, technology and knowledge—would be at the service of human happiness, by dismantling the racial, ethnic and religious barriers. Then we would rediscover the paths that lead to the Garden of Eden."[8]

We do not want to discuss here whether we are going through the crisis of the utopias or watching the victory of a utopia—the capitalist utopia—over all the others. Neither do we want to discuss here if it is possible for human beings to arrive at the Garden of Eden, that is, to build a fully just society, or even if the theories of quantum physics could be so directly applied to the field of human and social relations. What we want, in this essay, is to call attention to the weight and importance of the concept of historical subject in modernity, especially for Latin American Christians committed to the liberation of the poor.

The concept of historical subject has its roots in the Judeo-Christian tradition, which developed a notion of God as the subject of history, that is, of a God who stands outside history, and outside the world, yet directs or determines history. The transcendental God, who is beyond the limits of the human world, was seen as the subject of history; and history was seen as the object of God's will and action. Our modern world replaced this notion of God as subject of history with the notion of the human being as the subject of history. In this sense, secularization can be understood as a process of disenchantment of the world and of re-enchantment of the human being. Modernity usurps from God the image of subject and transfers it to the human being. As Alain Touraine says: "Upon entering modernity, religion explodes, but its components do not disappear. *The subject, ceasing to be divine or to be defined as Reason, becomes human, personal,* transmuted into a kind of relationship of the individual or group with themselves." Touraine also points out that "the subject of modernity is no other than the secularized descendant of religion."[9]

With this deep transformation, which is an authentic anthropological revolution, history begins to be seen as an object in relation to the human being. In the construction of the subject of history, there happens, at the same time, the construction of the concept of history as an object to be built by the human subject. During the primordial times of humankind, the predominant notion was the one of destiny written by the gods or by the spirits of nature, since there was not yet any notion of history. As time went by, there appeared the notion of an ethical evil, sin, and with it the notion of human freedom, from which sprang the notion of history. The Hebrew Bible is an example of this cultural rupture in the vision of history as a tension between God's will and human will. However, human history was perceived mostly as defined by the gods or by reason. With modernity comes this novelty: the perception of history as being constructed by human subjects.

Agnes Heller says that a dynamic concept of man plus the notion of history as that of personal and society's development appeared with the Renaissance. With this notion "the relation between individual and situation becomes fluid; past, present and future are transformed into human creations. However this 'humanness' becomes a generalized and homogeneous concept. It is then that 'liberty' and 'fraternity' are born as immanent ontological categories. Time and space are humanized; the infinite is transformed into a social reality."[10]

In the construction of history by the modern human subject, reason has a central role. The individual becomes a subject to the extent that he or she creates a world ruled by a rationale that is intelligible to human thought. This creation of a rational world is seen as the achievement of the progress that would lead us to the "Garden of Eden." God, the ordainer of the world and history, is replaced by the human subject, the ordainer of the world and history, according to reason.

This changes not only the concept of human being, the concept of subject, and the concept of history but also the "localization" of "paradise," the utopian horizon. The historical subject is the builder of history, which, in its turn, must flow into plenitude. The medieval paradise, which was to be found beyond human history, is placed in the interior of history, in the future. Here one finds a process of making medieval eschatology immanent. The human subject "constructs" history and "ordains" it so as to enhance, through progress, not only the abolition of all human and social contradictions but also the achievement of full harmony between human beings and nature. Karl Marx calls this the construction of the kingdom of liberty, and many Christians call it the construction of the kingdom of God.

I believe that the insistence on maintaining, recovering, or reformulating the concept of historical subject without questioning its presuppositions is tied to this deep desire to see such a utopian horizon shaping up in the interior of our history.

Some authors like Franz Hinkelammert and Hugo Assmann have criticized the transcendental illusion of believing that it is possible to construct, with finite human actions, a holistic world that presupposes infinite knowledge, time, and spaces. This type of illusion lies at the real center of neoliberalism's projects of perfect markets, the Soviet model of socialism's perfect planning, and even of many projects of construction of the kingdom of God. The problem with this illusion is not limited to the theoretical field. It also generates sacrificial systems, that is, social systems and institutions that demand sacrifices of human lives as the "necessary price" for reaching the "paradise," or the redemption of history and humankind.

Besides this transcendental illusion and its sacrificial logic there is an underlying theological problem that we want to consider briefly. The notion of God that is at the origin, and in some ways continues to undergird the notion of the human being as the subject of history, is a notion of God as the ordainer of the world and history. All fullness, all fully harmonious social or natural order, is conceived as an order free from evil and conflict.

Western thinking, or much of it, was influenced by a key characteristic of Greek philosophy: the search for God as the foundation of order. From this perspective Greek philosophy thought that human beings lived out their destiny to the extent that they held their place in the cosmic order, submissive to the God-established and God-ruled universal order. However, ethical indignation does not result from the awareness of lack of materialization of destiny or preestablished order. Ethical indignation—let me emphasize the ethical character of the indignation—is born out of the recognition of the humanity that is being denied to persons in relationships and/or social systems. It is the face-to-face experience that comes out of the contestation of the injustices and evils of the world. Indignation that results from any theory, without this face-to-face element, is not sustainable. It is soon forgotten or vanishes amid some pragmatic rationalization.

It is from the experience of mutual recognition of the subject-subject relationship, irrespective of any necessary institutionalization in society, that is born the conviction that in this ethical indignation we experience the grace of the God who is Love. The experience of God as Love, which may only happen in relationships of gratuity and liberty, cannot be explained and systematized by either philosophies or other theories that, by their own nature, are dependent on necessary logical relationships. The God experienced by the biblical people is different from the gods of philosophers and even theologians who only know the concept of God, and only look for God as the foundation of the perfect order.

As José Comblin says, "In the Bible, everything is different, because God is Love. Love does not establish order, but disorder. Love breaks the whole structure of order. Love establishes liberty, and, therefore, disorder. Sin is the consequence of God's love."[11] To say that God is Love is to say that the human vocation is liberty and that we fulfill ourselves as human beings as we live in liberty and love.

Liberty only exists when we face the possibility of being wrong. Love only exists when we are able to forgive the wrongdoings of our loved ones. The perfect social order, the new society without suffering, oppression, and injustice, the one of perfect harmony, not only cannot be constructed in the interior of history but also must not be desired. Yes, indeed! We must not desire the construction of such "perfect" social order. What we desire is a *utopian horizon* of God's kingdom, and we must always remind ourselves that such a horizon, like all horizons, can only be reachable by the eyes of desire; it is impossible to reach by human efforts. What we can and must construct is a more just, more human, and more fraternal society, but there will always be, in such a society, whether intentional or not, the possibility of errors and problems.

Christianity is not a proposal for running away from the world and the inherent contradictions and possibilities of the human condition. It is precisely the opposite. It is a proposal for loving our human condition and for living out love and liberty inside the boundaries of such condition. It is the proposal of faith in a God who

> emptied himself,
> taking the form of a slave
> being born in human likeness (Phil 2:7).

This is the scandal of Christianity!

Sometimes I have the impression that we in liberation theology, due to our renewed emphasis on the Exodus in Christian theology, often overestimate historical possibilities. One of the greatest contributions of the Hebrew Bible to the history of thought was its repositioning of the center of God's revelation from nature to ethical relations, that is, by moving it from a conception of destiny to the notion of human history. No more was God primordially looked for in nature but rather in justice relationships in the interior of human history. An important departure of Christianity from Judaism was not a return to nature or destiny but rather the acknowledgment of the limits of human history. In other words, by acknowledging that a defeated one, a crucified one, is the Risen One, the promised messiah, Christianity acknowledges that God does not undo the boundaries of history and human condition. Christianity acknowledges that God's promised liberation cannot undo human liberty and human condition, because, if that were the case, such liberation would neither bring us liberty nor be enjoyed by human beings. Christianity is built on the paradox of a crucified God, of a defeated liberator-messiah, and so too is our struggle's proposal for the life and dignity of the victims of the prevailing—that is, victorious—political systems and social relations, no matter if we end up with more defeats than victories. In other words, instead of reading the Jesus Christ event from the perspective of the Exodus paradigm, we should read the Exodus from the perspective of the crucifixion-resurrection event of Jesus of Nazareth.

If these reflections have any foundation, we are obliged to rethink seriously the concept of historical subject in our theology as well as in our social and pastoral endeavors.

SUBJECT AND SELF-ORGANIZATION

A second problematic aspect of the notion of historical subject is that the concept of subject appears counterposed to the concept of object of history. History is seen as an object to be built or molded by human action. The social sciences have for a long time criticized this notion, which undergirds many political and social theories. History (or society) is a very special object, to the extent that the subject of the relationship is part of it, inside it, and at the same time, both influenced or determined (depending on the stream of thought) by it, no matter if such object is one of study or transformation. Thus the concept of subject-object relationship could not be applied to the field of history and society, as a whole.

New concepts are gaining strength in the field of social and natural sciences and are further questioning this notion of historical subject, or of a "history builder" subject. These are concepts such as self-organization, self-regulation, self-making, and dissipative structures, coming from several fields of knowledge, including biology, physics, chemistry, and cybernetics. They are influencing the human and social sciences.[12] It is not the purpose of this essay to develop reflections about these new theories; for lack of space, we only highlight some of them here.

Hugo Assmann, in the excellent glossary that is the central part of his book *Reencantar a educação*, starts an entry note on "self-organization" by pointing out that such concept refers to the "dynamics of spontaneous emergence, in a system, of patterns of order and chaos, due to recurring internal relations and/or interactions with the environment. The unveiling of these emerging qualities is accompanied by an increase in complexity."[13] Strange language for those not acquainted with these new theories.

These concepts and theories are being utilized either as new metaphors or as instruments of analysis of social phenomena and social dynamics. But let us remember that the theory of spontaneous order is very old and has a long tradition in the history of social thought. It precedes Darwin's concept of evolution, even though it has gained strength in social thinking only since the 1970s. This theory is based on the notion that most of the things that bring about general benefits in social systems, or enhance their reproduction, are the result of unintended human actions, that is, of actions that are not under one's direct conscious control or conscious planning.

This notion of self-organization, or spontaneous order, raises a very important question for the challenge of rethinking the underlying notion of subject in our endeavors (previously known as the practice of liberation) in behalf of the life and dignity of victims, and also for our theologies.

For brevity's sake, let me quote a provocative text by Assmann, while assuming the risks it sets forth. Assmann, who during the 1970s was radically against the market, states:

> Among the undeniable realities, in the field of human interactions in complex societies, is the existence and functionality of partially self-regulating dynamic systems related to human behavior. In economics, this question has a name that, to this day, barely acquired any traction in sectors of the left: the market. Do we know how to connect social consciousness and ethical subject with the (partial) self-regulation of the market? The critical but positive acceptance of the market, without the loss of solidarity goals, demands a new reflection even about the conception, whether individual or collective, of the ethical subject. . . . This means to concurrently consider the ethical and individual options as well as the material and institutional objectification of

values, in the form of normalization of human conviviality, with strong self-regulating connotations.[14]

So, to prevent possible misunderstandings, it is important to point out here a fundamental difference between the use of the concepts of self-organization, self-regulation, and spontaneous order, as stated by Assmann, and their use by neoliberals or liberals such as Paul Krugman. For these, the market is a spontaneous order that always produces the best possible result. Assmann recognizes the existence of self-regulation in complex (social or natural) systems and their positive aspects, while at same time criticizing the neoliberal blind faith in the market, a blind faith that does not allow neoliberals to see the negative effects of this same process. That is why he criticized the *idolatry* of the market, that is, the sacralization of the market, but not the market, as such.[15]

SUBJECT, SOCIAL ACTOR, AND LIBERATION

We saw above that the experience of subject-subject relationship, face-to-face relationship, is one of the fundamental aspects of the founding experience we have been considering and represents one of two ways of understanding the concept of subject in the praxis of liberation. We dealt mainly with the notion of the subject as builder of history. Now we want to go back to some aspects of the notion of the subject as related to this face-to-face relationship.

To speak about the subject as subject, namely, of the subject that we experience in face-to-face relationship, is an impossible task. This is so because "when referred to as the subject, it is treated as an object, even when referred by the subject itself. When one labors in the realm of institutions, one is dealing with people transformed into object of the institutions, even when dealing with a person singled out as the superior of the whole institutional system."[16]

This does not mean that it is impossible for one to live out the subject being, but only that any theory and any institution is, in a way, bad theory and bad institution, because it treats the human being subject as an object. Yet, since we cannot live without language and institutions, what we can and should do is to distinguish the concept of subject from the social actor, that is, from the individual "living out" a social role in a given institutionalized relationship. The human being, the individual, is a subject that transcends all his or her objectifications in language and institutions. The individual cannot live without social institutions and roles, but the subject is not the sum total of these roles and does not identify himself or herself with a single role. Totalitarian oppressive institutions strive to deny the subjectness (the quality of being subject) of the individual, reducing the person to a social role or a set of roles, thus objectifying him or her in the interior of the system.

Let us take, as an example, the reduction of the individual to an economic actor. When the capitalist market system tells a person excluded from the market that he or she does not have the right to eat for not being a consumer (without money to act out the role of consumer), what is really happening is the negation of the subjectness of this person and his or her reduction to an economic role. The same happens when a worker is treated as a simple object in the chain of production. In the face of such a situation the following kind of protest of the poor is not uncommon: "I am poor, but I am a child of God's too!" This is someone claiming to be a subject prior to any and all institutionalizations that objectify him or her into a social role.

The subject being does not unveil himself or herself in our everyday life, when we act out our social roles as parents, husbands or wives, teachers, or consumers. The subject unveils himself or herself by resisting being reduced to a mere social role or to a set of roles. This is good both for those who hold high places in a given institution and for those who stand at lower levels.

For this to happen the person must deny the legitimizing rationalizations produced by the institutions. Such rationalization is in fact irrational, because it reduces the subject to object. This is why some authors, like Hinkelammert, are considering the concept of liberation not only as an anticipation of the kingdom of God through the construction of more just societies, but also as the recovering of the human being as subject. In the words of Hinkelammert: "When we talk, today, of the return of the repressed and crushed subject, we are talking about the human being as subject of this rationality who confronts the irrationality of the rationalized. In this perspective, *liberation* becomes the recovering of the human being as *subject*."[17]

When individuals unveil themselves and experience themselves as subject in the resistance against oppressive relations, they can recognize themselves as subject, and at the same time, recognize the subjectness of other persons irrespective of any social role. This is what we previously referred to when we considered the experience of gratuity in the face-to-face relationship. If we cannot talk about the subject as subject or build institutions where persons will not be objectified, we can at least live out our subject being in a resistance as well as in subject-subject relationship.

This means that the subject being is intimately linked to the resistance and struggle against objectifying and domineering institutions. The problem is that in order to struggle we need to channel our resistance and struggle through some social or ecclesial group or movement. In other words, for us to live out our subjectness in the resistance and struggle against oppressive institutions, we need, first, to participate in one or another institution, that is, we need to act out as social actors. Obviously, we must struggle for such an institution to be less oppressive and domineering than the social institution or system we are fighting against. Yet, to participate in an institution is to act out a social role and to obey, at least minimally, the institutional rules that objectify us. By doing so, the subject reduces himself or herself again to a social actor, that is, to a transforming role of social relations, which is a "reducer" of the individual's subjectivity. This is a tension it is impossible to resolve. And it is why to be fully subject is not attainable in the interior of our history.

In the case of social groups, when people get together to protest and resist the negation of their human dignity, we can say, analogically, that they form a subject community. But when this social group begins to strive to make its rights respected, it also begins to behave as a collective social actor.

The only way to preserve our subjectness is for us not to accept being reduced to any social role—no matter how important, how "holy," or how "revolutionary" it may be—and not to accept the sacralization of any social institution or system. This relates to our need to criticize idolatry and fetishism, as previously stated in the quotation from Gutiérrez.

TENSION BETWEEN THE MICRO-SOCIAL AND MACRO-SOCIAL

The experience of being a subject in the face-to-face encounter, as well as in the struggle for the dignity of self and others, is a truly gratifying one, and a giver of deep human meaning to our existence, that is, a spiritual experience of grace. Certainly our most propitious environment for this experience is the communitarian one, and the one of local social struggles. It is where we have more opportunity to engage in face-to-face relationships, for the simple reason that we can only cultivate such relationships in smaller environments, those not involving many people.

Two kinds of temptations may result from this fact. The first is the temptation of closing ourselves in communitarian environments and in micro-social local struggles. To the extent that big institutions and big social struggles do not allow for immediate face-face relationships, we are easily tempted to believe that the solution for religious and social problems is to be found only at communitarian and micro-social levels. However, no matter how much we try to deceive ourselves, the reality of economic globalization, the global Internet, and other "globalized" relations will continue to affect our lives. For example, a financial-exchange crisis in the Far East may cause unemployment for members of communities in Brazil.

Another temptation is for us to wish that the big religious, economic, and political institutions will come to function as our small communities do, or to fight for the project of a society that will be merely a quantitative enlargement of our community relations. In other words, this is a wish for a harmonious society, where all persons will respect one another, and relate to one another as if they knew one another and lived in the same community, that is, a society with no need of laws and regulations and, therefore, with no oppressive institutions.

These two temptations are fully understandable, to the extent that these relations and experiences are understood as the basis of social commitment, the fountain of strength and sustainability of the struggle, as well as the "guarantee" that liberation is possible. However, we should return to the theme of incarnation and remember that our struggle for solutions should be carried out from inside human and historical conditions. The temptation we feel to shut ourselves in communities, or a micro-social environment, is the temptation to shut ourselves away from the Spirit who "pushes" us, who calls us to get out of our communities and face the challenges of the world.

As for the temptation of wishing for our society to be a community, it results from the error of not recognizing the qualitative difference between one level and another, that is, the error of making linear projections from the micro-social to the macro-social. When we go from one level to another, whether from a micro-social to a macro-social or from the physical to the biological, new properties emerge. And it is precisely this emerging of new properties that allows us to perceive our transition from one level to another. If we are capable of perceiving this transition, we will also be able to acknowledge that in this other level the system functions in a different way. That being the case, things that functioned well in the previous level do not function in the same way in the new level or may not even function at all.

These confirmations challenge us to think about the relation between our experience and actions at the community and micro-social level, on the one hand, and the macro-social aspects of our problems and solutions, on the other. It is clear that this question has to be thought through as one considers other emerging concepts, such as self-organization and self-making, as previously mentioned.

FINAL CONSIDERATIONS

Latin American theology is going through a moment of delimitation of its challenges, as indicated by the numberless gatherings of theologians, all over the continent, to evaluate and discuss such challenges. This also indicates that the first moments of the crisis have been superseded. Since no theological stream can deal with all questions, it is fundamental for us to know how to limit and define our challenges properly. In the course of this essay I anticipated some themes and questions. Now, in conclusion, I just want to touch upon some others that are related to the previous ones.

For many of those who have been longer in the journey, who in the name of shared faith, in the hope that meaningful liberation or changes—in church and world—were emerging, it is important to find answers to disenchantment. It is the same disenchantment of the disciples at Emmaus: "We had hoped that he was the one to redeem Israel" (Lk 24:21). We need answers for the crisis of the failed messiah, for the crisis of the failure of our expectations.

An easy answer, the one adopted by the disciples and many Christians of our time, is that if he failed, he was not the Messiah (as implied by the disciples on their way to Emmaus); or, if we lost, and there is no way to victory, we were mistaken (as expressed in the current attitude of many former militants). The disciples were able to go beyond the immediate and easy answer in order to understand the paradox of the defeated Messiah. Yet, even after two thousand years of Christianity, this second answer is not easy to understand. Our generation needs to come up with our own answer. The answer must be faithful both to the experience of the disciples and to our own experience. We need to find the meaning of the struggle in behalf of the lives of the "little ones" without certainties and promises of victory—and often without expecting either the understanding or the support of our churches.

To that end I think it is fundamental that we continue deepening our reflections, aiming at developing and reviewing concepts and ways of thinking that will help persons of good will perceive, in ethical indignation and in the struggle for the life of the "little ones," with all its contradictions and limits, how we can live the most profound of all spiritual experiences, the experience of the grace of God that is in our midst.

Finally, allow me to touch upon a challenge that comes from liberation theology's previous reflections. Latin American theology had, as one of its central themes, the notion of God as the God of Life. Much was written to show how the God of the Bible is the God of Life. Yet, the second part of the expression, "Life," was assumed to be something obvious. Certainly it is easy to distinguish those who are alive from those who are dead. It is more difficult to say what life is. I believe that we should, in dialogue with the sciences of life and human sciences, accept the challenge to a better understanding of what life is, and of how it functions (in the biological, personal, social, and ecological contexts). This may enable us to better understand the meaning of the expression God of Life, and help us defend, more effectively, the threatened life.

—TRANSLATED BY JOVELINO RAMOS

NOTES

[1] Hugo Assmann, *Teología desde la praxis de la liberación,* 2nd ed. (Salamanca: Sigueme, 1976), 40. H. Assmann wrote this text—probably one of his most quoted paragraphs, worldwide—in 1971. Over thirty years later the text continues to be relevant.

[2] Ibid., 63.

[3] Gustavo Gutiérrez, *A Theology of Liberation* (Maryknoll, NY: Orbis Books, 1988), 9.

[4] Ibid., 10. It is worth pointing out that the critique of idolatry and fetishism is not addressed only to oppressive systems but also to Christian communities and popular movements.

[5] Ibid., 9.

[6] Rubem Alves, *Da esperança* (Campinas: Papirus, 1978), 46–47.

[7] For some of these problems, see Jung Mo Sung, *Teologia e economia: repensando a TL e utopias,* 2nd ed. (Petrópolis: Vozes, 1995).

[8] *Interfaces* 1, no. 1 (July–December 1997).

[9] Alain Touraine, *Crítica da modernidade* (Petrópolis: Vozes, 1994), 324, 22.

[10] Agnes Heller, *O homem do renascimento* (Lisbon: Ed. Presença, 1982), 9.

[11] José Comblin, *Cristãos rumo ao século XXI: nova caminhada de libertação* (São Paulo: Paulus, 1996), 6.

[12] Examples of scientists utilizing or in dialogue with these concepts are N. Luhman, Paul Krugman, Pablo Navarro, and I. Wallerstein. The last two have several texts available on the Internet.

[13] Hugo Assmann, *Reencantar a educação* (Petrópolis: Vozes, 1998), 134.

[14] Hugo Assmann, *Metáforas novas para reencantar a educação* (Piracicaba: Unimep, 1996), 64.

[15] Hugo Assmann and Franz J. Hinkelammert, *A idolatria do mercado: ensaio sobre economia e teologia* (Petrópolis: Vozes, 1989).

[16] Franz J. Hinkelammert, *A crítica da razão utópica* (São Paulo: Paulinas, 1988), 282.

[17] Franz J. Hinkelammert, "La vuelta del sujeto humano reprimido frente a la estrategia de globalización," italics added. Available online. For a wider reflection about the theme, see Jung Mo Sung, "Sujeito como instrumentalidade ao interior da vida real," in *Sujeito e sociedades complexas*, ed. Jung Mo Sung (Petrópolis: Vozes, 2002).

2.

From Liberation Theology to Indecent Theology

The Trouble with Normality in Theology

Marcella Althaus-Reid

A FEW YEARS AGO I found myself sharing breakfast in Germany with a small group of fellow Latin American theologians. My happiness could not have been more complete for they were not only *compatriotas*[1] whom I had the pleasure to meet in a foreign land, but they were also people who belonged to that group which could be called the pioneer generation of liberation theology, a term that for obvious (feminist) reasons I prefer to that of fathers of liberation theology. It happened that we were gathered at an international conference to discuss some of the current issues of theology of liberation and globalization. The Latin American atmosphere at that breakfast table was one of friendship. Interesting anecdotes and little-known insights from the hard years of the struggle of the militant church in Latin America were shared, from the unknown stories behind the scenes of the historical meetings at Medellín and Puebla to illuminating accounts concerning the everyday lives of the Latin American militant Christians at the time. Listening to these stories, shared with humor and insightfulness, it occurred to me that I was a privileged witness of a gathering of old theological *compañeros de lucha* (comrades in the struggle). Yes, as old comrades that generation of liberationists had and still has many things in common: a political pursuit of economic justice, resilience and courage, and a Christian vision of transformation of the structures of oppression in Latin America that inspired multitudes who came after them. Theology was not to remain the same after them, neither in Latin America nor throughout the world.

That breakfast conversation was for me a reminder of *where* theology of liberation comes from. It comes from a troubling of the Pax Romana of its time, similar to what Jesus did when he disturbed the peace of the Roman Empire, which had claimed the right to impose values and forms of life and oppression on Israel. But it also comes from something else that sometimes appraisals of liberation theology tend to forget. That is to say, Latin American liberation theology comes first of all from theological acts of disturbance that are also acts of collective love. Moreover, those acts of love are acts of a subverting, transgressive kind of love.

The fact is that the early work of the liberationists consisted of loving actions that troubled the imposed normality of the "Pax Romana" imposed in Latin America by the then-dictatorial regimes in the continent and the Reagan administration. That passion and compassion inspired by the gospel troubled deeply not only the established ways of thinking and relating values imposed by repressive systems, but also became part of an almost unique self-critical theological and historical exercise from the churches themselves.[2]

During that breakfast I was also able to remember the price that that generation paid for its acts of love. For instance, I have a collection of clippings from newspapers from the 1970s in Argentina that form a testimony to the denigration church leaders and liberation theologians suffered at the hands of the media at that time. Even book shops were forced to withdraw stocks of *La Biblia Latinoamericana* (The Latin American Bible, originally published in Chile) as that popular translation of the Bible emphasized with clarity the original links between social justice and the message of God. For Argentinean society during the years of the Cold War there was nothing "normal" about the gospel and liberation theology. The Latin American Bible was a book whose reading incited people openly to transgress the military-imposed legal ordering of society. We might even say that the Latin American Bible was considered an indecent book. Therefore, we may call those theologians denigrated by the media or the church at the hands of dictatorial regimes "non-normal" or indecent theologians. They were theologians who worked outside the definitions of normality laid down by the system. Were the Latin American Bible and those theologians indecent, then, or should we say that they were portrayed as indecent by the media? I would like to claim that it was both.[3] The Bible was indecent because it incited people to challenge the imposed decency of the normative values that regulated society at a time when state terrorism considered it normal to throw pregnant women out of airplanes into the river below or to send children to concentration camps. It was because of the cruelty of the political persecutions that the militant courage of many churches made many people tremble at the audacity of love inspired by the gospel. It was fear that inspired many moral condemnations of liberation theology. In that sense liberation theology was also very indecent. The dictatorial apparatuses of mass media represented the Latin American Bible as indecent in the sense of unfitting or immoral. To read the Latin American Bible was not for normal, law-abiding citizens subjected to the dictators of the times.

It is in this sense that I should like to assert the indecent past of liberation theology. It is a past that comes from a love story to be read against the grain, against regimes imposed, a paraphrasing of Ché Guevara's claim about the origins of authentic revolutions. That love was and still is a transgressive, passionate, prophetic commitment toward the dispossessed. The first love of the liberationists was for the gospel, but above all, for people and for those whose lives were held in the chains of political and economic oppression. It was a love of such magnitude that many ended by sacrificing their own lives for it. For the few names of famous theologians who are remembered and honored, and for the handful of names belonging to faithful servants and martyrs of the churches such as Archbishop Romero from El Salvador or Monseñor Angelelli from Argentina, there are thousands of anonymous Christians who paid a deadly price for their commitment. The cost was not necessarily in dying for Christ but frequently in being condemned to live in obscurity and unemployment, ridiculed by the media and marginalized at times by the institutional church. They were condemned to live in fear in order that others would one day enjoy a life free from fear.

The disturbing of normality in liberation theology needs to be considered as the foundation of a praxis by which we not only unveil the constructed normality of the processes of ideological formation in a theo-social reflection, but a praxis also by which we engage in a creative liberative theological work. This is a praxis which understands that God is always a category of the possible, that God is not God's own limit, and that the path of theology is not continuity but nonconformity.

LIBERATION AND ITS LIMITS

I must add that I have been a foreigner living in strange lands long enough to know when it is appropriate to remain silent and that a meeting with liberation theologians from the first generation tends (sadly) to be one of these occasions. In my case it is a kind of knowing silence, for I recognize well what the Finnish theologian Elina Vuola has called the "limits of liberation" in Latin American theology.[4] People who live in exile know that sometimes they need to remain silent because they feel that experiences conveyed in a different language and without their context do not necessarily make sense to others. Somehow there is a risk of trespassing the limits of the construction of normality or the common order of other people in different contexts. How do I translate to feminist European theologians a tango such as *La Pipistrella* from Tita Merello?[5] How can I convey the everyday memories of a church struggling for human rights at a time when, as Rev. José de Luca puts it, *lives* and not ideas were at risk?[6]

It is curious and sad that for reasons of indecency, that is, of love and subversion of the normality of authoritarian theological regimes, it has not been possible among liberationists to share what I call the memories of many "other Medellíns" and countless "other Vatican IIs." It would be good to be able to sit with old theological comrades to share other moments, stories of small meetings and humble initiatives that contributed to many major *aggiornamientos* of the "other" on our continent, struggles which still continue. For instance, how are we to share with them the memories of times when a liberation theologian minister, Rev. Roberto González, distributed homemade leaflets in the gay bars of Buenos Aires, inviting gay people for the first time to prayer meetings? These were days when the first pastoral strategies for the sexually marginalized were drawn up and the first demonstrations of human rights and sexuality were organized. In these ways liberation theology continued its path by actions which affirmed that the private was also political. Acts of love in theology are intrinsically related, and uncovering one ideological construct may lead us to another. Sexuality as an ideology has much to say to liberation theology, from the understanding of the hermeneutical circle to the implications of the option for the poor. As a hermeneutical circle it provides insights into social exclusion and what such exclusion does theologically in terms of alienating people from God. It also provides alternative praxes of liberation, because other ways of solidarity and of organizing that come from different ways of thinking are necessary for the so-called project of the kingdom, the project of the excluded. Moreover, a critique of heterosexuality as ideology may provide valid clues for the way forward for theology and for liberation in Latin America.

"INDECENTING": A HERMENEUTICAL CIRCLE

[The prophetic church] uses critical thinking and does not consider itself neutral nor does it hide its options. For that reason it neither divides the mundane from transcendence nor salvation from liberation. It knows that it is not a question of "I am," "I know," "I liberate myself" or "I save myself." Nor is it a question of "I give you knowledge," "I liberate you" or "I save you." On the contrary, [the prophetic church] is about actions such as "we are"; "we know"; "we liberate ourselves in community" and "we save our own communities."
—PAULO FREIRE, *LAS IGLESIAS, LA EDUCACIÓN Y EL PROCESO DE LIBERACIÓN HUMANA EN LA HISTORIA*

Some years ago, when Freire visited Scotland, I remember a brief but insightful theological remark he made concerning what could be considered a dialogical church. I mentioned to him the difficulties that some of the then-refugees had in integrating themselves into the local Scottish congregations. Freire's response was to elaborate on why churches did not accept people as they are. The churches were not dialogical. They worked with some assumptions that led them to behave more like "banking" churches than liberative ones. This contrasted with the example of a Pentecostal minister from Chile who used to welcome people from his poor rural congregation into the church to discuss the price of grain among themselves. The church can be a space for rightful economic exchanges or a space for justice in life as long there is dialogue and diversity. The vision of the humble church consisting of peasants talking about the harvest and comparing bags of grain while sitting in the pews says something about a non-dualistic understanding of the world and the sacred. Freire was concerned about the right of the community "to be" in the church, without any of the pretenses that sadly submerge people in an idealist Christianity that never challenges the systems of oppression.

For a peasant, to go to your church with a bag of grain is a metaphor about bringing your full identity in the presence of God and community. It is about unveiling a theology of resignation and its hidden agenda that support international trade agreements and un-fair prices for cereals. It is a prophetic act of denouncing hunger, and as such it is about a project of unmasking ideological programs dis-guised as theology. I deliberately use the term *indecenting* here in re-lation to the unmasking of ideologies. *Indecenting* is a term that re-minds us that liberation theology's first act of love was that of troubling the status quo, and that it was part of a provocative and heavily contested transgressive discourse. It also reminds us that some of the evident domestication of liberation theology may be due to the fact that over time liberationists tended to become "decent" (approved by authoritative systems). Capitalist ideologies tend to adapt or inte-grate critiques into their systems in order to neutralize them, and lib-eration theology has not been an exception to this rule. Theology, in times of a market economy, is also a product.[7]

In liberation theology "indecenting" was part of the style of shar-ing stories that was much more than simple bonding sessions for com-munity development. Sharing stories in community made liberation theology credible; stories provide theology with its credo as shared faith (or *confianza*), the memory of Christian belief. It has been a shar-ing linked to common memories, that is, memories of other people's struggles. Somehow we all need to become witnesses and to partici-pate in the act of giving testimony, of sharing our experiences of pain and joy. It is this act of giving testimony in community that makes the sharing of experiences (such as exclusion) not only translatable but also gives them the quality of salvific events. Experiences shared in community are meant to be more than an informative exercise; they are part of self-affirming processes, almost hermeneutical in the way that they search for the meaning of personal suffering in com-munity. In the process of sharing stories we reach for the "other" and we enrich the struggle for liberation by becoming witnesses of the suffering of the "other." Solidarity grows from these indecent encoun-ters, for the "other" is always marginal. However, there are stories of suffering that liberation theology has been reluctant to hear. By si-lencing those who do not fit the theological definition of the poor in liberation theology, we have not only broken communion but have deprived popular theology of the valid knowledge that liberationists wanted to seek in the first place, the knowledge of the "other," the only one who can challenge structures of oppression while at the same time providing alternatives.

It happens that I belong to a community traditionally made into foreigners by liberation theology. This category of otherness arises from gender and sexuality and keeps multitudes of fellow Latin

Americans, Christians and non-Christians, in exclusion and suffering. Liberation theology has not heard their stories, and many theologians have lost the opportunity of becoming witnesses in the story-sharing of multitudes. I am referring here to the multitudes of people, Christian and non-Christian, hidden in the closets of militant churches and faith communities or in the struggle of everyday life. It is sad to say that in the lands of liberation theology there is for many a continuous experience of exile from brothers and sisters, alienated from bad ecclesiologies and even from God—not by God but by even worse theology. In the twenty-first century liberation theology still cannot come to terms with simple issues such as gender roles in the church or women's theological education. It cannot find a way of incorporating so-called women issues into mainstream theology as opposed to the occasional contribution from a "woman theologian." What can we say then about sexuality? There is a fractured collegiality when fellow comrades know that they cannot speak. There is a process that turns upside down the strategy of sitting at the table with others, that very place where we should experience Jesus' befriending strategies of love, when a fellow theologian cannot introduce a lover to comrades in the struggle.

The problem is one of limits, and the limits of liberation theology are a result of ideology. The sophisticated analysis of class ideologies has produced a hermeneutical circle of suspicion that no doubt has had such an impact that theology has never been able to be the same again. However, the ideological construction of gender and sexuality in Latin America has been considered normal and normative. The trouble with normality in Latin America is that it has been constructed by centuries of ideological alliances forged in the history of exploitation of our continent. When Gramsci spoke of the strategy of common sense within ideologies, he referred to the way that we take normativity for granted in our societies. In theology we do not question what we consider to be normal, for instance, issues of gender organization and sexual identity. Thirty years ago feminist theology started to denounce the pervasiveness of patriarchalism in Christian theology, not only related to the behavioral expectations of women and men in church life but deeper than that, in the doctrinal consequences of (mainly Western and white) gender thinking. Mariology in Latin America, for instance, is close to *Marianismo*, which can be considered the gendered foundation for Latin American churches and societies. What Gramsci then called an ideology of common sense, I call decency. The dialectics of decency and indecency in Latin America is a complex set of rules and regulations that organizes the lives of men and women according to behavioral expectations but also ways of understanding community. When Gustavo Gutiérrez wrote his theology for the "man-cactus" *(hombre cactus)*, he was referring to the desire to make the subject of theology the "underdogs" of history, that is to say, the reified subject of classical theology. This reification process, denounced by Marx in capitalism (literally, making of people "things"), rendered human beings as passive objects of ideological discourses. Theology has also proceeded in this way. But liberation theology has not questioned the historical construction of sexual normality in Latin America. Concretely, heterosexuality is also an ideological construction that reifies people in even more profound ways than class. At least we can say that heterosexuality as an ideology is not politically innocent or economically naive.[8] Its way of conceiving and organizing both families and societies has ramifications for larger issues such as the destruction of the environment and the colonial/neocolonial way of understanding life through expansion, destruction, profit, and exploitation. In fact, to begin to understand how heterosexually based theologies work, one needs to understand first the history of colonialism and its strategies of the marginalization of otherness, which make the colonial normality normative, desirable, and sacralized. Indecenting as a hermeneutical circle is in a way a call to deviancy from centers of knowledge and faith to the margins, without returning to the center. It is an attempt to claim the marginal knowledge of God as a foundation for an alternative theological praxis of liberation.

INDECENT THEOLOGY

It is well known that theological projects are, by definition, communitarian projects. Indecent theology is no exception. Indecent theology is a path from liberation theology, that is, the continuation of the *caminata* (walk) undertaken by people who bring together an option for the poor and an option for the right to come out of the closet imposed by heterosexual thinking in theology. Moreover, the option for the poor is in itself an option for a coming out, in the sense that cultures of poverty and a Christianity from the poor claim recognition for what they are, not mere adaptations of some central theological model. The name indecent theology came from a desire to subvert the axis of decency/indecency that in Latin America is built around a complex web of class, race, gender, and sexuality. It is a recognition that normality in Latin America is sexually constructed, and that the spaces of the proper and the improper are more than fashion and display. They are symbolic spaces in which the public and the private areas of life are negotiated. Christian theology has a lot to say about the construction of these identities, which results in the organization of values, political strategies, and the possibility (or not) of alternatives for transforming the everyday life horizon that has been sacralized (approved by God). When indecent theology attempts to demystify the foundational sexual ideology behind liberation theology, one of the objectives is to expose, for instance, the connections in Latin America among poverty, illiteracy among women, and Mariology. Or among *machismo*, church hierarchical systems, and systems of authoritarianism. The point is that only by understanding the extent of the influence of heterosexuality as an ideology can we begin to address the injustice in our midst, oppressive elements to be found in theology that should not go uncontested.

However, indecent theology is much more than a gay/lesbian/bisexual Latin American theology in the sense that it goes beyond claiming the right of gays and lesbians to be respected and nurtured in a Christian community. That is in itself a crucial element of any liberation theology that understands that the core of social justice and what has been called the principle of the dignity of life are not negotiable elements in Christian theology. But to use an example taken from feminist theologies, just as the issue of women in the church goes far beyond women's ordination or the use of inclusive language in the church, indecent theology goes beyond the act of accepting gay Christians in worship. The mere dynamic of accepting or of being tolerant of others implies that there is a central ideological definition of what is right, in this case a sexual normality that cannot be challenged. The fact is that any discourse of acceptance in theology betrays hegemony. To accept or to adopt are gestures of incorporation, but not of welcoming the different. The agenda of indecent theology is not the incorporation of non-heterosexual lives into heterosexual ideologies. We must pursue a revolutionary, not a neoliberal agenda. Indecent theology is concerned with sexual modes of thinking, or sexual epistemologies and how they understand critical reality.

To use a concept from the Argentinean social psychologist Pichón Riviere, the passion of the early liberationists was somehow indecent because it was focused in the "emergent discourses" of their time in order to identify those discourses that unveiled fractures in our ideological (and theological) universes.[9] In other words, during the 1970s these were the discourses that kept pointing us in directions where a given normality was contested. For instance, the normality created by dictatorial regimes went beyond the justification of a neoliberal economy. It extended to norms concerning the family and the gender distribution of roles in society. It went so far as the prescription of the exquisite details of punishing with jail sentences the use of clothes that were considered not proper; indecency could be measured by the length of a man's hairstyle. The first wave of liberationists pioneered a theological praxis based on that emergent discourse. Its questionings and alternatives made liberation theology what it was— and is. The normality of dictatorial regimes and the politics of hunger and persecution were confronted. It is tempting to see this as a generational thing, that new emergent discourses are produced by different generations according to the challenges of their times. But that is not the case here. Issues of class, race, and sexuality have coexisted in a complex web of oppression in Latin America for many centuries. They have been reinforced, or in some cases re-created, by theology. The problem has been the disconnection between the emergent discourses; they did not talk to one another, and the connections that could have informed a real and alternative praxis of transformation were not made. Without denying the foundational validity of the Latin American theology of liberation, it seems that its praxis has the same relation to postcolonial and sexual theologies that trade unions now have to the new social movements that inform Porto Alegre and the carnival against capitalism. Or the distance between *Subcomandante* Marcos of the Zapatistas and the urban guerrillas of the 1970s. Indecent theology is part of the walk of liberation theology toward the margins of heterosexuality. Therefore, it reflects on the spiritual praxis presented in, for instance, the experiences of transvestites struggling to organize themselves in cooperatives, or the meaning of loving friendship among lesbians. It reflects critically on all the suppressed forms of loving relationships in our communities and considers what, theologically speaking, we have to learn from them. It is a humbling exercise for a Christianity heavily compromised by heterosexuality and a bold gesture of liberating God from current ideological sexual masks.

WITH WHOM DO WE DO THEOLOGY? QUESTIONING THE POOR

To be lesbian or gay presupposes . . . the option for a lifestyle, but in El Salvador just to be able to live with dignity is a privilege. In El Salvador we are merely surviving, only at a physical level, and not yet at the level of human rights.[10]

What, then, went wrong? Why were the connections not made among emergent, marginalized discourses? Indeed, in cases such as sexuality and gender, why were they actually prevented in liberation theology? That is the claim of the Salvadorean who wrote the lines quoted above during the war in that country. Anyone could become a guerrilla, but how about a *gay* guerrilla? During the war, gays and lesbians added new closets to the existing closets. Similarly, a gay liberation theologian, a minister or member of a militant church, can take part in a public demonstration claiming human rights but cannot claim his or her sexual human rights. The problem may be related to some aspects of the modernist paradigm of theology of liberation and its construction of the subject. That is, with whom are we doing theology? How do we define the poor? How do we identify the desires of the poor? What constitutes a liberationist? I am claiming that part of the problem lies in the fact that liberation theology was conceived from a modern paradigm. First of all, liberation theology carried a nostalgia for the past. It was a past with a memory and a self-critical reflection. It acknowledged that the church has supported oppressive regimes throughout the continent, while at the same time highlighting also the historical presence of prophetic voices of resistance. It was a subversive, liberative memory located in a mixture of mythical (biblical) and historical moments with a clear nostalgia for power. For instance, Las Casas received and no doubt deserved a place of privilege as the prototype of the influential priest who stood against the institutional church during the *conquista* of America. The Jesuit missions received similar treatment as an example of the counter-power inside the church, mobilized to defend and protect the poor and marginalized. However, present in all these events and in their interpretation as part of a liberation theology for the twentieth century is a narrative of church power. This power is counteracted or opposed or negotiated, but nevertheless it is firmly located in the subject as constructed from the narratives of the church. This also depends on the subject location within the structure of the church. As I have argued elsewhere, the liberative memory of liberation theology was built on dependency. Unless the negotiator of liberation (understood here as a priest and/or theologian positioned in the church) agreed with the terms of liberation, the real subjects of liberation, namely, the poor and marginalized, can do very little. The problem is that the nostalgia for the past in liberation theology is a colonial nostalgia in the sense that it is built around a centrally defined knower, negotiator, and authoritative pattern, which unfortunately do not recognize emergent discourses but construct the subject according to nostalgia. And for the colonizers, nostalgia is build around the sentimental appeal of normality, where issues of sexuality and gender do not appear because those discourses have already been subsumed under a category of redemption. The fact is that sexuality in the church is an object of redemption and not of dialogue.

This takes us to the category of "the poor." It was a discourse loosely developed around a patriarchal identity, heavily influenced by Paulo Freire's "poor but polite" student peasants, with a strategy roughly sketching the world of a socialist proletariat. For instance, many distinguished liberationists engaged themselves in giving workshops and writing pieces for discussion among urban factory workers. These inbuilt processes of conscientization in liberation theology came from a mixture of old narratives of the left, stories from the worker-priests movement, and men in their factories and women struggling to feed their families. These were straight stories in more than one sense; they were direct and simple narratives of the construction of poverty and normality under the Christian ethos of Roman Catholicism in Latin America. What was forgotten was Enrique Dussel's claim that the poor are a dialectical category.[11] However, dialectical categories are not given but built. Liberation theology made the category of the poor a straight category in more than one sense, because it assumed a dual universe of rigid identities between poor men and poor women without introducing any "hermeneutical suspicion" in its general sexual assumptions. Additionally, these assumptions were not the product of empirical knowledge but of decades of prejudices—European prejudices. Like all straight narratives relying on dualist universes for support, they were also false and relied curiously on power.

There was no black or indigenous consciousness in liberation theology because there were no blacks or indigenous people in the structures of power. For the same reason there were no discourses of women or gays. Liberation theology had built a concept of the poor within parameters taken from a strictly defined site of authority—as moral discourses tend to do. There was a vast and rich tradition of sexualities and intriguing relationships between local peasant economies and pre-Christian approved forms of love, but this was not explored. The conservativism of liberation theology was in evidence. It was forgotten that a theology rooted in people's experiences needs to take into account changes in these experiences and in the ways of analyzing and reflecting on them.[12]

Graham Ward has said that Karl Barth (a theologian of vast influence on the first wave of liberation theology) introduced theological categories such as crisis (as judgment) in order to confront the secular world.[13] Liberation theologians did not confront secular structures of oppression but structures permeated by religion. However, they too introduced a similar crisis technique by using categories such as prophetic, the kingdom of God, and justice. But as Ward reminds us, there is a tendency in the system to absorb criticism, or to create mechanisms of adaptation that devalue concepts, words, and strategies of change, or at least remove from them any revolutionary tendency. In order to find real alternatives for change, liberation theology needed to go a step beyond universal tendencies, beyond dualism, beyond normality. Too much faith in modernism and too little risk or self-criticism can be fatal for any theology that advocates serious acts of transformation. As Alistair Kee says, "We might adapt Marx to read as follows: Liberation Theology has only interpreted the world of the poor in various ways, the point is to change it."[14]

Theology is and always has been a sexual reflection, from stories of creation that are symbolic discourses of the patriarchal appropriation of birth, to narratives of the love story between God and a young girl in Palestine and their son. As an ideology, sexuality, and specifically heterosexuality, has had centuries of rendering life and especially religious life meaningful. That is to say, heterosexuality gives us an ideological structure through which we perceive phenomena and render them meaningful. Sexual understandings that come from the limited consciousness of stories from the Bible, mixed with centuries of making links among identity, biology, and power, are as much part of theology as anything else. Our faith comes with a sexual frame of thought that gives meaning to life and to God in our life by understanding destruction, justifying crime, or making reproduction a necessary virtue. By moving from the phenomenological to a more poststructuralist approach, gender itself loses its importance, because it is the positioning of (hetero)sexuality as an ideology that allows us to understand as we understand and to believe as we believe. Social stratification and gender stratification are related, as the destruction of nature is related to the oppression of women and femininity and colonial processes. Indecent theology is also, then, a postcolonial critique on the subject of liberation theology as colonially constructed.

The tragedy is that liberation theology has not taken seriously the rich traditions of the sexually different in Latin American. We are no strangers to bisexual gods, as in Peru, or to different amatory traditions between men and women.[15] Latin American popular traditional festivities, such as *Las Locainas* (the mad festivities) in Venezuela, are examples of the need and skill of the poor to destabilize ritually class and sexuality during their early carnivals. For instance, in *Las Locainas* some men became cross dressers while others traditionally dressed as priests. The whole community engaged in acts of defiance of a gendered and sacred order. These acts included ceremonies of mocking marriages between cross dressers and the whipping of priests.[16] We have in Latin America enough cultural and religious resources from the poor to enable us to reflect theologically, drinking, as Gutiérrez would say, from our own wells, including sexual wells. Not only that, but drinking from the wells of people's narratives of rebelliousness and troubling of the normality of church, theology, and society alike.

It can be argued that Christian base communities (CBCs) owe their success not to the strength of the liberation theological argument, but to the fact that Latin Americans have a power/knowledge manifested in ways of relating, befriending, and loving one another, of being community. Latin Americans have a communitarian spirit that flourished marvelously in the CBCs and enriched the church. CBCs were a gift of the poor to the church, not vice versa. What might have happened if, instead of the church reinforcing the usual elements of domestication by gender and sexual ideologies, theology had been able to take on board the more liberative experiences of the poor and disposed? Instead of that, the church reinforced the dualistic, authoritarian, patriarchal patterns from which the poor suffer in Latin America as much as anyone else. One way for liberation theology to have proceeded would have been to dismantle the process found in the church of conferring theological legitimacy on patriarchal ideology. That is, it could have recognized that when injustice, hunger, and violence are normal, the voices of transformation come from those rendered "abnormal" by the system. To be abnormal (or indecent) in this way is a human right. For instance, in the expansion of capitalism through globalization, to refuse to partake of a consumerist identity is abnormal. To claim the right to love and befriend people outside the metaphysics of the market, that is, outside a pattern of profit or advantages, may be more than abnormal. In the market, solidarity is an indecent value.

What if we were to say now that liberation theology needs to reclaim the right of not being normal? To understand the implications, let us reflect further on solidarity. Solidarity has been a very important value among liberationists, but unfortunately it has been built around notions of "homosolidarity," that is, the solidarity that links men to themselves and their own projects while excluding or at most merely "integrating" women and sexual dissenters into their ideas. That takes us back to my breakfast with liberationists in Germany, because there that homosolidarity was present and it was powerful. Homosolidarity is not a negative concept, but it is an exclusive one. Liberation theology had homosolidarity with women, but obviously with restrictions. First, they needed to be women as the concept is understood, essentialized, and universalized in the church. For instance, women's identity revolved around their biology as virgins or mothers outside any cultural and political experiences. Second, this exercise of homosolidarity was premeditated, in the sense of not negotiable. As in the case of an International Monetary Fund adjustment plan, solidarity with women in liberation theology comes from above. That process enforces patriarchalism in theology and society while breaking women's collective power. Women struggling in the crisis of their communities tend to be subsumed into the "bigger picture," into the "important struggle," which dismisses their particular concerns as marginal. In reality, these concerns bear on the core of patriarchal power and are able to offer alternatives in the struggle. The leadership of women in CBCs proved precisely this point: women are able to provide alternative ways of thinking, relating, and finding strategies in the struggle against oppression. That is not to say that women always know best, but they do know *differently*. It is not that a gay can have *better* friendships, but there is a pattern of gay/lesbian friendship that has a lot to teach heterosexual people whose lives are ordered by that medieval economic organization called marriage.[17]

STRANGERS AT THE GATE

Can we then speak of feminist liberation theologies or lesbigay/ bisexual liberation theologies (or transvestites, or transsexual . . .) as such? I should like to say that when I was reflecting with my community of struggle, which is known as indecent theology, we realized that we were moving beyond a feminist liberation or a lesbigay/bisexual theology in the classical sense of these concepts. What we are doing is attempting to find a strategy of solidarity in diversity that is wider than the men/women heterosexual construction of life, one that is inclusive of diverse sexualities. What we are doing is opening the doors to the strangers at the gate of theology of liberation. Feminist liberation theologies are very critical of essentialisms, but they still tend to assume the normativity of the heterosexual experience or the discourse of such experience, for both are different things. Heterosexuality is not a coherent, solid discourse but an ideology that does not reflect real lives, not even among non-heterosexual people.

These unwelcome guests are the "others" who are different because they do not follow the path of heterosexual ideology and are therefore perverted subjects, or have taken "another version" or another route for their journey.[18] This per/verted journey in theology also takes us to alternative, different understandings and hermeneutical approaches not only to the scriptures but also to the themes of our systematized theology: faith, redemption, grace, Christology, the meaning of the Cross. This is the subject of indecent theology, but it should also be the subject of any liberation theology that is still searching for the face of God in the "other," an unfamiliar, strange face that should take something from the identities of the rejected in history. Instead of homosolidarity we are now in the presence of the solidarity of the strangers at the gate of theology. This is what I have called elsewhere the communion with the failures (*fracasados*) of the scriptural stories, the marginalized who have received the solidarity neither of acceptance nor of belonging.[19]

Therefore, we are talking here of more than a women's theology or a gay or lesbian theology or a theology from the poor. We are talking about the diversity that exists in sexual identity, refusing to reduce an experience of, for instance, bisexuality or transvestism to the realm of the private, to the realm of the politically or theologically irrelevant. On the contrary, our claim is that by subverting liberation theology's uncritical (hetero)sexual ideology and thus allowing the silenced praxis of "love/knowing" to come forward and be considered critically, we liberate our praxis from forms of oppression "normalized" by patriarchal heterosexuality. We are able to engage in transformative practices which lead us toward strategies of peace and justice, liberating God at the same time. For in theology God has also become a prisoner of heterosexual ideologies. How can all this be achieved?

CLUES FOR INDECENT PRACTICES IN THEOLOGY

The following are just a few clues for a theological practice that may be able to disentangle the web of ideological oppression constructed around sexuality and economics.

1. Acknowledging the edges of the construction of the theological subject. The ideological limitations and strategies of power to domesticate or delegitimize those who do not partake of heterosexual ideology. By heterosexual ideology we mean much more

than a form of relations between men and women. We mean a construction of identities as if they were fixed, delimited, without ambiguities or changes. As if people were born with given sexual identities instead of societies constructing them. By heterosexual ideology we also mean the way in which these dualist and fixed identities are then given value, restricted agencies (in association with gender roles, for instance), and established in a framework of power dynamics. Sexual identities are not just constructed in the lives of individuals, though, but they are institutionalized. They function as a way of life, of thinking, hoping, desiring, and basically acting.

2. Acknowledging the relation between sexual ideologies and class and race ideologies; that is, seeing the relationships between poverty and sexuality. Stories of, for instance, transvestite collectives in Buenos Aires organizing themselves for economic survival but also for human rights issues carry with them a spirituality of liberation that is untamed, genuine, and effective.

3. Learning to engage in a theology of story, where people can "come out" as they are. This would give a different meaning to communion, because communion cannot happen among colonial subjects but only among friends.

4. Reading the Bible and our church traditions sexually. This implies asking new questions or organizing a different hermeneutical circle that might ask, for instance, about the relationship between the ethics of profit and the heterosexual understanding of a woman's reproductive identity. Exploring the sexual "unmaskings" in the scriptures requires the same suspicious attitude as understanding the Bible in terms of relationships of production.

5. Finally, exploring themes of God and sexuality beyond heterosexual metaphors. We have already denounced the "God-King" of the *conquistadores* and the "God the Father" of colonial processes, which tended to render their conquered nations as minors, thus encouraging parental metaphors for their relationships (such as mother churches). We now need to denounce the heterosexual God embedded in dualistic values, narrow understandings of human relationships, and faulty perceptions of worlds divided between the center and the periphery.

In the end, this liberation of God and God's people has been the core of liberation theologies. For that reason I claim that indecenting theology is not a novelty but is the obvious path forward in the process initiated many years ago when the church in Latin America was confronted with injustice and violence. The fact that liberation theology never produced a sexual ethics speaks of the limitation of a project of liberation in a continent where the poorest of the poor are women and where non-heterosexuals have their human and political rights limited by their love life. A sexual ethics is necessary, not just to restore the dignity and joy in the lives of many brothers and sisters, but also to examine the value system of the church and to acknowledge with honesty the sexual roots of theological thought. For although dualist thinking in Christianity has divided the world from the spiritual realm, liberationists know better. And they know that it is in the world that we encounter the presence of God. And it is Christ's spirit who moves through history. Unveiling sexuality as an ideology within theology helps us to remain more faithful to our faith not only as a negative exercise of denouncing theological manipulations, but also by rediscovering the presence of God and God's wisdom in the communities of those outside heterosexual ideologies.

NOTES

[1] *Compatriota* is the Spanish word for a co-national, in this case a co-national of the "bigger nation" *(patria grande)* of the Latin American continent.

[2] For elements concerning the self-criticism of the churches and the changes, even structurally, that this produced, see, for instance, Pablo Andiñach and Daniel Bruno, *Iglesias Evangélicas y Derechos Humanos en la Argentina 1976–1998* (Buenos Aires: La Aurora, 2001).

[3] In a recent conversation that I had with Professor Jaci Maraschin from the Methodist University of São Paulo, Brazil, he made the following point: "Can any theology be anything but 'indecent' [in the sense of transgressive or challenging]"? Paulo Freire once reflected on the term *education for liberation*, saying that if education was not for liberation, then it could not be called education. For Maraschin, the same can be said about theology. Unless theology transgresses the limits of ideology, it cannot be called theology.

[4] Elina Vuola, *Limits of Liberation: Praxis as Method in Latin American Liberation Theology and Feminist Theology* (Helsinski: Suomalainen Tiedeakatemia, 1997).

[5] *La Pipistrella* is a tango that tells ironically the story of a poor young woman from Buenos Aires who is a prostitute. Yet, for an Argentinean Christian that tango can evoke many things: the socioeconomic and historical context of its time and the culture of surviving that empowered many poor women in Buenos Aires.

⁶ Andiñach and Bruno, *Iglesias Evangélicas y Derechos Humanos en Argentina 1976–1998*, 141.

⁷ For a discussion on this point, see Marcella Althaus-Reid, *Indecent Theology* (London: Routledge, 2001), 27–33.

⁸ I use the concept of heterosexuality as an ideology rather than patriarchalism. Patriarchalism is not necessarily confined to contexts of compulsory heterosexuality. It can be present also within gay cultures.

⁹ For this concept, see Pichón Riviere, *Del Psicoanálisis a la Psicología Social* (Buenos Aires: Galerna, 1971).

¹⁰ *Planeta Marica: Periódico mensual de sátira maripolitica*, February 8, 1998, 2. Available online (in Spanish only).

¹¹ See Enrique Dussel, *Ethics and Community* (Maryknoll, NY: Orbis Books, 1988).

¹² Alistair Kee, "The Conservatism of Liberation Theology: Four Questions for Jon Sobrino," *Political Theology* 3 (2000): 37.

¹³ Graham Ward, "Introduction: Where We Stand," in *The Blackwell Companion to Postmodern Theology*, ed. Graham Ward (Oxford: Blackwell, 2001), xvi.

¹⁴ Kee, "The Conservatism of Liberation Theology," 34.

¹⁵ I have developed this point in the analysis of a "bisexual town" in Peru (see Marcella Althaus-Reid, *The Queer God* [London: Routledge, 2003]).

¹⁶ For an analysis on the festivity of the *locainas,* see Yolanda Salas de Lecuna, "La Inversión de lo Simbólica de lo Sagrado y lo Secular en las Locainas," *Montalban* 16 (1985): 47–70.

¹⁷ Cf., for instance, Elizabeth Stuart, *Just Good Friends* (London: Mowbray, 1985).

¹⁸ Per/version is a concept that I use in relation to the hermeneutical option that liberation theology advocates. *Pervertere* is a Latin word that means "to turn the wrong way" (from *per-*, "deviation," and *vertere*, "to turn"). Radical interpretations from orthopraxis usually challenge the orthodoxy (right dogma) of Western theologies. Therefore, they proudly can be called per/verted interpretations, and per/verted theologies, too.

¹⁹ See Althaus-Reid, *The Queer God.*

3.

Liberation Theology and the Search for the Lost Paradigm

From Radical Orthodoxy to Radical Diversality

Nelson Maldonado-Torres

LATIN AMERICAN LIBERATION THEOLOGY was born in the midst of social and political upheavals in many regions of Latin America during the decade of the 1960s. For Latin American Catholics this situation provided the context in which to apply the maxims of the Second Vatican Council in the region. Protestants in the United States and Latin America responded to the difficult times by creating a theological discourse that more directly addressed the situation of the many peoples under regimes of fear and death at the time. It was in this context that Latin American theologians boldly decided to highlight the relevance of praxis in the Christian faith and to take hold of the social sciences in order to diagnose and criticize the sinful institutional structures of domination. They opposed the preeminence of orthodoxy in Christianity by articulating a counter-discourse based on the relevance of orthopraxis. Correct action, and not purely correct belief, defined the horizon of the new theological, institutional, and spiritual practice.

Latin American liberation theology achieved no less than a paradigm shift in theology. Gustavo Gutiérrez's articulation of critical reflection on praxis and the development of the idea of the preferential option for the oppressed changed the face of theological method and inspired theologians and religious thinkers throughout the globe to give expression to the radical political insights in their religious views.

Particularly innovative in Latin American liberation theology was the way in which theology was brought together with social-science discourse. Whereas much of traditional theology had been constructed with philosophy at its side, liberation theology focused its attention on the social sciences. The reason for this is clear; the emergence of the Latin American social sciences, particularly dependency theory, helped liberation theologians to interpret poverty and injustice in the region as sinful, and not only as the natural or temporary outcome of modernization. The social sciences thus helped to demystify modernization theory and provided an optic through which Christian theology could more intelligently diagnose and criticize problematic economic and political structures.

Since liberation theology's emergence in the late 1960s, Latin American liberation theologians have refined their discourse and have inspired biblicists and religious leaders to either ground or give concrete expression to the Christian imperative of social critique and loving praxis. Today, however, many question the relevance of liberation theology. They seem to think that it was not only a contextual theology (only workable for Latin America or parts of the Third World) but also a theology with only a temporary significance. It could be said that since the 1970s the world has entered a period of readjustment. In the last thirty years the prospects of revolutionary action have been eroded along with the credibility of dependency theory. Liberation theologians have tried to remain faithful to the paradigm shift that they initiated by continuing to reflect on the links between theology and the social sciences. They have tried either to revive dependency theory or to use economics in combination with discourse analysis that investigates critically the founding myths of the West. Yet there has not been much reflection about the ways in which the very idea of addressing liberation through a combination of theology and the social sciences represents a problem by itself—not because it is too liberating but because it may not be liberating enough.

I will explore in this essay two critical approaches to liberation theology. The two are critical of liberation theology's relation with the social sciences. But while one goes in the direction of radical orthodoxy, the other pushes liberation theology toward "radical diversality."[1] I first focus on two neo-orthodox proposals that undercut liberation theology's mode of critique and dialogical tendencies: John Milbank's theology and Slavoj Žižek's Lacanian Hegelian Marxism. I critically examine Milbank's account of liberation theology and point to connections of his orthodox turn to other such turns in the contemporary intellectual arena. It is in this context that I analyze

Žižek's work on politics, psychoanalysis, and religion. I argue that Milbank and Žižek's intellectual efforts undo liberation theology's relative achievements in theology, politics, and social theory by reintroducing an unbearable form of Eurocentrism that disguises identity politics in a project of universalized provincialism. Liberation theology's achievements, however, appear quite limited and problematic when looked at from the perspective of women and peoples of color in the Americas. While liberation theologians have invested much time trying to communicate with Marxists and other secular activists and political thinkers, they have not invested the same time trying to forge links with peoples with non-European cosmologies. The very identification with *Latin* America points to the ideological marginalization of people with non-Latin cultures in the region. Intellectual production that highlights the complex character of colonial, racial, and gender differences reveals a problematic face in liberation theology's epistemological breakthrough. The turn from orthodoxy to orthopraxis appears limited in the context of demands for radical diversality. Radical diversality appears as an epistemological move that can more effectively mobilize liberation theology against the new orthodoxies of our time. It also promises to help liberation theology move beyond the epistemological impasse that it now faces.

LIBERATION THEOLOGY AND RADICAL ORTHODOXY

The project of radical orthodoxy was officially launched in 1999 with the publication of a collection of essays entitled *Radical Orthodoxy: A New Theology*.[2] This call for orthodoxy occurs at a point in which secular discourse demonstrates its own failures to sustain meaning in the modern world. While many secular ideologues for a long time represented secularism as the overcoming of Christianity, radical orthodoxy makes a shift in perspective by arguing that after the secular adventures have been all tested, Christianity is, as it were, waiting for them at the end. Radical orthodoxy is Christianity coming back with a vengeance: "In the face of the secular demise of truth, it seeks to reconfigure theological truth." It regards the "nihilistic drift of postmodernism" as a "supreme opportunity" to reconstruct privileged topics of secular interest according to an uncompromising Christian theological framework.[3]

Radical orthodoxy is orthodox in its "commitment to creedal Christianity and the exemplarity of its patristic matrix" as well as "in the more specific sense of reaffirming a richer and more coherent Christianity."[4] Like liberation theology, radical orthodoxy includes theologians of both Catholic and Protestant confessions. The main goal of the project is to recover and extend "a fully Christianized ontology and practical philosophy consonant with authentic Christian doctrine."[5] The concept of radicality reaffirms this orthodox trend; *radical* means primarily a return to the patristic and medieval *roots*. But radical also means the deployment of this orthodox vision to the critical inquiry of society. Here radical orthodoxy finds itself aligned again with liberation theology. However, in contrast to liberation theologians, radical-orthodox theologians attempt to find the sources and criteria of critique not in the social sciences but in the Christian tradition itself. This does not mean that they uncritically accept the whole of the Christian tradition. They just believe that the orthodox core of Christianity provides the necessary elements to criticize both society and also the weaker dimensions or expressions of Christian dogma.

Although radical-orthodox theologians have different confessions, they all share a theology of "participation." The theological idea of participation "refuses any reserve of created territory, while allowing finite things their own integrity."[6] This means that however the condition of being in the world is defined, for radical-orthodox theologians it can only be preserved in its integrity by appealing to permanent standards or metaphysical stability. Without reference to such eternal stability one ends up with the *aporias* of modernist epistemological humanism or postmodern ontological nihilism. Instead of the violent liberal subject or the negative theology of postmoderns, radical orthodoxy seeks to offer the one and only perspective that avoids nihilism and thus maintains the integrity of finite reality. The wider project of radical orthodoxy consists in reconstructing theories and re-envisaging particular cultural spheres from its orthodox and participatory theological perspective. The project is highly ambitious; its declared adherents aim to frame every discipline from a theological perspective. Otherwise, for them, such disciplines will be grounded in nothing. Participation thus provides the ground for a critical engagement with secularism and the social sciences. Such a critique is strongly articulated by the leading representative of radical orthodoxy, John Milbank.

The radical rejection of the social sciences as an instrument of critique appears in John Milbank's eloquent and ambitious book *Theology and Social Theory*.[7] *Theology and Social Theory* is a tour de force against the predominance of secular reason in the modern world. It argues that scientific theories of society are no more legitimate than the Christian orthodoxy they oppose and claim to overcome. For Milbank, the problem with social science is that it replaced rather than properly overcame theology—which for Milbank would be simply impossible. The social sciences are theologies or anti-theologies in disguise.[8] These secular theologies are highly problematic because they are complicit and help to legitimate a perverse ontology of violence. This ontology is predicated on a conception of the self as an irremediably interested entity whose only business is self-preservation. Milbank believes that this ontology of violence is at the heart of the very definition of the secular as a separate and distinct sphere. The social sciences in some sense provide the rationality of secularity and thus reduplicate the presuppositions of such a problematic order. But in truth, Milbank argues, they are no more justifiable than the Christian theologies that they seek to replace.

Theology and Social Theory seeks to restore the role of theology as queen of the sciences. For Milbank, only Christian theology, *beyond secular reason*, can provide the parameters of social analysis and critique. Milbank's conclusion is simple and straightforward:

> Theology has frequently sought to borrow from elsewhere a fundamental account of society or history, and then to see what theological insights will cohere with it. But it has been shown that no such fundamental account, in the sense of something neutral, rational and universal, is really available. It is theology itself that will have to provide its own account of the final causes at work in human history, on the basis of its own particular, and historically specific faith.[9]

The allusion to "historically specific faith" makes clear that Milbank does not have in mind the assertion of old metaphysics. If Christian theology can at all pretend to become a social science it is only because Christian faith is itself eminently practical. As Milbank puts it, "There can only be a distinguishable Christian social theory because there is also a distinguishable Christian mode of action, a definite practice. The theory explicates this practice, which arose in certain precise historical circumstances, and exists only as a particular historical development."[10] It is the history of the practice of the Christian church that provides the basis and criteria to develop a particularly Christian critical theory of society. It is history, and not the social sciences, that, for Milbank, should serve as a beacon to Christian theology. Of all histories it is the history of the church that will provide the central elements for theology. In this sense Christian theology becomes for Milbank first and foremost *ecclesiology*. From here that theology acquires a peculiar role: "The task of such a theology is not apologetic, nor even argument. Rather it is to tell again the Christian *mythos*, pronounce again the Christian *logos*, and call again for Christian *praxis* in a manner that restores their freshness and originality."[11]

In liberation theology terms, the radical-orthodox turn defended by Milbank redefines orthodoxy in terms of ecclesial orthopraxis. Like liberation theology, radical orthodoxy accepts that one of the permanent tasks of theology is critical reflection on praxis. But it differs with liberation theology in that, for it, the methods and criteria of such critique are to be based solely on the praxis of the church and not on social science. For Milbank, the main problem with liberation theology resides in its indebtedness to Karl Rahner. Rahner proposed a version of "integralism" that "naturalizes the supernatural." For Milbank, the thrust of this form of integralism "is in the direction of a mediating theology, a universal humanism, a *rapprochement* with the Enlightenment and an autonomous secular order."[12] Milbank argues that liberation theology opted for this theological vision. In doing so liberation theology "remains trapped within the terms of 'secular reason,' and its unwarranted foundationalist presuppositions. Marxism is embraced as a discourse which supposedly discloses the 'essence' of human being and a 'fundamental' level of human historical becoming."[13] In this way, what for liberation theology appears as a paradigm shift in theology, for Milbank is no more than "another effort to reinterpret Christianity in terms of a dominant secular discourse of our day."[14]

While Milbank's critique of liberation theology and the social sciences may point to certain weaknesses in liberation theology's epistemological breakthrough, there are two obvious problems with Milbank's reading of liberation theology. First, his interpretation seems to presuppose that liberation theology is exclusively a Catholic phenomenon. He seems to ignore that the Latin American theologian who first articulated and partly developed liberation theology was a Protestant. It was Rubem Alves who first coined the concept in his dissertation at Princeton, *Toward a Theology of Liberation*, in 1968. James Cone, also a Protestant, proposed black theology of liberation before the Catholic Gustavo Gutiérrez published his *Teología de la liberación: perspectivas*.[15] Neither Rahner nor Marx counted as Cone's principal sources. Although these facts do not invalidate by themselves Milbank's critique, they point to the inadequacy of taking Rahner's theology of integrism or Marx's political economy or philosophy to criticize the theology of liberation as a whole.

Another problem with Milbank's reading is that he exaggerates the role that Marxism and the social sciences as a whole play in Latin American Catholic liberation theology. He does not consider, for instance, that for a group of Catholic Argentine theologians it was philosophy and Emmanuel Levinas rather than Marx or the social sciences who appear most centrally in their writings.[16] Indeed, theologians like Enrique Dussel openly criticized Marx and Marxism with Levinasian categories.[17] Since Levinas's philosophy is strongly tied to Judaism, it can perhaps be said that the mistake (if there was any) of these theologians was not to succumb to secular reason but to Judaic reason. Indeed, liberation theologians turned many times to the Hebrew scriptures to find examples of biblical categories of liberation. Accounts of creation and the Exodus as well as their interpretations in base communities form part of the kernel of liberation theology. Although these features of liberation theology can create problems of their own, they can hardly be explained by a collapse of theology into secular reason.

In an essay published just a year after Milbank published *Theology and Social Theory*, Enrique Dussel examined the links between liberation theology and Marxism.[18] In that essay Dussel argues that "theology originates in Christian praxis. For this reason we should search in the historical praxis of the relation between Christians and Marxists in Latin America the condition of possibility for the theoretical use of Marxism in Latin American liberation theology."[19] While Dussel points out that liberation theology's epistemological revolution consisted in for the first time using the critical social sciences in theology, it is clear that for him the absolute center of theology is the praxis of Christians and not the social sciences themselves.[20] Dussel approaches Milbank's own position; it is not only contemporary or revolutionary praxis but the *historical* praxis of Christians that he considers fundamental. One must take Dussel very seriously on this point. He alone was responsible for organizing a massive edition of the history of the church in Latin America and the Caribbean.[21] It may be true that liberation theology has not paid enough attention to the church fathers and theologians of the Middle Ages, but this does not mean that they have left the history of the church out of sight. They are just interested in another history, and it is from this history that reflection on the relation between theology and the social sciences makes sense. For liberation theologians, Bartolomé de Las Casas more than Aquinas represents an example of Christian stewardship and incessant critique. In part, then, the difference between Milbank and liberation theologians is that they are reflecting from a different history of the church. What appears in their work is thus not only the *theological* difference but also the *colonial* difference, which remains hidden for Milbank and for the project of radical orthodoxy.

Walter Mignolo defines colonial difference as

> the space where coloniality of power is enacted. It is also the space where the restitution of subaltern knowledge is taking place and where border thinking is emerging. The colonial difference is the space where *local* histories inventing and implementing global designs meet *local* histories, the space in which global designs have to be adapted, adopted, rejected, integrated, or ignored. The colonial difference is finally, the physical as well as the imaginary location where the coloniality of power is at work in the confrontation of two kinds of local histories displayed in different spaces across the planet.[22]

The theology of liberation asserts theological difference from the space of enunciation of the colonial difference. Liberation theology thus cannot be accounted for completely with reference to European theologies of integralism. The relation between theology and the social sciences in Latin America follows another route as well. As Dussel points out, it was not any kind of critical social theory or the whole body of the social sciences that interested liberation theologians. The social sciences that made the most impact in liberation theology were Latin American social sciences, which also gave expression to the colonial difference. It is thus arguably the colonial difference at work in the history of the Latin American church that leads liberation theologians to use the tools of the critical social sciences that begin to emerge in the space of enunciation marked by the colonial difference. Liberation theologians used the Latin American social sciences to clarify from a theological standpoint an operating logic in the history of the Latin American church. Instead of simply reinterpreting Christianity in terms of a dominant secular discourse of their day, as Milbank argues, they subsumed the social sciences in their theological framework. The framework was provided by a historical context marked by the colonial difference.

Another problem in Milbank's critical account of liberation theology and in his position as a whole is that he relies too heavily on postmodern conclusions about secular Western culture. He fails to realize that while postmodernism can help to elucidate the problems with secular reason, it cannot equally uncover the problematic aspects of Eurocentric reason. Another way to put this is to say that post-modernism has not been able to see or detect the colonial difference. By relying too heavily on a postmodern critique of the social sciences, Milbank is unable to differentiate epistemological problems that derive from a more or less exclusive focus on European modernity from problems that appear in modernity's darker side. That is why he cannot elucidate crucial aspects of liberation theology. Milbank's account is thoroughly Eurocentric. Since he only has Western secular reason on the horizon, he believes that asserting *theological* difference is enough to respond to the challenges of Western modernity. For him, the only significant history of epistemological significance is that of the encounter between Christian theology and Western secular reason. Liberation theology insists, on the contrary, that both secular *and* theological reason by themselves can remain caught up in the logic that asserts *colonial difference*. Liberation theology thus not only attempts to respond critically to the devastating effects of secular reason, but also to the historical framework and the epistemologies that sustain the colonial difference. While it may be true that liberation theology has to clarify further its relationship to secular reason after postmodern excesses and critiques, radical orthodoxy has to closely examine its complicity with the order of things that begets the colonial difference.

Gregory Baum points out other problems in Milbank's critique of the social sciences and their use by liberation theologians. He asserts that there are moments in the scriptures that anticipate sociological theory. He gives the example of Samuel's warning to the Jews about the implications of having a king (1 Sm 8:10–18). Baum argues that in Samuel's speech he "applies the theory that monarchies produce class distinction and class exploitation to the particular historical situation of the Israelites."[23] Liberation theology would point out something similar about the Exodus narrative and about Las Casas's critique of Spanish treatment of indigenous peoples and African slaves in the Americas.[24] It can be added, as Dussel points out in his study of theological metaphors in Marx's work, that to some extent it was Marx who first relied upon and further refined critical theological categories imbued in the Bible and not the other way around.[25] That is, liberation theologians are not drawing on completely foreign literature when they use Marxism as a tool of analysis. Not using social-science categories that partly rely on the Bible would imply, from this perspective, avoiding advancing critical theological thinking only because of a quarrel of European theology with its archenemy, modern Western secular reason. This gesture would be an extension of a long legacy of impositions of criteria of analysis from the "core" of the West to its epistemological periphery.

Baum further adds, in line with liberation theology's claims, that the church has much to lose if it fails to use both critical analysis and sociological theory. Baum mentions Augustine's failure to recognize the reasons behind the Donatists' rejection of the bishops who had betrayed their faith during the persecution.[26] Baum's examples highlight the relevance of sociological theory, and, even when he does not mention it explicitly, of ethnic studies in the analysis of the Donatists' reactions. Baum explains:

> The Donatists were drawn from the ethnic population of North Africa that had been pushed by the Roman colonists from the fertile stretches of land along the Mediterranean coast to settle in the mountains, less fertile regions of the interior. These people refused integration in the culture of the Roman Empire. They stood aloof from the assimilated Christians of North Africa, who, like Augustine, spoke Latin and were proud of the best of Roman culture. While the Latinized Christians looked upon the idolatrous surrender to the Emperor in times of persecution as a sin that could be forgiven, the Donatists judged this apostasy as an irreparable break with the church, pouring into this judgment their historical resentment against the material and cultural oppression inflicted upon them by the Empire. Because he lacked such analysis, Augustine was unable to address the Donatists in a manner that acknowledged their suffering.[27]

Put in a different way, Baum's argument is that theological difference can cause blindness to colonial or racial difference. To be sure, the same can occur with the social sciences. That is why liberation theology resists the temptation of reducing the problems of the age to a tension between theology and secular reason. Their internal tensions and oppositions help to conceal the contours of the colonial difference. Liberation theology does not use the Latin American critical social sciences because it conceives of the secular as purely autonomous. If that were the case, the European social sciences would suffice to make the necessary enquiry. Liberation theologians use Latin American social sciences because they help to illuminate the forms of power relationships that maintain the colonial difference. In addition to this consideration, Baum points out, liberation theology insists on the incompleteness of the redemption of the world and the absolute priority of the "preferential option for the poor," a form of *practice* that seeks to undermine the colonial difference.[28]

In addition to alluding to moments in the history of the church when sociological theory could have helped theology to better understand social dynamics and to become more critical of society, Baum applies the same insight to Milbank's project itself. Baum brings to light the "dark side of Christian practice," which he thematizes in relation to the negation of Jewish existence.[29] Baum's point is that not only secular ontologies but "Christian practice itself, almost from the beginning, contained dimensions of violence."[30] For Baum, Milbank's project is in line with such tendencies. His exclusivist Christology "re-introduces the traditional negation of Jewish existence into Christian theological discourse and interrupts the recent conversion of the Church to universal solidarity."[31] Baum further adds, "Throughout his book Milbank reads history with the old Christian prejudices."[32] For an example, "When Milbank praises the 19th-century Catholic socialists who criticized capitalism on Christian, ethical grounds (and not, as the Marxists did, on ground of its inner contradictions), he does not mention that the vision of a just, Christian society they entertained generated anti-Jewish resentment among the people who followed them."[33] Another possible approach to this issue would be to examine the repercussions of the Christian socialists' views on women or people of color in the European colonies. Theological reason by itself hardly provides the only means for the criticism of society. As Baum asserts, without entering "into dialogue with emancipatory secular reason and listen(ing) to God's Word addressed to them through the voices of society's victims," theologians are bound to be complicit with structures of power of domination and control.[34]

For Baum, Milbank's orthodox (re)turn has three main problems: (1) dependence on doubtful postmodern conclusions (which coexist with the opposition to postmodernity as a whole), (2) reliance on Christian prejudices of old, and (3) resistance to dialogue. Milbank's Christology is preeminently exclusivist. Milbank may believe that his intervention is uniquely theological, but a look at the philosophical production of the times shows that orthodoxy is hardly only a theological move nowadays. Indeed, the general withdrawal by many groups today from the dialogical gestures of Western intellectuals and Christian theologians in the aftermath of the Holocaust and the visceral reaction to the struggles by racial minorities and women in the 1960s make one wonder whether the call to orthodoxy does not fall precisely into the same error that, according to Milbank, irremediably stains the project of liberation theology, that is, of becoming simply "another effort to reinterpret Christianity in terms of a dominant secular discourse of our day."[35] In truth, it is probably more correct to say that neither liberation theology nor Milbank's project simply reinterprets Christianity in terms of dominant secular ideologies. What they both do is to respond from a Christian perspective to what they consider as the urgent social and political issues of the day. Radical orthodoxy is hardly an expression of theological difference alone. Orthodoxies are emerging in our times in ways similar to liberation thought in the late 1960s. The difference is that while liberation thought attempted to politicize the dialogical turn in Western thought, orthodoxies withdraw from dialogue and the ethical encounter with the "other" in order to assert the primacy of a unique and supreme tradition of praxis and critique. A problem with this posture is, as Baum points out, not only the withdrawal from dialogue but also the repetition and legitimization of Christian prejudices of old. This is evident in Milbank's work as well as in the recent critical theorizing of the Lacanian Marxist Slavoj Žižek.

SLAVOJ ŽIŽEK'S LEFTIST ORTHODOXY

A significant example of the orthodox turn in critical thinking today is the more recent work of the Lacanian Marxist Slavoj Žižek.[36] Žižek's project combines what Baum highlights as the most problematic features of Milbank's work, that is, an exclusivist attitude, resistance to dialogue, and reliance on old Christian prejudices. Žižek's project is a critical response to what he considers to be the predominant philosophical and social problems today: the postponement or evisceration of the political in the name of ethics or culture, the propagation of New Age and new spiritualities, and the distorting dimensions of subaltern dialectics. The rapprochement of Marxist and Christian orthodoxy is evident in Žižek's work. He believes that "Christianity and Marxism *should* fight on the same side of the barricade against the onslaught of new spiritualisms."[37] The complicity between orthodox Christianity and a new Marxist orthodoxy is no clearer today than in Žižek's latest book, *The Puppet and the Dwarf*. Reflecting on the Catholic thinker G. K. Chesterton's 1908 *Orthodoxy*, Žižek asserts:

> Chesterton's basic matrix is that of the "thrilling romance of orthodoxy": in a properly Leninist way, he asserts that the search for true orthodoxy, far from being boring, humdrum, and safe,

is the most daring and perilous adventure (exactly like Lenin's search for the authentic Marxist orthodoxy—how much less risk and theoretical laziness, is in the easy revisionist conclusion that the changed historical circumstances demand some 'new paradigm'!).[38]

Like Chesterton in his time, Žižek responds critically today to the rupture of a paradigm of Western and Christian epistemological superiority. The first chapter of *The Puppet and the Dwarf*, inspired by Chesterton, is a neo-Orientalist positing of intrinsic and irreducible difference between a backward "Orientalist spirituality" and a progressive and radical Christian tradition. Instead of investigating the material conditions and the discursive mechanisms that led to the idea of a fundamental divide between East and West, as some scholars in religious studies are trying to do today, Žižek reifies the divide and thus perpetuates its racist and colonial basis.[39] Instead of exploring the ways in which adherents of Buddhism or Islam articulate forms of critical thinking and legitimate radical political praxis, Žižek declares the whole of "Orientalist spirituality" as irremediably apolitical or complicit with war.[40] The efforts of activist Buddhist monks like Thich Nhat Hanh or the works of radical Islamic women are all elided in the name of Christian and European exceptionalism. Žižek's intensions are thoroughly exclusivist. As he asserts:

> My claim . . . is not merely that I am a materialist through and through, and that the subversive kernel of Christianity is accessible also to a materialist approach; my thesis is much stronger: this kernel is accessible *only* to a materialist approach—and vice versa: to become a true dialectical materialist, one should go through the Christian experience.[41]

As Baum notes in relation to Milbank's exclusivist Christology and his historical interpretations, Žižek's orthodoxy also follows the path of undoing Christian attitudes of universal solidarity, including nonreductive readings of Judaism. The last two chapters of *The Puppet and the Dwarf* are dedicated to asserting the epistemological superiority of the "Christian breakthrough" beyond paganism and Judaism. Judaism appears as no more than a transitory but utterly necessary moment between pagan wisdom and properly Christian universality. Žižek criticizes Christian anti-Semitism with an epistemological framework that promotes, if not is in itself, anti-Semitic:

Christian anti-Semitism is, in effect, a clear sign of the Christian position's regression into paganism: it gets rid of the "rootless," universalist stance of Christianity proper by transposing it onto the Jewish Other; consequently, when Christianity loses the mediation of the Jewish Law, it loses the specific Christian dimension of Love itself, reducing Love to the pagan "cosmic feeling" of oneness with the universe. It is only reference to the Jewish Law that sustains the specific Christian notion of Love that needs a distance, that thrives on differences, that has nothing to do with any kind of erasure of borders and immersion into Oneness. (And within the Jewish experience, love remains on this pagan level—that is to say, the Jewish experience is a unique combination of the new Law with pagan love, which accounts for its inner tension.)[42]

The irony of Žižek's declaration is that while for him Christian love thrives on differences, it is itself predicated on the construction of strong hierarchical differences. The only problem that Christianity confronts, for Žižek, in regard to the expression of love is that of not correctly assuming the lower hierarchies that constitute it, specifically the Jewish "unplugging" from the social realm. Žižek's Christianity is one that preaches love and subordination to the Christian narrative of love at the same time. Other epistemological positions are in themselves unsustainable and ultimately decadent. One wonders if the communities that attach themselves to those ideas will be judged to be sustainable while their religious and social ideals are considered otherwise.

Žižek's conjunction of Christianity and Marxism includes reading Saint Paul as a Leninist and Lenin as a sort of saint. For Žižek, Paul's conception of the Christian community is thoroughly Leninist: "The key dimension of Paul's gesture is . . . his break with any form of communitarianism: his universe is no longer that of the multitude of groups that want to 'find their voice,' and assert their particular identity, their 'way of life,' but that of a fighting collective grounded in the reference to an unconditional universalism."[43] Like Lenin and the proletariat, Paul is the representative of radical political universality: "We, the remainder, were nothing, we want to become All."[44] This Christian political conception breaks through previous ideas of community life, particularly the pagan and the Jewish. Žižek is aware that Jewish scholars like Paul Boyarin have depicted Paul not as a Christian thinker but as a radical Jew.[45] Žižek comments that he agrees with this approach but notices that, if taken seriously, it has catastrophic consequences.[46] Žižek's idea is that if Paul is looked at as a Jew, then Judaism reaches its very end with him. Although he may be a Jew, his conception of universality does away with the Jewish concept of community.[47] Boyarin would not reject some of these implications.[48] But he adds that Paul's reaction to Jewish communitarianism had some excesses of its own, which include the devaluation of ethnic and gendered bodies.[49] This problem was not unique to Paul, but also to the Jewish thinker Philo. For Boyarin, the best way to understand Paul is precisely through reference to "a religious-cultural formation contiguous with other Hellenistic Judaisms."[50] The problem with this Hellenistic trend is that it tended to make particularity disappear under the shadow of the universal. But such disappearance could only lead to the universalization of a particularism, in Paul's case, to the universalization of male and Christian bodies.[51] Žižek's rescue of universality arguably goes in a similar direction. His conception of universality collapses into a defense of *universalized provinciality*.

The option for universalized provinciality has to be understood in the context of the crisis of the Left in Europe and elsewhere. Communist utopia is now replaced by a return to the origins. In this situation allegedly "rootless" universalism gives ironic expression to an orthodox search for roots. Universalism is supposedly the opposite of the search for roots. But not in the European experience. In it, conceptions of particular identity are intimately tied to the hubris of universality. The trick of Eurocentrism is that it matches identity politics with the search for the universal, and then it opposes identity politics elsewhere as vicious forms of victimization. The search for the universal is thus tied to exclusivism and the affirmation of particularity: the highest religion, Christianity, corresponds with the highest civilization, Europe—a point clearly sustained by Chesterton in his opposition to Buddhism, Islam, and other religious expressions.[52] This ideological framework has been part and parcel of Western modernity. Christianity, liberalism, and Marxism for the most part define themselves within this scheme of things. Christian and Marxist orthodox oppositions to secular liberalism are thus the outcome of an intra-modern struggle for the heritage of Western exceptionalism and universality. The overall result is the *recolonization* of entire areas of thought and the suspension of dialogue.

Boyarin's intervention is refreshing in this context. For while the disputes among Christianity, liberalism, and Marxism seem to corroborate Fanon's suspicion that Western dialectics have become paralyzed, Boyarin attempts to revive the dialectic between Pauline universality and Rabbinic particularism for cultural critique.[53] When

Boyarin reclaims Paul for Judaism, it is not to universalize the Jewish particular but to work critically through the limits of the dominant Western conception of universality from a Jewish perspective that is informed by different strains of Judaism and by struggles from other ethnic groups and women's demands for liberation. Ethnic and women studies play an important role in Boyarin's articulation of his conception of (Jewish) diasporized identity. His use of these more recent fields of study in the academy is not gratuitous or incidental; they address precisely what the Pauline universal and its secular renderings tend to make invisible—the role of race, ethnicity, and gender in social and cultural formations. In his study Boyarin thus addresses both the limits of the Pauline universal in its Christianized form and the limits of its secular expression in the modern social sciences. From this perspective both Christianity and the social sciences are much closer than they appear in Milbank's critique of secular reason. From this perspective the challenges of liberation theology also appear to be different. Now the question is not so much the extent to which liberation theology betrays *theological* difference in its use of the social sciences but exactly the opposite: to what extent has liberation theology been able properly to neutralize the negative aspects of the universal as they appear in both its *Christian* theological vocation and in its embracing, critical as it is, of the social sciences? This is the challenge that liberation theology confronts today, not from its European theological peers, but from Christian women as well as black and indigenous peoples in the Americas.

FROM ORTHODOXY TO RADICAL DIVERSALITY

Latin American liberation theology confronted trouble early on regarding its reliance on sociological categories of poverty and marginalization. Massive poverty was understood in relation to capitalist dynamics elucidated through the concept of class. U.S. black theologians and Latin American theologians have discussed at some length the problems with the category of the poor from the perspective of race. Feminist theology raised a similar challenge to Latin American liberation theology from the perspective of gender. As Elina Vuola has elucidated, Latin American liberation theology's concept of the poor hid the specificity of women's struggles.[54] Liberation theology also failed to develop a consistent account of praxis; questions regarding sexual ethics and the liberating praxis of women did not form part of theological accounts. In these respects Latin American liberation theology seemed to stay within the limits of the Christian and secular European account of the universal in terms of gender and race.

While liberation theology critically responded to the hegemonic European universal from the perspective of the colonial difference, it failed to realize the complexity of the coloniality of power, in particular, the situation of *colonial heterogeneity*. The coloniality of power does not create a homogeneous field of colonial difference but instead a set of interrelated forms of oppressions articulated not only through class but through race and gender as well. Colonial heterogeneity designates the structurally heterogeneous space in which the colonial difference is born. That is to say, the coloniality of power not only creates epistemic colonial difference but also social and political colonial heterogeneity, which has an impact on epistemology as well. The political, social, and epistemological space marked by coloniality of power is full of tensions, contradictions, and ambivalences, which, as María Lugones so aptly illustrates, pose unique difficulties to the political dynamics of subaltern peoples.[55] This explains the inconsistencies in the formulations and expressions of epistemic colonial difference. Much of the early Latin American sociology of dependency was blind to the complexity of the coloniality of power.[56] Latin American dependency theory arose out of one specific vector of the colonial difference, that of displaced (for the most part male) Latin American intellectuals who investigated the realities of their region through modes of analysis that were ultimately complicit with the situation of poverty and dependency in Latin America. The struggles and demands of certain groups of women and black and indigenous peoples remained in the periphery of their concerns. In this way liberation theology became complicit with an elite mestizo Latin American consciousness that gave only partial expression to the needs for liberation in the region. Liberation theologians' epistemological breakthrough was thus limited from the very beginning. The introduction of the philosophy of Emmanuel Levinas in liberation theology did not help things much either. The concept of the "other" did not help to clarify the specificity of gender and race relations. Although there are exceptions, it is fair to say that for the most part the efforts to cultivate and deepen the paradigm shift that liberation theology represented has most often functioned as a straitjacket of sorts. Although there have been noticeable advances, for the last thirty five years liberation theology has for the most part remained caught within its own revolutionary epistemological breakthrough.

Liberation theology has an important role to play today against the terrifying Christian support of neo-Orientalist perspectives and the onslaught of new orthodoxies. Its focus on questions of poverty and marginalization, along with the option for dialogue, gives it strong resources to combat the nihilism of postmodern culture and the cynicism of neoliberal reason. There are at least three activities that liberation theology could do today to overcome its paradigmatic impasse. First, it needs not only to support but also to let itself be taken up by Christian women and people of color. This is not only a question of representation. As works from Christian women like Elsa Tamez and Silvia Regina de Lima Silva demonstrate, the next epistemological breakthrough in liberation theology may well depend on the leadership of theologians and biblical scholars like them.[57] Second, liberation theology has to renew its social-science and philosophical tools as well as to incorporate ethnic studies, gender studies, and sexuality studies in its analysis. The emerging sociological, cultural, and philosophical studies around conceptions such as transmodernity, border thinking, and coloniality of power offer a possible new venue of exploration. The concept of coloniality of power itself emerges out of the tradition of dependency theory in Latin America.[58] Coloniality of power seeks to bring together political economy and cultural analysis in a single theoretical framework. Transmodernity refers to a horizon of dialogical relationships among subjects beyond monological modern or postmodern paradigms. The concept has been formulated by the Argentinean Mexican philosopher and theologian of liberation Enrique Dussel.[59] Border thinking emerges in the theorizing of Chicana women like Gloria Anzaldúa.[60] Border thinking refers to the epistemological formations that emerge in physical, emotional, and epistemological *fronteras*. Scholars like Walter Mignolo, Freya Schiwy, Catherine Walsh, and others have been working on the conjunction and further elaboration of these concepts.[61]

Border thinking points to the third activity that Latin American liberation theologians could do today to break through the limits of their own epistemological revolution. They have to sit, listen, and learn. As Baum points out, the dialogical dimension of liberation theology has been defined by its inclusivist Christology. Baum applauds such inclusivism in face of Milbank's exclusivism. But inclusion poses limits to dialogue. Inclusivism does not solve the problem of which epistemology includes which. Liberation theologians have for the most part talked about poverty, but they have failed to address the non-Christian epistemological sources of the poor and the dispossessed. The turn to orthopraxis questioned some of the excesses of orthodoxy but hardly broke with the monolingual and monological implications of the meaning of *ortho*doxy (*correct* belief) or *ortho*praxis (*correct* praxis). Given that colonialism was not only material but also cultural and epistemic, one wonders to what extent social justice can be achieved without epistemic justice. Should one think not only in terms of orthodoxy or orthopraxis, but also in terms of heterodoxy and heteropraxis? Perhaps only in that way would one sit and listen to the "other," let oneself be subsumed by the "other," rather than putting oneself in a position of exclusive includer. Must one choose, like a sort of Leibnizian God, the best of all worlds? Or is it possible to imagine, as voices from the Zapatistas to the World Social Forum insist, "un mundo donde hayan muchos mundos" (one world where there are many worlds), "un mundo donde quepan todos" (a world where all are included), or "la sociedad que las mujeres soñamos" (the society of which women dream). Here one departs radically from an orthodox point of view and approximates what I call radical diversality. Radical diversality is an ethico-political perspective that criticizes the excesses of global capital, the pathos of postmodern nihilism, and the facile relinquishment of politics to ethics in the neoliberal world. Radical diversality is the conjunction of a politicized form of dialogical ethics with a universalistic rendering of the implications and repercussions of the coloniality of power and the colonial difference. That is, it takes the imperative of articulating macro-narratives and micro-narratives from the perspective of coloniality as a universal imperative with profound ethical and political implications.[62] Radical diversality conceives of material, cultural, and epistemic *decolonization* as a universal ethico-political imperative. In this sense, radicality makes reference here not to the search for roots but to the critique of imperial and colonial roots.[63]

The concept of radical diversality is close to interculturality, an idea that has been theorized by intellectuals who worked in the context of the indigenous Universidad Intercultural in Ecuador.[64] An interesting point about the Universidad Intercultural in Ecuador is that it emerged after frustration with decades of "assistance" from Marxist activists and committed Christians in line with liberation theology. If liberation theology wishes to promote "un mundo donde quepan otros mundos" (a world where all worlds are included), it has to be able to learn, not only from social theory, or from "poor" Christians in base communities, but also from the epistemic contributions of those who have been disavowed by both the Pauline and the secular universal. The consistent opposition to the devastating effects of orthodoxies old and new as well as to the limits of sociologically informed orthopraxis may reside in a radical dialogical move of this kind. We'll have to sit, learn, work, and be ready.

NOTES

[1] For the concept of radical diversality, I am indebted to Walter Mignolo's discussion of diversality (see *Local Histories/Global Designs: Coloniality, Subaltern Knowledges, and Border Thinking* [Princeton, NJ: Princeton University Press, 2000], 26, 244, 274).

[2] John Milbank, Catherine Pickstock, and Graham Ward, eds., *Radical Orthodoxy: A New Theology* (London: Routledge, 1999).

[3] John Milbank, Graham Ward, and Catherine Pickstock, "Introduction: Suspending the Material: The Turn of Radical Orthodoxy," in Milbank, Pickstock, and Ward, *Radical Orthodoxy*, 1.

[4] Ibid., 2.

[5] Ibid.

[6] Ibid., 3.

[7] John Milbank, *Theology and Social Theory: Beyond Secular Reason* (Cambridge, MA: Blackwell, 1991).

[8] Ibid., 3.

[9] Ibid., 380.

[10] Ibid.

[11] Ibid., 381.

[12] Ibid., 207.

[13] Ibid.

[14] Ibid., 209.

[15] See James H. Cone, *Black Theology and Black Power* (New York: Seabury Press, 1969); James H. Cone, *A Black Theology of Liberation* (New York: J. B. Lippincott, 1970; Maryknoll, N.Y.: Orbis Books, 1986). Gutiérrez's *Teologia de la liberación* was published in 1971.

[16] See in particular the many works of Enrique Dussel and Juan Carlos Scannone.

[17] See Enrique Dussel, *Philosophy of Liberation*, trans. Aquilina Martinez and Christine Morkovsky (Maryknoll, NY: Orbis Books, 1985).

[18] Enrique Dussel, "Teología de la liberación y marxismo," in *Mysterium Liberationis: conceptos fundamentales de la teología de la liberación*, vol. 1, ed. Ignacio Ellacuría and Jon Sobrino (San Salvador: UCA Editores, 1991); English translation *Mysterium Liberationis: Fundamental Concepts of Liberation Theology* (Maryknoll, NY: Orbis Books, 1993).

[19] Dussel, "Teologia de la liberación y marxismo," 115.

[20] See ibid., 123–24.

[21] See Enrique Dussel, *Historia General de la Iglesia en América Latina*, vol. 1, *Introducción general a la historia de la iglesia en América Latina* (Salamanca: Ediciones Sígueme, 1983). For a more recent collection, see Enrique Dussel, ed., *Resistencia y esperanza: historia del pueblo cristiano en América Latina y el Caribe* (San José, Costa Rica: Editorial Departamento Ecuménico de Investigaciones, 1995).

[22] Mignolo, *Local Histories/Global Designs*, ix.

[23] Gregory Baum, "For and against John Milbank," in *Essays in Critical Theology* (Kansas City: Sheed & Ward, 1994), 59.

[24] See Enrique Dussel, *The Invention of the Americas: Eclipse of "the Other" and the Myth of Modernity*, trans. Michael D. Barber (New York: Continuum, 1995); and Gustavo Gutiérrez, *Las Casas: In Search of the Poor of Jesus Christ*, trans. Robert R. Barr (Maryknoll, NY: Orbis Books, 1993).

[25] See Enrique Dussel, *Las metáforas teológicas de Marx* (Estella, Spain: Verbo Divino, 1993).

[26] Baum, "For and against John Milbank," 60.

[27] Ibid.

[28] Ibid., 65, 67.

[29] Ibid., 70.

[30] Ibid.

[31] Ibid., 71.

[32] Ibid.

[33] Ibid.

[34] Ibid., 72.

[35] Milbank, *Theology and Social Theory*, 209.

[36] See specially Slavoj Žižek, *The Fragile Absolute, or, Why Is the Christian Legacy Worth Fighting For?* (London: Verso, 2000); Slavoj Žižek, *On Belief* (London: Routledge, 2001); Slavoj Žižek, *The Puppet and the Dwarf: The Perverse Core of Christianity* (Cambridge: The MIT Press, 2003).

[37] Žižek, *The Fragile Absolute*, 2.

[38] Žižek, *The Puppet and the Dwarf*, 35.

[39] For works in religious studies that go in this direction, see Carl W. Ernst, *Following Muhammad: Rethinking Islam in the Contemporary World* (Chapel Hill, NC: The University of North Carolina Press, 2003); Richard King, *Orientalism and Religion: Postcolonial Theory, India, and 'The Mystic East'* (London: Routledge, 1999); and Anouar Majid, *Unveiling Traditions: Postcolonial Islam in a Polycentric World* (Durham, NC: Duke University Press, 2000). For a critique of Žižek's discourse on religion from the perspective of postcolonial critical theory of religion, see William D. Hart, "Slavoj Žižek and the Imperial/Colonial Model of Religion," *Nepantla: Views from South* 3, no. 3 (2002). There are important exceptions to Žižek's orthodox turn in critical theory. See, for instance, Susan Buck-Morss, *Thinking Past Terror: Islamism and Critical Theory on the Left* (London: Verso, 2003).

[40] See Žižek, *The Puppet and the Dwarf*, 25–33. For Buddhist perspectives on social ethics and liberation, see Christopher Ives, "Protect the Dharma, Protect the Country: Buddhist War Responsibility and Social Ethics," *The Eastern Buddhist* 33, no. 2 (2001); Christopher Queen and Sallie B. King, eds., *Engaged Buddhism: Buddhist Liberation Movements in Asia* (Albany, NY: State University of New York Press, 1996), Christopher Queen, Charles Prebish, and Damien Keown, eds., *Action Dharma: New Studies in Engaged Buddhism* (London: Routledge, Curzon Press, 2003).

41 Žižek, *The Puppet and the Dwarf*, 7.

42 Ibid., 120.

43 Ibid., 130.

44 Ibid., 130–33.

45 See Daniel Boyarin, *A Radical Jew: Paul and the Politics of Identity* (Berkeley and Los Angeles: University of California Press, 1994).

46 Žižek, *The Puppet and the Dwarf*, 9.

47 Ibid., 130–31.

48 See, for instance, Boyarin, *A Radical Jew*, 32.

49 Ibid., 8, 38.

50 Ibid., 13.

51 Ibid., 38.

52 G. K. Chesterton, *Orthodoxy* (New York: John Lane Company; London: John Lane, The Bodley Head, 1908), 240–52, 73–76.

53 Fanon's sentence reads: "Aujourd'hui, nous assistons à une stase de l'Europe. Fuyons, camarades, ce mouvement immobile où la dialectique s'est muée en logique de l'équilibre" (Frantz Fanon, *Les damnés de la terre* [Paris: Editions Gallimard, 1991], 374).

54 Elina Vuola, *Limits of Liberation: Praxis as Method of Latin American Liberation Theology and Feminist Theology* (Helsinki: Suomalainen Tiedeakatemia, 1997).

55 María Lugones, *Pilgrimages/Peregrinajes: Theorizing Coalition Against Multiple Oppressions* (Lanham, MD: Rowman & Littlefield).

56 One important exception is Anibal Quijano, who not only formulated the concept of coloniality of power but who from early on also articulated the notion of structural heterogeneity that provides the background to understand the concept of colonial heterogeneity (see Anibal Quijano, *El proceso de urbanización en América Latina* [Santiago, Chile: CEPAL, 1966]).

57 For their contributions, see Elsa Tamez, *La sociedad que las mujeres soñamos* (San José, Costa Rica: Editorial Departamento Ecuménico de Investigaciones, 2001). Also relevant here is the work of Sylvia Marcos (see, among others, Sylvia Marcos, ed., *Gender/Bodies/Religions* [Cuernavaca, Mex.: ALER Publications, 2000]).

58 For the concept of coloniality of power, see Anibal Quijano, "Colonialidad del poder, cultura y conocimiento en América Latina," *Anuario Mariateguiano* 1997; idem, "Coloniality of Power, Eurocentrism, and Latin America," *Nepantla: Views from South* 1, no. 3 (2000); and idem, "Globalización, colonialidad y democracia," in *Tendencias básicas de nuestra época: globalización y democracia*, ed. Instituto de Altos Estudios Diplomáticos "Pedro Gual" (Caracas: Instituto de Altos Estudios Diplomáticos "Pedro Gual," 2001).

59 See Enrique Dussel, "Modernity, Eurocentrism, and Trans-Modernity: In Dialogue with Charles Taylor," in *The Underside of Modernity: Apel, Ricoeur, Rorty, Taylor, and the Philosophy of Liberation*, ed. Eduardo Mendieta (Atlantic Highlands, NJ: Humanities, 1996).

[60] See Gloria Anzaldúa, *Borderlands: The New Mestiza=La frontera* (San Francisco: Aunt Lute Books, 1991); idem, ed., *Making Face, Making Soul=Haciendo caras: Creative and Critical Perspectives by Feminists of Color* (San Francisco: Aunt Lute Foundation Books, 1990); idem, *Interviews/Entrevistas*, ed. Ana Louise Keating (New York: Routledge, 2000); and Gloria Anzaldúa and Analouise Keating, eds., *This Bridge We Call Home: Radical Visions for Transformation* (New York: Routledge, 2002).

[61] See Mignolo, *Local Histories/Global Designs*. See also Santiago Castro-Gomez, Catherine Walsh, and Freya Schiwy, eds., *Indisciplinar las ciencias sociales* (Quito: Editorial Abya Yala, 2002).

[62] In this sense radical diversality takes on the dimensions of what I have called elsewhere transgresstopic critical hermeneutics (see Nelson Maldonado-Torres, "Post-Imperial Reflections on Crisis, Knowledge, and Utopia: Transgresstopic Critical Hermeneutics and the 'Death of European Man,'" *Review: A Journal of the Fernand Braudel Center for the Study of Economies, Historical Systems, and Civilizations* 25, no. 3 (2002).

[63] I have articulated this point in Nelson Maldonado-Torres, "The Topology of Being and the Geopolitics of Knowledge: Modernity, Empire, Coloniality," *City* 8, no. 1 (2004).

[64] Due to Ecuador's and Spanish's marginal place in the academic marketplace, the work of thinkers such as Walsh, Patricio Noboa, and others has not received the attention it deserves in the United States. In conjunction with José David Saldivar and Ramón Grosfoguel I am currently preparing a volume—tentatively titled *Coloniality, Transmodernity, and Border Thinking*—that would make their work better known to the U.S. academy. Raúl Fornet-Betancourt theorizes about interculturality from a philosophical perspective (see Raúl Fornet-Betancourt, *Hacia una filosofía intercultural latinoamericana* [San José, Costa Rica: Departamento Ecuménico de Investigaciones, 1994]; idem, *Interculturalidad y globalización: ejercicios de crítica filosófica intercultural en el contexto de la globalización neoliberal* [Frankfurt: IKO; San José, Costa Rica: Departamento Ecuménico de Investigaciones, 2000]).

4.

From within Ourselves

Afrodescendant Women on Paths of Theological Reflection in Latin America and the Caribbean

Silvia Regina de Lima Silva

TRANSGRESSING, PUSHING THE LIMITS, speaking from within ourselves . . . not recognizing the place historically assigned to us by the racist and patriarchal world . . . being a theological actor. This is part of the task of theology emerging from Afrodescendant women in Latin America and the Caribbean.

This article is a small contribution that seeks to make these faces known. A word added to other theological words and reflections by Afrodescendant women from different countries in our Great Homeland, Latin America. It is also a voice joined to many other voices that rise up, crying out that another world is possible and that in that other possible world other faces of God will be manifested. The chapter is divided into two main parts.

First, we present some elements that characterize Latin American feminist theology. The language is descriptive, but behind every word, every concept, we find life leaping, moving, challenging the rigidity of Western academic theology.

The second part is permeated by the bodies, life, and everyday experience of black women. We black women also do theology. What we share is very little in comparison with what the women of our people have to say.

A LITTLE HISTORY

Theological production coming from women in Latin America, especially in its early years, has been a space of dialogue between academic theological production and the women's movements of popular and ecclesial organizations. That same is true of black theology, as we will see further on. This process of group reflection was marked by spaces of reflection and regional, national, and continental meetings that brought together women theologians, community leaders, theology professors, and pastors.[1] Theological reflection emerging from women began within liberation theology. Keeping the same starting point and methodology as liberation theology, Latin American feminist theology has maintained a close relationship between theology and political, economic, social, and ecclesial reality. The challenges experienced by women in their everyday surroundings and in their relationship to the overall social context have been a locus and subject matter for theological reflection. Believing and proclaiming faith in the God of life means being committed on a daily basis to decent living conditions for everyone. This characteristic was to be part and parcel of the theological activity of women at its different stages. Today this requirement is regaining importance vis-à-vis the current market system.

To continue reflecting on the different ways of doing feminist theology in response to history and reality, we want to present three different stages that we also regard as characteristic of our theological endeavor. They are treated as stages because they arose at particular moments in history in response to challenges that were coming from reality itself. But they are also characteristic of our work because they remain part of current theological experiences. We now turn to one of the three moments.[2]

Feminist Consciousness in a Context of Poverty

Feminist theological thought emerged in Latin America in the 1970s. In the cry of the poor was heard the cry of women for decent living conditions. This process was experienced within liberation theology. The context of poverty, the condemnation of injustice, the commitment to human dignity that was being insulted and offended in the life of impoverished women identified this first moment of theological reflection by and from women. At that time there was no talk of a feminist theology. Some groups on the left and some sectors in the

church, even the liberationist church, saw in the word *feminist* an elitist movement that fomented division between men and women at a
time when everyone, male and female, had to be united to stand up
to the system of economic domination. This and other prejudices and
misconceptions about feminism kept this theological reflection from
being identified as feminist. At that time it was decided to call it a
theology of woman. During that period, theology and rereading of
the Bible sought to strengthen women in their political and social commitment and in their ecclesial commitment. There was a certain awareness and acknowledgment of the situation of domination and subordination experienced by women in society and in the churches. But
the concern and orientation of the struggles of women were aimed
particularly at large-scale structural changes. The understanding of
female and male identity did not allow for a radical critique and for
overcoming in theory and practice the situation of domination and
subordination created by machismo. Deep internal contradictions
were experienced. For example, it was not recognized that the places
occupied by women in the churches and in social-movement groups
were in most cases an extension of what they did at home, that is, the
same functions assigned by the patriarchal system. The important step
at this time was when, even in the midst of contradictions, there developed a capability of discovering the woman's face as a distinct
face, one with its own history, a different voice within the cry of the
poor. A second step was the affirmation of this face and this place as
a theological locus. Within that perspective what stands out is the
commitment of women to community-development struggles. Demands for decent living conditions are an expression of faith in the
God of life who cares for God's people. At this time important topics
were developed that are still with us: woman and church, female spirituality, women and political participation. Biblical rereading was
devoted to highlighting the participation of women in the liberation
struggles of the people of Israel. It also sought to give visibility to the
presence of women in the biblical text. This was a significant contribution to the search for recognition and empowerment of women.

Theology from Women or Theology from the Female Standpoint

In the 1980s it became clear that women were more present in the
world of academic theology, as the female presence in theological
institutes, seminaries, and universities increased. This factor was to
mark significantly the second moment of theological reflection by
Latin American women. Women were no longer one more face in the

midst of the poor but a voice distinct from others, a voice expressing a thinking of its own, a reading, an interpretation of life but also of God. Theological production by women went on to focus on recovering the feminine dimensions of God. This was the moment of affirmation of difference. God is male and female, Father and Mother. But such a claim came loaded down with an essentialist vision of female and male identities based on a relationship of complementarity between them. In theological terms this is a feminine theology that complements masculine theology, which is patriarchal theology. Hence it understands itself as "theology from women's eyes."[3] This theology does not imply a critique accompanied by the dismantling of patriarchalism, at least in theory, but rather it is satisfied to be a complement to patriarchal interpretation and theology in a reconstruction of patriarchalism. It was during this time that the first Latin American Woman and Theology meetings took place. A more critical view of this theological perspective recognizes that at this time highlighting the feminine and recognizing differences were not accompanied by analysis of the power relationships that establish the differences and that are structured on the basis of these differences. From this standpoint the differences are reduced to the biological and are identified as part of God's creation. Aspects that may be retrieved as a contribution from this theological perspective are different images of God and the active role played by women in biblical history, which was already present in the previous period.

Feminist Latin American Theology

By feminist theology we mean the theological reflection that arose in the 1990s. An important element at this stage of reflection is the mediation of the categories of gender as instrument of analysis, as a broader conceptual framework for analyzing issues of identity, power relationships, and the relationship with the cosmos. "This perspective places theology in a holistic, systemic, and ecological paradigm."[4] It is a different conception of the human being, of how our identities are formed, and of power relationships. Gender is the category used to interpret reality, identities (woman-man), and the relationships between them and with nature. It is a conceptual framework by which we approach reality and theological endeavor. For our reflection it is important to retrieve in gender thinking the assertion that female and male identities are not the results of a biological determination but are constructed in history; they are socially constructed relations. This means that we learn to be men and learn to be women, and it is from that place that we are going to see the world, build our relationships, and produce meanings in life. Patriarchal society has been built based on the masculine, and the world has been thought about from that particular locus, attributing a status of universality to that thinking. Hence we say that patriarchal society is based on asymmetrical relationships where the interests, perception, power, values, and sciences (including theology) are built from the masculine; that (masculine) particular is called universal. Gender theories challenge us to destabilize traditional theoretical assumptions and to build new non-dualist and more inclusive rationalities with a holistic conception of the world. Given its radicality, gender reflection is identified as a proposal for a new paradigm; in other words, it is not one more issue to be reflected on theologically, but rather a questioning of all theological production because it unmasks the myth of neutrality and concepts such as objectivity, impartiality, and universality, which are fundamental in patriarchal theological discourse.

On the basis of gender categories, theology assumes that task of theological deconstruction. It questions and dismantles the foundations of patriarchal theological discourse as a single discourse and proposes distinct forms of interpretation and approach to the mystery that is God. We share some of these new understandings that we utilize in theological reflection.

God as Reciprocity

God is no longer conceived as a being outside, solitary, above us, but as relationship and reciprocity—a God who is revealed in relationship with the other. As Ivone Gebara points out, this is a God who, while transcendent, also works from within women to build bridges, to establish connections. Indeed, creation itself is a result of God's relational power. Jesus' ministry is understood on the basis of this relational dynamic, as passion for the other manifested in healing and liberating encounters. A relational spirituality affirms life and creatively makes possible relations of respect and reciprocity aimed at happiness.

Theology of and in the Everyday

Feminist theology comes out of a particular place, believes in situated objectivity as a way of building knowledge; it reaffirms the importance of the everyday as a theological locus. The everyday with its contradictions emerges as a hermeneutical category that allows the overcoming of a dualistic and dichotomous view of life. The everyday is the site where God is experienced and where new relations are built affirming the dignity and human life of women and men.

Theology and Affirmation of the Body

Situated objectivity leads to the recognition of subjectivity as a part of reflection, as possibility of approach to and knowledge of the world. That allows the recovery of the female and male body in the theological task. The body is the place of experience and encounter with the other, with oneself, and with God. This bodily experiential knowledge unmasks the fallacy of neutral knowledge that sought to be a disembodied knowing, a knowledge for everyone, and hence "universal." In Latin American feminist theology the body is present in different forms. It is in the form of a cry against the violence that humiliates and kills women. It is the body that protests against a system that is imposed as sole and ultimate word, to the detriment of our right to a decent life, even denying us the right to dream of a world with different relationships. We cry out against a sacrificial theology that continues to demand that women deny themselves. Yes, because we experience so many forms of death in daily life, we resist a theology that affirms the suffering of those who are in situations of powerlessness as a route of salvation. We insist on the affirmation of the body as place of enjoyment, pleasure, and sharing life. That is why we recover celebration and festival as places of encounter, celebration, and manifestation of God.

Theology with Warmth and Feeling

A theology that undertakes the task of breaking with the gender identities assigned by patriarchalism recovers feeling as part of human life. It launches the challenge and the right to a spirituality of tenderness, especially to men who were alienated from this possibility of loving and manifesting love. Tenderness is presented as a way of being in the world, and it serves as a way to discover sisterhood, God's friendship with humankind—God as the sustaining and accompanying female friend.[5]

Theology as Experience of Reencounter with the Universe

One of the contributions of the present moment of feminist theological reflection in Latin America is the recovery of a holistic world view in which humankind is discovered to be part of a whole, integrated into the vital energy of nature. The holistic dimension of theology has been especially focused in ecofeminism, a theological expression developed in recent years.[6] Ecofeminism in Latin America reaffirms fundamental elements that were already present in theologies from aboriginal peoples, from Afrodescendants, and from peasant theology. Within this theological perspective is the awareness of the relationship of interdependence, where as human beings we can no longer conceive of ourselves as separate, above the created universe. We are part of the universe. We carry part of the universe in our body, and hence we assume an attitude of reverence, care, and responsibility toward all created beings.

These are some characteristic elements of Latin American feminist theology. One of the treasures of the present moment is the pluralism of thought, of perspectives that are appearing among women theologians themselves. Today's feminist theological reflection is a pluralist reflection. Different faces of women can now be discerned, that is, different feminist theologies emerging from the ethnic, cultural, and religious diversity that is part of the wealth of our continent.

Within this diversity there some common elements, such as those mentioned in the previous section. There are accents, specific approaches that arise out of each context. Black feminist theology is one of these faces. In the reflection below we present some of the contributions and characteristics of this theology.

THEOLOGY FROM AFRODESCENDANT WOMEN

I was born a black woman, society made me a man and white;
Today I cry out and struggle in order to be black woman.
                    —BENEDITA DA SILVA, BRAZIL

Black feminist theology in Latin America emerges from a double challenge. First, like feminist theology, it has the challenge of questioning and deconstructing the patriarchal theology that in Latin America and the Caribbean has assumed a male, white, and elitist face, fostering an ethnocentric, class-based, macho theology. This hegemonic patriarchal theology is an expression of the colonial power in the past and is still in complicity and participating in today's systems of domination.

The other challenge assumed by black feminist theology is that of reflecting on the experience of faith lived by black women. We ponder theology as a new theological locus where black women may come together in order to share, to think, and to proclaim their liberating experiences and presences of God. This is what we seek to share in the pages that follow.

From the Margins of the Theological Locus

Where does our theology emerge? We are Afrodescendant women in the African diaspora. We carry an Africa in our heart. More than a real Africa, we bear a mythic, symbolic Africa, a utopian construction that nourishes our dreams and desires of liberation, of a decent life. This is a theological locus that we are sketching and reconstructing in community. It portrays the world that we desire and that we seek to build.

We are black women in a racist society. We are women in an androcentric and sexist world. We experience a "non-place."[7] Being a black woman is part of a process of rebuilding our own identity. Black identity is part of a project of affirmation in the face of denial and exclusion. In the past we encountered a theology that legitimated slavery and racism. Today we seek not only the delegitimization of that theology, but we also want to recover theology as a contribution in the process of affirmation of identity and in the retrieval of black citizenship. The "non-place" becomes a place of shouting, protest, demand. It is also the place from which we build new relationships. It is the place of empowerment, of affirmation, of the discovery of a God who is accomplice and female companion in this journey of seeking our own face and life with dignity. Theologically, we seek recognition of the black face as image and likeness of God.

> I can now say that I am a black woman and I am proud of being a black woman. But it wasn't always that way. Before I accepted how I am I had a confrontation with my God for having made me like this, black and woman. He seemed an unjust God to me. How could I have been created only for suffering . . . whole peoples of black women and men condemned to suffer eternally.[8]

The struggle against discrimination and racism roots this theology in movements and organizations of impoverished women and men, and it is united to other groups who are similarly excluded. Conscious of the growing exclusion fostered by neoliberal globalization, we offer blackness and feminist commitment from the world of the poor, and together we seek the other world that is possible, the society that respects life, protects those who are weakest, allows everyone, female and male, to exist with dignity amid differences. Believing in and anticipating the other possible world is another important theological locus from which black feminist theology emerges.

From the outset black feminist theology has dealt with the rigidity of patriarchal theological discourse. For us, doing theology has meant entering into someone else's building, one that was very well built, with firm unshakable foundations, but at the same time a building that was uninhabitable and little frequented. It had narrow corridors and tight rooms where often our exuberant bodies didn't fit or, if we did go in, we found it hard to move. Even so, we think it is important to go there, to be familiar with the theology that has ignored us and discriminated against us for centuries . . . but not to stay there. We believe in the need to do theology from a different place. That means taking on the double challenge stated at the beginning of this essay, that is, the deconstruction of hegemonic patriarchal theology and the proclamation of new understandings about God, an alternative theology that will allow us to recover the human person with dignity and other revelatory images and experiences of God. We share some of the elements that spring up from this theological activity of ours.

Retrieval of the Body as Place of God's Manifestation

In Latin American feminist theology we find the affirmation of the body as a theological locus. In black theology it reappears as the black body. The experience of racial discrimination is the negation of the black body. The association of black with what is evil, dirty, with the negative dimensions of life, makes many black women and men deny their blackness by wishing to be whitened. Wishing to be whitened is ultimately wishing one's own extinction as person and as a people. Unwillingness to assume one's blackness means aspiring not to be, not to have been.[9] The black woman is challenged to rediscover her own bodiliness, to be reconciled to her black body, to reencounter it as the beautiful work that came from the hands of the Creator. Beauty is accompanied by the feeling of dignity and awareness of rights as a citizen, as daughter of God. Black theology recovers the importance of the body, recognizes it, celebrates it. It retrieves the body in its everyday relations. The questions that emerge from life, from the experiences we have in our body, the searching, dreams, daily needs—and also hunger, health, pleasure, desire, reproduction, and love—are part of our theology.

History and Memory

An important task of black theology has been taking part in the process of retrieving the history and memory of the black people. We discover ourselves as part of a people of a community with roots, with a past. Integrating ourselves into this history of the past means discovering ourselves as subjects who make history today. We also discover our history as a place of encounter, of manifestation of God. The history of black women and men is also place of revelation. Rediscovering history is an important step in the retrieval and affirmation of memory. We understand memory not simply as a lifeless recalling of the past, but as the living power of the past that is manifested in the present, filling it with meaning and transcendence. This memory is kept in the depths of the heart, hidden in the secrets of grandmothers, taught through the wisdom of elders, deposited in the foundations of religions from Africa. It is liberating memory, for it holds principles of black identity and dignity at the same time as it is updated in ongoing dialogue with the challenges presented in each new situation in history.

Encounter with the Religious Experience of Our Ancestors

The encounter with history and the retrieval of black memory have enabled many women to encounter their ancestral religious experience. That has meant approaching something that in some fashion we thought we knew, the God of our ancestors. We have called this experience intra-religious dialogue, because it takes place within us. We feel loved and embraced by the God of our grandfathers, by the Goddess of our grandmothers, by our ancestors. It is the encounter with a particular experience of God/Goddess, "of a God who is not a single gate, not a single path, but who makes many paths possible."[10] This has been something liberating for the life of women. We do not renounce the experience of Christian faith, but we enrich it on the basis of the encounter with this different countenance of God/Goddess. A God/Goddess who also has a female countenance, who is closer to nature and sometimes merged with it. Land, ancestors, rivers, food, the *axé* (Yoruba tradition: energy, vital power) are part of historic religious memory, part of our experience of God, and foundations of a theology with a black countenance. This is an ecumenical and macro-ecumenical theological experience incarnate in the challenges of society. The retrieval of our roots gives us the strength to continue to be a prophetic voice against inequality, discrimination, and racism. In theology we are called to reflect on the basis of this double belonging, of this God who has different countenances but an enormous heart that loves us and gathers us in.

CONCLUSION

For Afrodescendant women, doing theology is an act of transgression. It entails thinking of God beyond the codes and codices of the patriarchal, racist world that excludes. We travel one portion of the route of Latin American feminist theology. But we also enter through other paths, by our own ways. Along this route there are two orientations that are present in the different efforts at black theological production. I see them reflected in my own theological journey.

When I began my studies, I firmly intended to think of God with the head of a woman, a black woman. My concern was to understand the experience of the faith of the black people, especially of black women, and to reinterpret it using the concepts of Western Christian theology. The aim was to seek the rationality of black faith and to find a place for it within theological thought. To begin with, it was an effort to reconcile the irreconcilable. Moreover, the effort to understand black theology with concepts from Western Christian theology set up Western patriarchal theology as the main, and in some instances only, interlocutor of our theological endeavor. We were doing theology to answer the questions and challenges coming from white Western theology. Slowly we began to become aware that black feminist theology and other liberation theologies in Latin America operate within a different rationality. They seek to respond to questions coming from other places. As traditionally understood, theology is invited and challenged to extend its borders so as to make room for other actors who until that moment have been excluded from its process and method of theological reflection. That even demands a change in our understanding of what *theology* means to us. Looking at the initial inspiration that led me to theological study, I discover that I think of God not only with my head. I am a living-thinking-loving-enjoying body. The experience of God passes through my entire body and through the bodies of other women and men. Theology takes on another meaning. In theological reflection we no longer feel committed to give explanations of God but to seek to give new significance to life. Theology is part of inquiry into the meaning of life. We find it in the realm of desire, pleasure, dreaming, striving for happiness.

Doing theology means recovering our right to name ourselves and to speak a word that may be little, but is a word of our own about God/Goddess. To do so one has to be convinced that no people or human gender possesses the whole truth of God. What theologies can do is open a space, a broad space, to reveal God/Goddess's diversity of expression, with its many and different countenances. This is a theological and political task, one committed to changes in human and social relations. It involves unmasking all those who seek to hijack God and reduce God to themselves, to their interests. At the same time it returns to each person and human group the right to be in difference, a creature, a people created in God's image and likeness.

—TRANSLATED BY PHILLIP BERRYMAN

NOTES

[1] The three major Latin American meetings were held in Mexico (October 1979), Argentina (1985), and Brazil (1993). These gatherings also marked each of the three characteristic phases of feminist theology of liberation. Other meetings—San José (1981), Bogota (1984), Buenos Aires (1985), Mexico City (1986), Rio de Janeiro (1993), Bogota (1999)—were sponsored by EATWOT (Ecumenical Association of Third World Theologians). See Maria Jose F. Rosado Nunes, "La voz de las mujeres en la Teología Latinoamericana, *Concilium* 263 (February 1996).

[2] This periodization has been extensively worked by Ivone Gebara, "Aportes para una teología feminista," in *Tópicos 90* (Chile) (1993), 71–133. Elsa Tamez analyzes it from the standpoint of hermeneutics (Elsa Tamez, "Hermenéutica Feminista de Liberación," in *Teología Feminista Latinoamericana*, ed. Maria Pilar Aquino and Elsa Tamez (Quito: Ediciones Abya Yala, 1998), 78–110.

[3] See Margarida Luiza Ribeiro Brandao, ed., *Teología na ótica da mulher* (Rio de Janeiro: Pontificia Universidad Católica, 1990).

[4] Yolanda Ingianna, "Teología, liberación y paradigma de género: apuntes en marcha para la reflexión colectiva," in *Vida y pensamiento* (San José, Costa Rica: Seminario Bíblico Latinoamericano) 14, no. 1 (1994), 5.

[5] Sallie McFague, *Modelos de Dios—Teología para una era ecológica y nuclear* (Santander: Sal Terrae, 1987), 259–99. English translation: *Models of God: Theology for an Ecological Nuclear Age* (Philadelphia: Fortress Press, 1987).

[6] See Ivone Gebara, *Intuiciones ecofeministas, ensayo para repensar el conocimiento y la religión* (Montevideo: Doble Clic Soluciones Editoriales, 1998).

[7] This expression was used by a colleague, Maria do Carmo Lima, participating in a group of black women in the Baixada Fluminense, in Rio de Janeiro.

[8] *Beber de fuentes distintas: Teología desde las mujeres indígenas y negras de Latinoamérica* (Quito: World Council of Churches/CLAI, 2002), 1.

[9] Neusa Santos Amaral, *Tornar-se negro* (Rio de Janeiro: Graal, 1983), 4.

[10] *Beber de fuentes distintas*, 2.

5.

Ethic of Life
and Option for the Poor

German Gutiérrez

THE DISASTROUS IMPACT of structural adjustment programs, the neoliberal model, and so-called globalization in Latin American have been obvious. We can indicate some of the destructive effects produced by almost three decades of neoliberal domination in our Latin American societies:

1. growing impoverishment and exclusion.
2. pauperization of professional middle strata and of small and medium business people, especially those involved in production in agricultural, agroindustry, and industry.
3. heightening of conflicts within social groups (competition) and among different groups in society (social conflict) for survival and access to available resources.
4. gradual dismantling of institutions and public spaces that foster ties within society.
5. growing commodification of all spheres of social life and of its institutions; commodification of politics, culture, and even religion (religious marketing, electronic churches, theologies of prosperity, and so on).
6. transnationalization of decisions and public policies of a strategic character, *and* growing loss of sovereignty of states and autonomy of governments.
7. appropriation of social and natural national resources by large national and international capital.

8. monopolization of the symbolic cultural universe by big money in the culture industry and communication (TV, film, information technology, and so on) and reduction of people's own cultural forms to folklore.
9. aggravation of the desperate and rudderless search for alternatives to the crisis by groups or individuals in a situation of vulnerability or impoverishment.
10. increase of violence and of illegal, parallel, underground, or high-risk activities; spread of actions and behaviors that threaten the life of other human beings and one's own life and even the commodification of human life (paid assassination, market for bodily organs, trafficking in youth for drug traffic networks, prostitution, and so on).
11. strengthening and professionalization of police control of states complemented by the privatization of citizen security and the paramilitarization of social life.

If we wished to group these effects in a more general manner, we would say that the neoliberal structural adjustment associated with the process and project of globalization now under way:

1. has directly affected the survival of a large portion of the population; worsened and/or diminished the living standards and quality of life of the vast majority of the population.
2. has reinforced the trend toward the destruction of institutions, spaces, and practices of shared social life; fostered fragmentation, economic and social warfare; concentrated economic, social, political, and cultural power as never before in ever smaller elites isolated from, and insensitive to, the reality of the rest of society, further polarizing conflicts; proven to be absolutely the enemy of any possible space of national life and notion of common good.
3. has fostered indiscriminate and voracious exploitation of nature.

The popular and social response to neoliberalism has been continuous and ever more widespread rejection. This response has had to confront state terrorism, media manipulation, ideological and cultural assault by big money, psychological warfare, and many other forms that from a position of power have tried to undermine social resistance.

Recently the crisis to which the neoliberal process has brought our societies and the advance of popular protest have converged, and that has given rise to a significant change in the Latin American political map. This is especially the case in South America, where left-wing political parties, social organizations, and mass movements of protest and resistance have been able to establish new governments that under very vulnerable conditions are seeking (1) to transform the public policies inherited from neoliberalism and imposed by international lending and finance institutions and (2) to implement social policies to reverse the destructive effects left by the neoliberal wave. Still pending is the transformation of the structures of inequality set up by neoliberalism.

The conflict that marks the current Latin American context, between the imposition of a globalization strategy that combines market messianism with imperial domination strongly colored by fundamentalist and Manichean theological discourses and growing media and military intervention on the one side, and resistance and demands for life, dignity, peace, and true democracy on the other, is not a conflict that is merely regional in character. It is present throughout the Third World, and also in the First World, taking a specific shape in each region and country.

In this sense we can say that in contemporary society there is an ethical conflict in which three major ethical paradigms with global implications are involved: that of the functional ethic of the market, that of the ethic of a gang of robbers, and that of the ethic of life.

FUNCTIONAL ETHIC[1]

Adam Smith formulated it in his *Theory of the Moral Sentiments:*

Though among the different members of the society there should be no mutual love and affection, the society, though less happy and agreeable, will not necessarily be dissolved. Society may subsist among different men, as among different merchants, from a sense of its utility, without any mutual love or affection; and though no man in it should owe any obligation, or be bound in gratitude to any other, it may still be upheld by a mercenary exchange of good offices according to an agreed valuation.

. . . If there is any society among robbers and murderers, they must at least, according to the trite observation, abstain from robbing and murdering one another. Beneficence, therefore, is less essential to the existence of society than justice. Society may subsist, though not in the most comfortable state, without beneficence; but the prevalence of injustice must utterly destroy it.

... [Beneficence] is the ornament which embellishes, not the foundation which supports the building. .... Justice, on the contrary, is the main pillar that upholds the whole edifice. If it is removed, the great, the immense fabric of human society, that fabric which to raise and support seems in this world, if I may say so, to have been the peculiar and darling care of Nature, must in a moment crumble into atoms.[2]

In speaking here of justice as a pillar of social life, reference is made to the existence of a system of laws with a strong coercive capability:

The most sacred laws of justice, therefore, those whose violation seems to call loudest for vengeance and punishment, are the laws which guard the life and person of our neighbor; the next are those which guard his property and possessions; and last of all come those which guard what are called his personal rights, or what is due to him from the promises of others [i.e., contracts].[3]

Friedrich von Hayek, a neoliberal, expresses it even more bluntly when he says that we live in civilized societies because in a historical process we have learned to assume in a non-deliberated way habits and moral norms of adaptation to the mercantile order that are imposed on us as a condition for the reproduction of our lives and for the selection of lives.[4] Here is how he formulates this ethic, which selects human lives:

A society requires certain morals which ultimately come down to maintaining lives: *not to maintaining all lives,* because it could be necessary to sacrifice individual lives to preserve a larger number of other lives. Therefore, *the only moral rules are those that carry the "calculus of lives*: property and contract."[5]

In the expression of these authors we have the basic features of the functional ethic that now reigns supreme in the current globalization process.

We could sketch the broad outlines of this functional ethic as follows. Each human being is responsible for his or her own survival and operates within the framework of a series of relationships of interdependence coordinated by normative systems that enable individual actions that are partial and performed out of self-interest to produce opportunities for others and in their entirety to help reproduce an order called society. The most effective normative system for coordination is the market, and hence its basic rules (those that constitute it as market, not those applied to it from a particular morality), which are respect for private property and for contracts, are the normative framework within which social actions are valid. Within this normative framework the participants may act with complete freedom in seeking their own interests without impairment to the general interest of society. The latter is guaranteed by the market mechanism itself and not by a particular or group intention of social benefit. In principle, all participants have free room to achieve their ends and projects (hence the functional ethic claims to champion the greatest ethical pluralism known) and the normative framework does not seek to legislate about ends. Provided the general guidelines are respected, all possible means to assure achieving the ends may be used. To the extent that all participants are struggling for particular ends, the normative framework defines a competitive environment of action. And in that environment, although the majority finds its own ends more or less attained, there are greater and lesser awards. The latter is the responsibility of each individual, and each must carry out his or her action ever more efficiently and competitively in order to achieve his or her ends. Given this situation, efficiency and competitiveness are defined as maximum values and criteria for good action. Within this setting of social action, there is a variety of ways of living and understanding the life that is lived.

Hence we have a functional system of ethics comprised of norms of action, the corresponding values and rationality, theory about ends, and their corresponding moral and ethical quality.

However, when this ethic is imposed broadly in a society, as is happening today with the new neoliberal order, the result is not the achievement of all social ends in competitive harmony, but what we have noted at the beginning of this article: polarization of society between an ever more economically powerful minority and an impoverished, pauperized, or excluded social minority; a growing and conflictive fragmentation of society with strong features of anomie and self-destruction. When this market ethic becomes *the* ethic of society and is absolutized, it leads society itself to fragmentation, anomie, and violence, if not to self-destruction.

For neoliberalism there is only one ethical alternative. Obey the rules of the system or die. Here the explanation of poverty is that some groups in society refuse to assume the morality of the market and remain tied to backward moralities of altruism, solidarity, compassion, and cooperation. From this angle the system guarantees and governs the life and death of people.

Human beings want to live, and if they can do so only in institutional and normative frameworks that they have not chosen and in the face of which they lack the individual capability of making change, they will usually submit to these mechanisms of superior force; they will consider such mechanisms as natural or impossible to understand or transform, and they will consequently seek to pursue their life projects within the realms of freedom and decision that those structural frameworks offer or allow them.

In this sense we can say that the system and its founding ethic are maintained and strengthened not by an assumed autonomous and systemic self-regulating capacity, but as a result of the activity carried out by members of the society to reproduce their life *under conditions of subjection to an already established mercantile social order*, and before which each of them as individuals or small groups can only struggle to adapt. That is why social organization is so much under attack within neoliberalism, because that is the only way that human beings can act on the mercantile social order.

THE FUNCTIONAL ETHIC OF THE MARKET
AS ETHIC OF WAR AND OF A GANG OF ROBBERS[6]

In the framework of neoliberal ideology the functional ethic is nothing but an ethic of social and economic competition unleashed in the context of a system of law that is built on that ideology. That is how the law defines the field of action and becomes its guarantor, while war (or competition) within that framework is what drives social relations. Efficiency is supposedly the criterion of selection between the fallen and those who are saved. The award for one who falls is exclusion, loss of self-esteem, and the feeling of defeat. The award for one who is saved is survival, power, and paranoia. And the direction of society as a whole is in the hands of the "astuteness" of mercantile reason, which, freed from its own dynamic, leads society to self-destruction.

The everyday life from which people experience a feeling of uncertainty, chaos, and competitive paranoia anticipates the uncertain direction of this "astuteness." However, it does not grasp the existence of the order concealed behind the chaos of experience. This order is that of a gang of robbers.

It is striking that Adam Smith in his attempt to ground a normative order as a condition of survival for society returns to this very figure of the gang of robbers:

If there is any society among robbers and murderers, they must at least, according to the trite observation, abstain from robbing and murdering one another. Beneficence, therefore, is less essential to the existence of society than justice.[7]

In his line of argumentation, Smith tries to show that even a gang of robbers, in order to subsist, must respect basic norms such as not killing one another, not stealing from one another, and respecting agreements (the three basic norms of what he calls justice and Hayek calls market morality). He thereby intends to say that these norms of justice are so universal and constitutive that even in societies of a very questionable moral condition, such as a gang of robbers, or in relations of mercantile exchange of resources, such as the market, those norms must be observed.

Nevertheless, when Smith identifies these three norms of a gang of robbers with the norms of justice without which the building called society "crumbles," and at the same time when he declares any ethical standard for action to be a decoration that embellishes but does not support the edifice of society, the question emerges whether Smith is not ultimately identifying society with a gang of robbers that is occasionally embellished by acts of benevolence that are always private. Thus the ethic of the gang of robbers here appears as the paradigm, the foundation of justice, and the condition of survival of society.

Nevertheless, in addition to respecting these three rules, a gang of robbers, in order to survive as such, must secure the material goods that enable it to survive and to constitute a minimum of group cohesion. It is not enough for the robbers not to rob or kill one another. They must have material means to survive—and hence the existence of an "other" to rob. That means the existence of human groups who have an economic surplus that will be the booty to be expropriated by the gang of robbers. It means a working population that, in addition to being the target for stealing, can keep reproducing so that they can continue to be robbed, or an unlimited population that will allow the gang of robbers to occupy itself with new human groups.

This means that the ethic of the gang of robbers is broader than the ethic of the market. In the former it is fundamental that the members of the band have their needs met and that there be a minimum principle of solidarity that goes beyond prohibiting the violation of certain norms. These are the two things that keep the group together, while the prohibition of the violation of certain norms is a stabilizing element. It could be seen as a conflict between legitimacy and legality within the gang of robbers. In the market ethic, on the other hand, there is no principle of solidarity or responsibility for providing material goods, because the "invisible hand" is believed to do that. In that sense the market order performs "godfather functions" (sharing of goods or provisioning and principle of solidarity).

There is another point to consider. The gang of robbers knows that it needs the population that it targets for stealing, and it knows that its expropriation must not be total because the band lives off that population. Even in Plato the *polis* is organized as a gang of robbers vis-à-vis societies outside it. But in the global society the "other" is within society. How then to think about social order on the basis of a gang-of-robbers ethic, ignoring the dimension of provisioning and cohesion, and not having an "other" to expropriate and who is inside the market society?

This means that the norms postulated as the basis for society are actually not such, but rather are the discourse for legitimizing a social order built on the logic of a gang of robbers, which conceals from the rest of society the material character of the norms of justice (provisioning for some and expropriation for others), establishes the law as basis of social life and of universal compliance (so that the band may deceive and rob based on the universality of compliance), and reduces the common interest or common good to the level of the decorative, the superfluous, or the inimical (so that there may be no occasion for raising a challenge with another logic different from that of the gang of robbers).

In liberal and neoliberal thought the market is the mechanism that enables the struggle for particular interests to lead to general benefit. According to that logic it could be said that, in neoliberal thought, the bands of thieves in the end contribute to the general good, thanks to the "invisible hand." In respecting the internal norms of shared life and in going out to do battle with everyone else, they all, without intending to do so, contribute to the good of the entire society. In this case the market would be the normative standard that all the bands of thieves must respect so that their struggle may be sustainable over time.

Neoliberal globalization is increasingly being shown to be the planetary extension of this kingdom of the gangs of thieves that have set out to plunder the entire planet in the framework of the gang-of-thieves law—except that the target of this plunder is most of the population and nations of the world.

In this sense the chaos that we are experiencing is the product of this new world order, which is the order of the bands of thieves in which the transnationals have taken command of the economy, international financial institutions, and governments. As the strategy of globalization moves into a new phase, in which military mechanisms of imposition are becoming stronger by the day, this thought about the gang of robbers must be examined now not from the economic but from the politico-juridical standpoint.

LEGALITY AND LEGITIMACY OF THE GANG-OF-THIEVES ETHIC

Juridical positivism, which was formulated by Hans Kelsen in the first half of the twentieth century, developed as a major current in legal thinking.[8] It conceives the legal norms of a society as norms established by an effective (de facto) authority through a system of imputation that consists of establishing relationships between acts regarded as unlawful and the corresponding sanctions. The normative system governs the life of individuals within that social order. Imputation presumes an act of evaluation, but insofar as it has been enshrined as a positive norm, it has taken root in the positive world as a fact to which one must adapt. The power of actual constitution gives imputation a force similar to that given by causality.

The question of the validity of the norms arises. And Kelsen responds, "The validity of a positive norm is simply the particular mode of its existence." The particular form of its existence behaves as principal aspects: the act of its creation, its application, and its efficacy, that is, its fulfillment. Since law is "a social technique used to induce men to behave in a particular way" consisting of "assuring that . . . a human behavior regarded as socially harmful is followed by an act of coercion, which may be used in order to attain any social end whatsoever, inasmuch as law is not an end but a means . . . law is a technique of social control very closely connected to a social order which it is its purpose to uphold."[9]

If what is specific about legal normativity (as opposed to moral normativity) is its coercive character, what distinguishes the juridical act from other coercive acts? What is the difference between a group of bandits collecting a sum of money from a merchant and the tax collector collecting the same amount of money from the same person? Or, putting it in other terms, what is the difference between carrying out a death sentence and a murder? According to Kelsen, subjectively there is none, because for the victims the acts have the same meaning. They are acts of coercion that take the same thing from them—in one case a sum of money and in the other life itself. The only difference, according to Kelsen, is exterior, and it lies in the valid juridical (legal) character of the actions of the state and in the non-juridical character of the crimes. This objectivity is likewise recognized subjectively.

But now there arises the question, why is the juridical act valid? Because it is derived from a juridical system. A juridical system whose validity in turn ultimately rests on a unique fundamental norm that is the common source of the validity of all the norms of the system and is at the same time the source of its unity.[10] This means the very first constitution; there is no way to go further back. And here there is an interesting reflection:

> Let us take the example of coercion exercised by one individual over another, depriving that person of freedom by incarceration. Why is that coercion a juridical act belonging to a specific juridical order? Because it is prescribed by an individual norm established by a tribunal. This norm is valid because it has been created in accordance with the criminal code. The validity of the criminal code in turn comes from the constitution of the state, which establishes the procedure for making laws and establishes the competent body for it. If we should now wish to determine what is the basis for the validity of the constitution on which the validity of the laws and juridical acts depends, we could go back to an older constitution, but we would finally reach *a first constitution established by a usurper or by any group of people whatsoever.* The will of the first party establishing a constitution must then be regarded as having a normative character, and this fundamental hypothesis must be the starting point for all scholarly research on the juridical order considered. . . . That act is thus the fundamental fact of the juridical order derived from this constitution. Its juridical character may only be assumed and the entire juridical order is based on the assumption that the first constitution was a collection of valid juridical norms.[11]

In other words, the validity of a legal system (and therefore of all the norms derived from it) lies not in its content (here meaning its reference to concrete human life) but in its having been set up by a de facto power that still has its ability to apply the norms that it has established, and therefore by its efficacy. As a result of this criterion the author is led consistently to reflect on revolutionary processes:

> The importance of the fundamental norm is manifested particularly in cases in which one juridical order replaces another, not

in a legal manner, but by a revolution. . . . If that happens, it means that the old legal order ceases to be efficacious, and the new one becomes so, for the conduct of the individuals at which these two orders are aimed is no longer generally conformed to the old one but to the new. The latter is then regarded as *a juridical order*, and acts that are in keeping with it are juridical acts, but this assumes *a new fundamental norm* that delegates the power of creating law no longer to the monarch but to the revolutionary government. . . .

If, however, the attempt at revolution fails, the new order does not become *effective* because the individuals at which it is aimed do not obey it, and we have before us not a new constitution but a *crime of high treason*. Norms are not being created but violated, on the basis of the old order, whose validity assumes a fundamental norm that delegates to the monarch the power to create law.[12]

In other words, the measure of the revolutionary or criminal act is success:

There is thus a relationship between the validity and effectiveness of a juridical order; the former depends to some extent on the latter. . . .

In order for a national juridical framework to be valid, it must be efficacious, that is, what is done must be to some extent in keeping with this order. This is a *sine qua non* condition, but not a *per quam* condition. A juridical order is valid when its norms are created in accordance with the first constitution. But the science of law verifies that that fundamental norm is only assumed, if the juridical order created in accordance with the first constitution is to some extent, efficacious.[13]

Even so, the *per quam* in the end comes back to depending on the *sine qua non*. Inasmuch as this theory was worked out in the context of at least two different social systems (capitalism and socialism), this pure theory of law seeks to elaborate a general theory of the state and law that can be applied to this dual reality. It also notes that in the field of international law all de facto regimes that assured their effectiveness, that is, that succeeded in maintaining themselves, had to be recognized.[14]

It seems to me that these few lines illustrate very well the topic we are discussing. From a formalist or functional viewpoint, *there is no substantive difference between a state governed by law and a gang of rob-bers.* There is no subjective difference (in agreement with Kelsen) and no objective difference (in disagreement with Kelsen, inasmuch as he states that the fundamental norm that makes the difference between one and the other is the product of an originating act of force of a usurper or a particular human group, regardless of the content of the founding action).[15]

Similarly it is obvious that the elaboration of mystifying discourses about the state governed by law is nothing but the ideological cover-ing under which the modern gang of robbers takes shelter. In ignor-ing any material criterion of judgment (that is, reference to concrete human life) the effectiveness of a juridical (and generally systemic) order is reduced simply to the cleverness of the gang of robbers in power and to its de facto power.

In Latin America this is easily understandable. Those who set up the military dictatorships of national security, those who carried out structural adjustments, and those who control what are now called processes of re-democratization, all claimed to be defenders of the rule of law and the government by law.

Kelsen ultimately posits international law as fundamental norm of every political and juridical order. He perhaps thereby intends to set limits to the relativism of his focus in accordance with which anyone usurping power by a de facto route could be legitimated. But what happens when the usurper thinks it has the power to impose a new international order, as is the case now with the U.S. government?

When political processes are detached from the material referents of human life, politics becomes a mere play of powers who base their legitimacy on pure legality or on brute force combined with the ca-pacity for deception, seduction, and submission. Legitimacies based on de facto powers, on force, on compliance with laws, or on carica-ture democratic proceedings have proven to be diverse ways of instrumentalizing our societies by real bands of thieves. But they also accelerate crises and reactions that increasingly threaten shared so-cial life and human life itself.

THE ETHIC OF LIFE

Faced with the functional ethic and the gang of robbers ethic, we can only oppose an ethic of life and of the common good. The pro-cesses of globalization and the planetary nature of the crises we now face do not allow for building societies set within in the framework of the gang-of-robbers ethic. Solutions must be common. That is the very idea presented in the Zapatista slogan of a society with room for everyone.

The way out of this crisis understood as chaos in the sources of life (nature, human labor, and pleasurable shared human life) cannot come out of the paradigm of individual interests and of the competitive society. And hence the ethic of life can no longer become an ethic of war for my life and that of my friends (the gang). Indeed, it is this very ethic that has led to the current predicaments. That is why so-called specific struggles, when they are not open to a common good perspective, are still to some extent an upside-down copy of this logic of the gang of robbers. Hence the urgent need for a new ethic of the common good raised up out of the excluded and oppressed majorities of the whole world. The option for the poor unrelated to the common good is limited to itself, just as reference to the common good without the discernment given by the option for the poor is often itself a device of power.

Today the ethic of life is expressed in countless resistances to this neoliberal globalization process in defense of the legitimate rights to life of different human groups. On the basis of these resistances and movements, today it is also said that there must be links and a common program of resistance to neoliberalism and to imperial totalitarianism, and for the construction of a new international order that will make it possible for all human beings, nations, peoples, and cultures to live and to share their life.

If we analyze well the dynamics and exigencies emerging from real resistance movements, we find that they are not rejecting the market, the state, or the legal order out of hand. Rather, they refuse to allow them ultimately to determine which human lives "deserve" to be respected. They refuse to allow these institutions or institutionalities to be totalized, to become "super-subjects" who grant life and death and determine the legitimacy of the right to life of every human being.

On the contrary, human life is the criterion over every institution, norm, action, or policy. Institutions themselves have emerged from the necessities of life, and it is out of this horizon of needs that their performance, their need for reform, and whether they are to be limited or eliminated are judged. This is a judgment out of the recognition of the very limits of human action and hence a judgment that has gone through stages of learning in which utopianisms and voluntarist absolutisms that claimed to be able to create the new society out of nothing and in absolute freedom are gradually being overcome.

In this sense the necessary change is no longer satisfied with imagining new modes of social and institutional organization, nor does it seek to invent modes of social organization absolutely without precedent in history. Rather, what is being said is that in addition to the need for new institutions and reformed old institutions, the humanization of a society rests on an adequate relationship between structures and institutions and the conscious action of social subjects. The aim is to think and build modes of open and flexible relations between subjects and institutions. And this is the basis for developing a non-formal, noninstitutional, open understanding of the democratic society for which we all yearn. The aim is a democracy that is not so much a formal political system as a society in which it is possible for all to live, one that allows the ongoing mobilization and interaction of social groups and diverse interests on the basis of giving priority to the weak so that all those different proposals for the "good life" that do not assault the life of others may flourish in endless dialogue.

ETHIC OF LIFE AND COMMON GOOD

In the context of this conflict between a functional market ethic (which has opened the way for the gang-of-robbers ethic) and an ethic of life, which is the ethical conflict of our present moment, conflicts of class, gender, race, ethnicity, larger and smaller nation, migratory population, region, community, and so forth are now taking place. These battles are being waged by the majority populations of our planet, but the system treats them as minority conflicts, both in geopolitics and at the state level.

It is a multiplicity of different conflicts in terms of space, time, economics, politics, culture, with greater or lesser degrees of fragmentation, but not thereby unrelated to one another; through them runs this ethic of life that urgently demands the establishment of an alternative horizon of the common good planetwide, but also regionally, nationally, and locally.

By contrast, the functional ethic deals with the complexity of the natural and social world in an utterly simplistic way: respect for the law and relationships of force. This is a sacralized law, identified a priori as a saving mechanism that seeks to "order" the world on the basis of a unitary, simple, abstract, and totalized principle that is mercantile and strategic-instrumental in nature and essentially a relationship of force.

In the framework of this conflict we face at least four broad lines of work in the ethical field (with the further qualification that these are transformations in the field of the ethical that must be connected to a process of major cultural and political transformations):

1. strengthening the ethics of resistance.
2. promoting social action upon the absolutized totalized functional market ethic, which leads to the strengthening of civil society and the struggle for the transformation of the state to intervene in the logic of the totalized market in behalf of the demands of life of the population affected by neoliberalization (90 percent of Latin American societies).
3. constructing an ethic of the common good for our times in opposition to the unilateral and violent logic of power.
4. transforming the cultural matrix of Western ethical thought, which means an epistemologico-cultural revolution of ethics.

Just as modernity declared itself to be a cultural age that was overcoming not only myths but also religions and the weight of traditions, declaring them all to be authoritarianism, the current state of this modernity now in a crisis of exhaustion shows that it not only did not end myths or religions, traditions or authoritarianisms, but that it has built within itself myths and religiosities, traditions and authoritarianisms that are much more powerful and oppressive over human beings. Many centuries have been needed to understand that the new society to be built cannot follow the path of modernity, whose presumptuous faith in formal reason has brought it to vast life-destroying processes, to the point where it finally realizes that everything it sought to overcome it has reproduced, much augmented. Respect for life must show respect for the myths, religions, and traditions of peoples, and the recognition of their strong rational dimension. That means revising our ideas of what is rational and what is irrational. Our problem today is not overcoming myths, religions, or traditions, but expanding our ideas of rationality and discerning among all the material and symbolic production of society that which helps reproduce, re-create, and re-enchant the life of all human beings as opposed to everything that contributes to and legitimizes the subjection and sacrifice of human beings.

ETHIC OF LIFE AND LIBERATION THEOLOGY:
THE OPTION FOR THE POOR AND THE COMMON GOOD

From the outset liberation theology was the response of a group of Christians to the ethical challenge of the impoverished multitudes of Latin America and their liberation struggles. Articulating that response theologically was an achievement that marked a milestone in the history of Latin American culture. It would not have been possible had it not been an ethical response to a challenge that was likewise ethical.

That was not how it was seen at the time. It was outweighed by the political context. Moreover, the prevailing conceptions of ethics at that time prevented such an understanding. But as the challenge from the impoverished people and the influence of liberation theology reached other realms of culture, it became possible for properly Latin American conceptions of ethics to develop.

The Latin American theology and ethics developed in the second half of the twentieth century were distinguished not only by how they related to social and economic sciences, but also because social and economic sciences in Latin America were different. Again, what was new about Latin American social science sought to be understood primarily from the standpoint of its politicization. Today we can see that its fundamental feature was not its degree of politicization but its ethical character. Politicization was merely a corollary of this character that was translated into a particular commitment.

The issue here is not to examine how these multiple relationships and determinations developed among the theological, ethical, and social science contexts in the Latin America of the 1960s and 1970s. Indeed, that was a historic moment when the entire social and cultural life of the continent underwent a genuine revolution. As time goes on, the dimension of this cultural change will be seen more clearly. It was the social praxis (broadly understood) of that time that wove all these complex interrelationships together.

Latin American thought has changed significantly since then. It is no longer conceivable that there should be any significant analysis that does not start from a recognition of the determined and specific context in which thinking, feeling, speaking, listening, and acting are taking place; that does not start with commitments explicitly assumed that determine the specific perspective of the analysis; and that does not understand itself as serving a social praxis or a specific social challenge. In other words, the ethical decision (which each one must make) is a constitutive part of social analysis, and it does not undermine the objectivity of analysis but rather makes it possible.

THE OPTION FOR THE POOR
AND THE ETHIC OF LIFE

In the 1990s much was written about the so-called inevitable crisis of liberation theology, if not about its fall, failure, and termination. Much was also written on the necessary changes in that theology.

As Gustavo Gutiérrez asks, *"Where will the poor sleep in the twenty-first century?"* Even if liberation theology should die, the question of the fate of the growing multitudes of impoverished human beings would retain its currency in the present-day world. For Gustavo Gutiérrez, the option for the poor is the fundamental theological option, not liberation theology understood as theological thought or as simple "theory" or discourse. In other words, liberation means either a practical (not simply epistemological) option for the poor, or it means nothing.

The radicality of this claim also affects social theory. Even if there were no set of analytical tools relevant to social analysis (a very widespread notion with the death of Marxism, socialism, dependency theory, and critical theories in general), the central problem would continue to be "where will the poor sleep?" This ethical challenge (the "cry of the poor") becomes the source situation of theology, and ethical sensitivity and response are the primary and fundamental theological response, without which the theological universe of an authentic Christianity—or at least one closer to the model praxis of Jesus—cannot be built.

With the heightening of the planetary crises over the last forty years, and awareness of them, liberation theology's call to the option for the poor and subsequently to the option for the God of life (not of the law) has taken on a dimension that is not simply Latin American or Third World, but universal.

The strategy of globalization has also accelerated the globalization of poverty and extreme poverty and has aggravated the threats hovering over the life of all human beings. The option for the poor has now become the foundation of the option for human life itself, and it is increasingly understood in the framework of a logic of the common good, of this struggle for a society where all human beings will have a place as human beings, all human worlds as cultures in terms of ways of living.

This means that the option for the poor as ethic of liberation is the way in which the universal cry for an ethic of life as foundation of social life is manifested.

Today these postulates of a Latin American theology or ethics have shown their validity and relevance beyond the boundaries of Latin American society. And that is why, when they see the direction to which neoliberal totalitarianism and its now war-mongering and fundamentalist forms are heading, liberation theologians ask, If things keep going the way they are, where will we all sleep?[16]

—Translated by Phillip Berryman

NOTES

[1] Cf. German Gutiérrez, *Etica y economía en Adam Smith y F. Hayek* (San José, Costa Rica: DEI, 1998); and idem, "Etica funcional y ética de la vida," *Pasos* 74 (San José, Costa Rica: DEI, 1998).

[2] Adam Smith, *The Theory of Moral Sentiments* (1759; reprint Cambridge, UK: Cambridge University Press, 2002), 100–101.

[3] Ibid., 98. By protection of life he understands the punishment of the individual and intentional murder, not structural murder, which in his conception is outside the scope of ethics, although he recognizes it openly when he says that the fluctuations of the market lead to the death of children of the poorer classes or stimulate their reproduction (Adam Smith, *The Wealth of Nations* [1776; reprint London: Everyman's Library, 1975], 57–78).

[4] Friedrich von Hayek, *La fatal arrogancia* (Madrid: Unión Editorial, 1990). "The idea that those who adopted the practices of the competitive market achieved greater population increase and displaced other groups who practiced different customs dates back many years" (192). "Only those groups that behave in accordance with this moral order are able to survive and prosper. . . . What decides which system is going to prevail is the number of persons that each system is able to maintain" (204).

[5] Friedrich von Hayek, in *El Mercurio* (Santiago, Chile), April 19, 1981, cited by Franz Hinkelammert, *Cultura de la esperanza y sociedad sin exclusión* (San José, Costa Rica: DEI, 1995), 78.

[6] For a reflection on the ethic of the gang of robbers in the tradition of Western thought from Plato, Saint Augustine, Luther, Adam Smith, and others, see Franz Hinkelammert, *El grito del sujeto* (San José, Costa Rica: Dei, 1998), 158–90.

[7] Smith, *The Theology of Moral Sentiments*, 100–101.

[8] Hans Kelsen, *Teoría pura del derecho* (Buenos Aires: Eudeba, 1960). *Translator's note:* This Spanish translation is evidently of the first German edition

Reine Rechtslehre, published in 1934. The English translation, *Pure Theory of Law* (Gloucester, MA: Peter Smith, 1989), is of the second German edition, published in 1960, which was a thorough revision of the 1934 original. Hence, the translation here is from the Spanish as cited by German Gutiérrez.

⁹ Ibid., 73–74.

¹⁰ "The validity of juridical norms does not come from their content. The law may have any content whatsoever, for no human content in itself is unsuited for being the object of a juridical norm. The validity of that norm is not affected by the fact that its content is in opposition to a moral value or any other value" (ibid., 386). "A juridical norm is valid if it has been created in a particular manner, that is, according to the rules laid down, and in accordance with a specific method. The only valid law is positive law, that which has been 'posited.' Its positivity lies in the fact that it comes necessarily from a creative act and is thus independent of morality and of any other analogous normative system. The norms of natural law and those of morality are, on the contrary, deduced from a fundamental norm, which by reason of its content, is regarded as though it appeared immediately evident, as an emanation from the divine will, from nature, or from pure reason" (ibid., 137).

¹¹ Ibid., 138, 140.

¹² Ibid., 140, 141.

¹³ Ibid., 141.

¹⁴ "In establishing the principle that in order to be valid a juridical order must have a certain degree of efficacy, we are limiting ourselves to formulating a norm of positive law that does not belong to this juridical order, but to international law. . . . International law considers a de facto power as legitimate insofar as the order of criterion established by that power is truly efficacious. . . . This principle of effectiveness, which is one of the rules of international law, constitutes the *fundamental norm* of all national juridical orders. The constitution established by the first constituent party is only valid if it is efficacious. . . . Even a government that has achieved power through a revolution or a coup d'etat is considered valid by international law if it is independent of other governments and is in a position to make the norms that it issues respected in a lasting manner. This means that a coercive order dependent on international law is a legitimate order and is therefore valid and obligatory for the territory in which it has become effective in a stable manner" (ibid., 143–44).

¹⁵ Nevertheless, Kelsen, much less ideologically than Adam Smith and Friedrich Hayek, eventually recognizes in his own way the ultimate material aspect of the juridical order. Ultimately a judicial order depends on its ability to eliminate all resistance of the human groups affected, and from there derives its own justification of validity. But over any juridical order there always hangs, like a sword of Damocles, the potential founding force of any new order that issues from the pressing needs of a subject population. In other words, the relative validity of any juridical order depends on the emergence of social forces capable of changing the social order, and that emergence

depends on how much that order responds to the needs of all the members of society.

¹⁶ In view of this question the option for the poor becomes the foundation of an ethic that is necessary, not optional, for guaranteeing the life of all human beings and is the criterion of specification of an ethic of life.

6.

To Speak of God from More Than One Place

Theological Reflections from the Experience of Migration

Nancy E. Bedford

Un círculo de mi vida se termina y otro círculo está a punto de comenzar y la respuesta no está clara, mientras el avión sube y sube hacia el aire turbulento y azul del exilio, rumbo de nuevo al Norte y el Sur comienza a retroceder hacia la memoria, no supe en ese momento tal como no sé ahora que escribo y traduzco estas palabras si ese círculo habrá alguna vez de cerrarse.
—Ariel Dorfman, *Heading South, Looking North*[1]

As anthropologist Néstor García Canclini points out, in the world of late capitalism, Latin Americans share the experience of being globalized: as debtors, as producers of culture, and as migrants.[2] All three of these signifiers are closely interrelated and richly suggestive as generators of theological questions. If we ponder debt, for instance, we can immediately bring to mind biblical images related to debts and debtors in the texts about the Jubilee and in the Lord's Prayer. As people whose countries are structurally in debt and therefore ourselves "structural debtors," the exercise of praying to a God who—in a context of institutionalized usury—forgives us our debts as we forgive our debtors resonates powerfully. Indeed, Latin American theology has a rich tradition of pondering both human and divine economies and how they might be interwoven.[3] Or, to take up the question of cultural production without forgetting the economic dimension, it is intriguing to ponder Latin American religious practices and theology inasmuch as they, too, constitute cultural production. We might ask: How have Latin American religiosity and theologies, their language and their symbols, been exported and imported across national and cultural borders? In what ways has the circulation of theologies had a bearing upon the praxis and language of Christian believers around the globe—that is, how are they being globalized?[4] As captivating as these questions are, I would like to focus here on some theological implications of the *third* way in which Latin Americans are being globalized according to García Canclini's analysis, that is, as *migrants*.

In truth, this last category should be read in a way that is intimately linked to the other two, because migrants are both economic actors and agents in the production of culture. Consider, for instance, the economic and cultural significance of remittances. Viewed over the last decade, remittances sent home by migrants have been a larger source of income for developing countries than official development assistance and more stable than the volatile investment monies that flow only to certain countries at certain times. Remittances to developing countries go first of all to lower-middle-income and low-income countries.[5] Migrants from Latin American countries living in the United States sent around $30 billion to relatives in their home countries in 2003; this figure far exceeds the $17.2 billion allotted by the U.S. government to foreign aid to all countries.[6] The money tends to go directly into the hands of relatives at home to aid in their subsistence and therefore to uphold a cultural ethos and a way of life. From a theological perspective, one important question that this flow raises is what it might mean concretely in the life of ecclesial communities in Latin America. I am reminded of Paul's report in Galatians 2:1–10 of the strictures by James, Peter, and John: that it was permissible for Paul and Barnabas to continue their itinerant (migrant) mission among the Gentiles as long as the poor were not forgotten; the offering of the Macedonian churches spoken of in 2 Corinthians 8 also comes to mind. Significantly, the remittances to Latin America by migrants did not diminish with the downturn of the U.S. economy after September 11, 2001, which means that many migrants give sacrificially to support their relatives back home even in the face of unemployment and sub-employment in the Unites States. Furthermore, some recent models suggest that though the physical loss represented by the emigration of persons cannot be reversed, the older metaphor of the "brain drain" was too unilateral, given what actually happens when—for instance—highly skilled people leave their countries of origin. Instead, what *can* emerge, given the right conditions, is a "brain exchange," "brain circulation," or "network" approach[7]—or to put it theologically, a more *perichoretic* model of service and exchange.[8] Thus the remittances themselves can become a metaphor for the sharing of knowledge by expatriate networks with people and institutions "back home"—to the personal and cultural enrichment of both sides.

The idea of Latin Americans as producers of culture can also be read productively in conjunction with the experience of Latin American migrants. One example of cultural production by Latinos/as in the Unites States is Chicana literature and feminist theory. Gloria Anzaldúa might be seen as paradigmatic in this regard; her work has the added value of highlighting that although in one sense her heritage might be seen as that of a migrant by the hegemonic logic of the Mexican–United States border, in another sense she is rooted in what is now U.S. territory in ways that precede present-day borders.[9] She writes, purposely mixing English and Spanish and providing no translation for the monolingual:

> Because I, a *mestiza,*
> Continually walk out of one culture
> and into another,
> because I am in all cultures at the same time,
> alma entre dos mundos, tres, cuatro,
> me zumba la cabeza con lo contradictorio.
> Estoy norteada por todas las voces que me hablan
> *simultáneamente.*[10]

The metaphor that she uses for this is *nepantilism,* from the Aztec word *nepantla,* which she translates as "torn between ways." Her work "interweaves autobiography, history of the Chicano/a Southwest, essay, autobiography, and poetry in a manner that defies traditional categorization"[11] and, along with other Chicana writers such as Cherríe Moraga and Norma Alarcón, is spurring on a generation of Latina theologians, somewhat as Alice Walker has done for womanist theologians.[12] By choosing these women as prime examples of producers of culture, I am purposely going against the socio-symbolic grain, because—as Ofelia Schutte points out—Latinas specifically tend to be coded stereotypically in U.S. society as hot blooded, temperamental, submissive, defiant, sexually repressed or sexually overactive, exploited, and so on, but *not* as producers of culture. At best, they are thought of as caregivers whose function it is to transmit but not to create culture.[13]

Another example of the cultural production of migrants from Latin America is their gradual transformation from Mexicans, Peruvians, or Uruguayans into *Latinos/as en USA,* a process full of ambiguities but perhaps also of promise, in which "nationalities are transgressed, extended, reformulated, and combined, giving rise to multiple identities."[14] One study of Peruvians in Paterson, New Jersey, shows their transnationalism, inasmuch as they move capital, goods, and ideas back and forth from Lima to New Jersey, but also how they at times become honorary Dominicans, Latin Americans, Latinos, or Hispanics, and adopt Colombians or Salvadorans as honorary Peruvians.[15] These kinds of processes are constantly being negotiated in Hispanic *iglesias evangélicas* (evangelical churchs) and *parroquias católicas* (Catholic parishes) in the United States and are suggestive theologically: in what ways can and should Hispanic churches claim or contest the image of what is sold and "packaged" as Latino/a in U.S. society? Should the gospel empower migrants to question dominant U.S. values and desires, to adapt to them—or perhaps to adopt a mixture of both? What of the racism suffered by migrants within and without Latino/a circles? What should the role of Spanish be in the services and in the culture of Hispanic churches? What of the migrants of Latin American origin who worship at English-speaking churches? These are not trifling questions. Several studies suggest that the retention of the language of origin—in this case Spanish—over more than one generation "is associated with high self-esteem, cultural pride, academic success and socioeconomic mobility among members of the second generation."[16] These matters certainly have a cultural component but also an eminently *theological* one, inasmuch as they have to do with power, with empowerment, and with ways of being in the world of human beings beloved by God. To subvert English monolingualism in the U.S. churches and in the academy without falling into a sectarian politics of identity that puts Latinos/as in competition with groups such as Native Americans, African Americans, and Asian Americans may be more of a theological statement—and achievement—than seems evident at first glance.

Within this context of proximity with the other two strands, but focusing primarily on the actual category of Latin Americans globalized as migrants, I propose to reflect upon this question: What might it mean for theology when—as a result of transnational migration—we begin to speak of God "from more than one place"?

TRANSNATIONAL LATIN AMERICAN MIGRATION

Migration is, of course, much older than what we now call Latin America. The first inhabitants of the so-called Americas probably migrated from Asia over the Bering Strait twenty thousand years or more ago, when it was a land bridge that scientists call Beringia.[17] There were probably several waves of migration of these "original peoples" *(pueblos originarios)*. The ancestors from the many different ethnicities in Africa, Asia, and Europe whose cultural roots and stories, together with those of the original peoples, are our own as Latin Americans today, were also migrants: some willing, some forced.[18] José Vasconcelos famously called Latin Americans *la raza cósmica,* the "cosmic race" made up of all other races, which may be poetic license but certainly holds some truth.[19]

Latin American or Latino/a is not a racial or ethnic category. Indeed, it is not even strictly a linguistic category. Not all so-called Latinos/as or Latin Americans speak Spanish fluently. Some belong culturally and linguistically to the original peoples who retained their languages against the onslaught of Spanish after 1492. Others are the second or third generation in a non-Spanish-speaking country. Still others hail from countries in Latin America or the Caribbean where Spanish is not spoken at all.[20] Hispanic as a widely cultural and to some extent linguistic, non-ethnic category implodes the ethnic categories so characteristic of U.S. discourse. When Hispanics try to describe themselves ethnically, they use a multitude of self-designations and are usually satisfied with none. As María Pilar Aquino, Daisy Machado, and Jeanette Rodríguez lucidly write about Latinas, "Our common bond is that we live in the United States of America (our physical reality), where we have all experienced racism, sexism, devaluation and exclusion by a culture and a society that cannot seem to move beyond the white/black focus of its national discourse on race and national identity."[21]

Although there would be much to say about the migration of Latin Americans from region to region or country to country within our own subcontinent or to Australia, Japan, and Europe,[22] here I focus on the situation of Latin Americans as migrants in the United States, primarily for three reasons: linguistic, geopolitical, and existential.

First of all, the United States now has the world's fourth-largest Spanish-speaking population,[23] as well as many immigrants from Brazil and the Caribbean. It has paradoxically become one of the most populous "Latin American" countries in a way that is both influential and significantly different than the reality of the (other) countries in "Nuestra América" (Martí). As Cervantes-Rodríguez and Lutz point out, Spanish (or more precisely, the Castillian language, *castellano*) was one of the major languages through which the modern capitalist world was articulated. It was employed to control and discipline subaltern groups and languages in some regions of Spain, the Canary Islands, and what is now Latin America, a process largely achieved by the end of the sixteenth century. However, the global rise of English subsequently transformed Spanish into a racial marker used to identify colonial subjects, first, and later minority or subaltern groups (such as Latin American migrants in the United States today). Spanish was pushed to the borders of Western cosmology as Spain's global hegemony declined; in its place emerged U.S. manifest destiny and its expansionism with regard to Latin America, beginning particularly with its war against Mexico in 1846 and its increasing racialization of the Hispanic population. This population is currently made up of migrants from Mexico, Puerto Rico, and Cuba—the three traditionally strongest groups of Latinos/as—and additionally of the so-called new Latinos from other countries in Latin America, who by the time of the 2000 census made up between 15 and 18 percent of the Latino population. The constant influx of migrants from Latin America and the rising influence of Spanish-language media such as Univisión and Telemundo ensure the continuation of Spanish in the United States as a presence not achieved by any other minority language. Nonetheless, to raise its status and attain symmetry with regard to English would require "reinforcing the use of Spanish as an empowering instrument of communication and knowledge for Latino and non-Latino groups."[24]

In the second place, the United States exerts imperial power with respect to Latin America and the Caribbean in direct and indirect ways.[25] One shorthand way of expressing this is to remember three dates: 1848, 1898, and 1973. I am referring respectively to 1848 as the year of the Treaty of Guadalupe-Hidalgo, in which much of what was previously Mexico was annexed by the Unites States;[26] 1898 as the year of the Spanish-American War, with its particular significance for Puerto Rico and Cuba; and 1973 as the year of the coup in which Salvador Allende was overthrown in Chile with U.S. support. Many other dates could be chosen to symbolize an interventionism in Latin America that is a way of life in Washington. It must perhaps be admitted that, as Walter Mignolo puts it, the emergence of global colonialism managed by transnational corporations redraws classical spatial distinctions between colonial centers and peripheries. He argues that the *colonial difference,* that is, the space in which coloniality of power is enacted, is now all over the place, in the peripheries of the center and in the centers of the periphery.[27] At the same time, there is a very real sense in which the United States continues to be at the center of power; the March 2003 invasion of Iraq made this particularly apparent. To live in the United States, the seat of world imperial power and the symbolic center of transnational finance, puts immigrants from Latin American countries in an ambiguous and theologically challenging situation. Perhaps this holds especially for Protestant (*evangélico/a*) immigrants, moving from places in which for decades they have been religious and theological minorities, often sociologically sectarian in character, to an immensely powerful country in which historically most varieties of Protestantism—even those that profess the separation of church and state—have been closely linked to civil religion and a symbolic place of power. This move happens in their lives at the same time that they move to minority status in another realm: that of being Latinos/as in a racial U.S. society. The question is whether Latinos/as will compensate for the second by strategically adopting a civil-religion version of Protestantism, and with it a religiously tinted ideology that works against the interests of their home countries and erases their prophetic voice.

In the third place, honesty requires mention of an existential reason for spotlighting migrants in the United States. Together with our three "cosmic" daughters, whose ancestors run the gamut from Cherokee and Choctaw to Comechingones, from English Puritans and Scots-Irish Protestants to Swiss, Spanish, and Italian Catholics, and who joyfully came to the world in our beloved Buenos Aires, my husband and I recently became additions to the strangely virtual category of *Latinos/as en USA.* The expression rolls strangely on our tongues; it challenges us and begs both for critical disarticulation and theological construction. We have always understood ourselves primarily as Argentines, and still do, yet we feel bound in solidarity by many shared interests and historical and linguistic ties to other Latin Americans in the North and South. Thus, as always, there is a sense of autobiography in my theology, in the fact that I am framing these questions in this way, at this time. Parting from this personal perspective, one of the questions that has become a burning one for me is how to rethink my theology *in this place,* here, in what Cuban-American theologians (and many others in the Spanish-speaking world) often refer to as Babylon.[28]

MERITS AND LIMITS OF THE METAPHOR
OF THE *LOCUS THEOLOGICUS*

The metaphor of the "place" of theology has been a rich and productive one for centuries. From its Aristotelian roots it grew during Scholasticism and branched out in the sixteenth century into Protestant and Catholic understandings. On the Protestant side the paradigmatic work was Melanchthon's *Loci communes rerum theologicarum* of 1531, which took the *loci* to mean "places" in the sense of "doctrines" that organized theological expression, such as justification, faith, grace, or sin. On the Roman Catholic side, the *loci* came to refer to the "places" in which the truths of faith could be found and appropriated, roughly following the understanding of Melchior Cano in his *De locis theologicis* of 1563. These "places" were subdivided by Cano in the *loci theologici propii* of the Bible, oral tradition, and Magisterium, on the one hand, and the *loci alieni* of reason, philosophy, and history, on the other.[29] It is the latter tradition that is preponderant in Latin American liberation theology, appropriated and transformed creatively by theologians such as Ignacio Ellacuría and Jon Sobrino.

With his usual vigor Ellacuría states that the poor in Latin America are a *locus theologicus* inasmuch as they constitute "the maximum and scandalous prophetic and apocalyptic presence of the Christian God and consequently, the privileged place of Christian praxis and reflection."[30] He then further refines his definition in a threefold fashion. He understands the poor as *locus theologicus* first of all as "the place where the God of Jesus is manifested in a special way because the Father has so willed it." This manifestation is a revelation that illuminates but also calls to conversion: to our conversion to the world of the poor. In the second place, *locus theologicus* is the most apt place for living out faith in Jesus and its corresponding praxis of following Jesus *(seguimiento)*. Just as a place of wealth and privilege constitutes a dangerous place for faith, the place of the poor is a privileged one for faith. Third, he considers the poor as *locus theologicus* as the most "proper" place (and here the faint echo of Melchior Cano's *locus propium* is certainly no accident) in which to carry out reflection about faith, that is to say, Christian theology. Ellacuría goes on to distinguish between the "place" *(lugar)* and the "source" *(fuente)* of theology, understanding the former as the place "from which" theological experience and reflection emerge and the latter as that which "in one way or another maintains the contents of faith." However, he refuses to make a hard and fast distinction between the two.[31]

Sobrino introduces a similar twist on Roman Catholic tradition by distinguishing between the *sources* of theology proper (such as scripture, tradition, and Magisterium) and the *locus* or place of theology par excellence, which he likewise understands to be the world of the poor. At the same time, the source and the place of theology are closely interconnected, inasmuch as the *place* can also serve as a *source* because it can provide conditions for the actualization of certain truths.[32] If, as Ellacuría and Sobrino state, there are privileged structures in and through which the Christian truth can express itself more clearly— such as the place in which the poor are[33]—then the people with whom a theologian identifies and the social location of the theologian are not indifferent to the depth of his or her insights. This conviction is at the heart of the most common usage of *locus theologicus* as a metaphor in Latin American theology.

A similar epistemological (though non-theological) move is made by some third-world feminist theorists such as Chandra Talpade Mohanty. She incorporates insights from the feminist-standpoint epistemology of thinkers such as Nancy Hartsock, Dorothy Smith, and Sandra Harding, according to which there is a link among social location, women's experiences, and epistemic perspectives, but she further refines them by locating her vision in the *particular situation of a given historical group of poor women* in the Third World. She considers this an epistemological move contrary to "special interest" thinking: "to see the world better it is necessary to read *up* the ladder of privilege, because privilege blinds us to reality." Thus, given their *locus*, most African Americans and Latinos/as are more conscious of environmental racism than most "white" people in the United States simply because three out of five African Americans and Latinos/as live close to toxic waste sites.[34]

The metaphor of place is both rich and suggestive, pointing as it does to geographical and social location and their fundamental importance for both the interpretation and production of theological discourse. However, the metaphor has one fundamental limitation that becomes evident when we look at it from the perspective of migrants: its *static character*. Certainly, we need to drink from our own wells, as Gustavo Gutiérrez has so vividly written.[35] But what happens when those wells are left behind, in a geographical sense, in a place of origin far away? From what wells should *migrants* drink? Do we carry bottled water with us—or will the water become stale? Do we drink virtual water using communication technologies—as when we read newspapers from home over the internet? Do we get inebriated on water from our wells when we are able to visit our places of origin? Can we dig new wells, and are they somehow less hydrating by virtue of the water quality abroad? What happens to us when, as a result of globalization and migration, our *locus theologicus* becomes blurred, in movement, unstable, not easily recognizable as a "place" socially and physically? Where or how can we situate ourselves to speak meaningfully of God?

TO SPEAK OF GOD FROM MORE THAN ONE PLACE

Characteristic of the experience of migration is a certain restlessness, a fluidity, a forced flexibility, and an inventiveness in responding to new situations in new ways. The experience of migration questions fixed ontological categories and tidy linguistic solutions. As migrants who are theologians and theologians who are migrants, our experience is by definition more that of a way or a path than of a place. We might think therefore in terms of a *via theologica* as a possible variation on the *locus theologicus*. This both is and is not a further elaboration of the *locus theologicus* theme found in what we might term classic Latin American liberation theologians such as Sobrino.[36] The fact that *following* Jesus *(seguimiento)* is so central to his theological method and indispensable for *knowing* God—that is, for his theological epistemology—is already very much akin to the fluidity and dynamism structurally present in migrant experiences. This can also be expressed christologically, as when he states about Jesus that "Christ is 'truth' inasmuch as he is 'way.'"[37] Clearly in Sobrino a theology done in solidarity with the place of the poor already involves a *way*. What I want to do here is make the point that for migrants (and particularly for the poorest among migrants, because they often bear the burden of an undocumented legal status and consequent high job insecurity) the *locus* for speaking of God is structurally, by definition, a *way*. The very fidelity to the place of this group of the poor that leads to speaking of God "from more than one place" points to both the merits and the limits of the *locus* metaphor as a sufficiently precise instrument for articulating the God-talk of liberation.

If the rule of prayer lays down the rule of faith, as in Prosper of Aquitaine's maxim,[38] one first test of this hypothesis could be to examine the prayers of migrants for hints of how they speak *to* God from more than one place. And indeed, to pray the *via crucis* from the fragile and fluid perspective of migrants seems to give it a depth and dynamism that point to a larger story of human and divine migrations, as the following liturgical rendition of the three stations of the cross where Jesus falls makes clear:

> Jesus falls under the weight of the cross. Help us not to fall under the weight of our crosses of each day: poverty, discouragement, ups and downs, a lack of hope. We the migrants go from one side to the other in this country and, because many times we have fallen, we are not welcome.
> Reader: Lord, you who fell under the weight of the cross.
> *All: Help us not to be bitter.*

> Jesus, the weight of the cross is too much and you fall again. My cross is very heavy, also, Lord. It is so hard. People call me "vagrant" and "lazy" as if I were a criminal. I want to return to my town, but I cannot, because the situation there has become even worse.
> Reader: Jesus, who got up the second time.
> *All: Don't let them marginalize me because of my condition as a migrant.*

> Jesus, your cross is so heavy, like mine, but you inspire me to continue on. My cross becomes so heavy when they tell me, "There is no work here." "Return to your town, to your country, because here you are a nuisance." And I can't do anything in the face of this.
> Reader: Lord, forgive them.
> *All: Because they know not what they do.*[39]

It leaps to the eye that christological considerations can in fact take on significant nuances from the fluid perspective of migrants. In the prayer above, it is evident that the migrant poor *have no place,* no fixed address; in a sense, their *locus* is defined as the lack of a *locus.* Jesus, who had no fixed place upon which to lay his head (Mt 8:20), is seen as a brother in suffering and dislocation. It is no coincidence that the *via crucis* with its narrative framework and its movement from station to station would lend itself to express prayerfully what we have tentatively called the *via theologica* of migrants.

It does not take much imagination to take the insight reflected in the prayers of migrants—such as the one above—and begin to develop it christologically. Indeed, this hermeneutical lens for Christology seems to be one that suggests itself quite naturally to theologians who are themselves, by virtue of their own biographies, conversant with the fluid place of migration. Hugo López, for instance, suggests that the work of Christ could be seen metaphorically as the "granting of documents for migration to those who would otherwise wander aimlessly in their exile."[40] The Incarnation itself can be read from the perspective of migration, as suggested by Korean American theologian Jung Young Lee: "The incarnation can also be compared to divine immigration, in which God emigrated from a heavenly place to this world. As an immigrant in the new world, Christ, like the Asian-American, experienced rejection, harassment, and humiliation."[41] Certainly, "migrant" theologians are not alone in coming to such an insight; Karl Barth already spoke of the "journey of the Son into the distant land"[42] in a christological transmutation of the journey of the prodigal son.

TOWARD A CHRISTOLOGICAL REFLECTION FROM A MIGRANT PERSPECTIVE

The Bible is full of stories of wanderers such as Hagar, Sarah, and Abraham; stories of foreigners such as Ruth; stories and psalms of exile coming out of the Babylonian experience; stories of pilgrims and strangers beckoned on their way by faith—as presented in Hebrews 11. Why, then, speak here of *migrants*? The main reason is methodological. I wish to start *from below*, from the concrete reality of Latin America. And many Latin Americans—indeed, many people from all over the world—live out the experience of migration to the point that it can be said, with García Canclini, that Latin Americans are being *globalized* as migrants. Rosi Braidotti examines the metaphors of exile and of migrant only to discard them as figures for her own feminist philosophy; she instead chooses "nomadism" and "nomadic subject" as a self-designation. Nevertheless, her analysis sheds light on why the figure of the migrant is attractive to a theological project closely attuned to the legacy of liberation theology. She points out the fact that "the migrant bears a close tie to class structure; in most countries, the migrants are the most economically disadvantaged groups." On the other hand, "the exile is often motivated by political reasons and does not often coincide with the lower classes; as for the nomad, s/he is usually beyond classification, a sort of classless unit."[43] Although these three categories often overlap and coincide more than Braidotti might concede, her comment makes it clear that the designation that points toward issues of class and poverty more clearly than the other two is that of *migrant*. It points to the present-day subtext of capitalist globalization and displacement of peoples more clearly than either exile or nomad.

Given the social reality that I have tried to describe in terms of a *via theologica* rather than a *locus theologicus,* what hermeneutical riches might the perspective of migrants bring to the table? As it turns out, their viewpoint does indeed contribute to the task of biblical hermeneutics, allowing readers to discover new riches in the reservoir of meaning of the biblical text.[44] Let us consider, for instance, the dialogue depicted in John 8:13–14:

> Then the Pharisees said to him, "You are testifying on your own behalf; your testimony is not valid." Jesus answered, "Even if I testify on my own behalf, my testimony is valid because I know where I have come from and where I am going, but you do not know where I come from or where I am going."

As Barth points out, in this dialogue Jesus' interlocutors fall into a two-dimensional flatness that misses the deeper (divine) dimensions of Jesus' frame of reference.[45] This lack of understanding on the part of the Pharisees can be better understood if we take into account that "hegemonic" language and theories are simply not adequate to express "foreign" experiences.[46] Exiles or foreigners often have only the options of remaining silent, complaining, or speaking and being misinterpreted.[47] As María Lugones puts it from the point of view of a Latin American immigrant feminist speaking to a white feminist: "You are ill at ease in our world; yet we have to be in your world and learn its ways, and when we are in your world you remake us in your own image."[48] When migrants, as in the case of Jesus in the passage above, refuse to be remade in the image convenient to the holders of power, and insist on framing their self-understanding in other terms, their message is rejected as not valid. In defense of the Pharisees, it should be said that to know someone in "collectivist" society such as the one they shared with Jesus meant to know where a person was *from* (Jesus of Nazareth, Saul of Tarsus) and in particular to be familiar with a person's family background.[49] In his humanity Jesus was indeed "of Nazareth" and as such known to his interlocutors. It is thus primarily with regard to his *divinity* that he should be imagined as a migrant; but if this is so, then conversely we should be able to postulate that migrants can also be imagined as icons pointing toward the Divine as manifested in Jesus Christ.

In the context of her experiences as a Cuban feminist philosopher in the United States, Ofelia Schutte describes situations similar to the one that the passage in John illustrates, in which there is a fundamental lack of dialogical understanding, on the basis of the principle of "cross-cultural incommensurability." She does not mean by this term that cross-cultural communication is impossible. What she does say is that for dialogue to succeed, two aspects are necessary: *understanding* what is being said, and *relating* what is being said to a complex set of signifiers that point to what remains unsaid.[50] Those two necessary factors are, however, too often absent from the experiences of migrants when they attempt any sort of complex self-representation. The speaker from the dominant culture often expects to be able to say, "Communicate with me entirely on the terms I expect, or I won't listen to you." The migrant, however, as a speaker from a subaltern culture, simply *cannot* communicate what he or she wants in those terms. Schutte gives the following example of this problem:

> Unfortunately, I have seen repeated cases of a Latina treated as if she were speaking nonsense, only because her accent, her sentence structure, and perhaps her vocabulary differ from that of ordinary English usage. Rather than taking the effort to listen to what the other is saying, the native speaker will treat the non-native speaker as if she were linguistically or intellectually incompetent. From the perception "I don't know what the other is saying," the dominant speaker will draw the invalid conclusion, "the other is speaking nonsense, the other is incompetent," "the other does not belong here" and so on. The relegation of the culturally different "other" to a subordinate position, as this exemplary exercise shows, may itself be diagnosed as a lack of culture. Cultural prejudice of this sort is indeed a sign of cultural deficit on the part of the dominant culture.[51]

Looking back at our text, we can see signs both of incommensurability and of a dismissal of what Jesus is saying on the grounds that it simply does not "make sense." From this side of the resurrection and with the eyes of faith, we read the attitude of the Pharisees as a deficit. They lacked the theological imagination to tackle the question of where Jesus came from and why that might be important. But they no doubt represented the majority culture; their position probably seemed flawless from a "common sense" perspective. "Why shouldn't they learn our language and our ways?"—people ask about migrants, it would seem rightfully. "After all, they are the ones who want to come live here." And yet, such a hermeneutical model is flawed because it is too short-sighted. Migrants do indeed make tremendous efforts to communicate—as Jesus does in John's gospel. But some of what they want to communicate—just as some of what he wanted to communicate—simply cannot be transmitted using the reigning pre-suppositions. And it may just be that the message that gets left out is a message of vital importance.

Granted, the analogy between the "home" from which Jesus comes and the "home" of migrants should not be pushed too far, since a careful reading of John shows that "the pre-existent state of the Logos is the lens through which the rest of the Gospel and the entire life of Jesus are to be viewed,"[52] and such a divine preexistent state is in a strict sense without analogy. Nevertheless, migrants can immediately relate to the question of not being understood because the persons to whom they are speaking do not know their origin or have the pa-tience to hear their stories. This apparent obstacle paradoxically opens up a way toward christological reflection. Precisely because they too are "on their way" (*via theologica* rather than *locus theologicus*) they can relate in meaningful ways to this One who "lived among us" (Jn 1:14).

What of the second part of Jesus' statement, when he says that he *knows* where he is going? Can migrants relate to that? Surely migrants, of all people, are those who by definition know little about where they are going. Is it back home? Will it be to stay? Here in this city, or in the next town, or even in another country? Can they expect a wel-come? They don't really know. They do know about *saudades*, about the kind of longing that cannot be really assuaged once they have put their foot on the path and begun walking. They do know something also about eschatological hope, about having "no lasting city, but . . . looking for the city that is to come" (Heb 13:14). Migrants may not know exactly what the Johannine Jesus has in mind when he speaks of the place where he is going—but it may well be slightly less in-commensurable to them than to those at home in a hegemonic dis-course incapable of listening to the "other." This "may well be" is a *kairos* of the migrant situation, one of its ambiguous yet promising possibilities. Perhaps a fruitful way to begin speaking of God from more than one place as migrants is, then, to enter into christological dialogue, trained into it by virtue of the migrant experience itself. I would go as far as to hazard that to live in awareness of the tensions of cultural *incommensurability* is a useful port of entry into reflection even on such christological doctrines as the hypostatic union and the *communicatio idiomatum*. A migrant accustomed to living in a way that brings together two incommensurable languages and cultures may not find even the logic of the definition of Chalcedon all that unfamiliar:

"the difference of the natures being by no means taken away because of the union, but rather the distinctive character of each nature being preserved and coming together to form one person and subsistence, not as parted or separated into two persons, but one and the same Son and Only-begotten God the Word, Jesus Christ."[53] The possibility of the simultaneous presence in one Person of two incommensurable dimensions, in this case humanity and divinity, cannot be very easily dismissed a priori by a migrant whose very life is a struggle to make sense of the coexistence in his or her own person of two or more very different realities. To reflect on Christology from a migrant perspective allows us to acknowledge, once again, from a palpable standpoint, both the *alterity* and the *affinity* of our existence in relation to that of Jesus.[54]

Later in John (14:4–6) Jesus says to the disciples, "You know the way to the place where I am going." Thomas is not so sure of that: "We do not know where you are going. How can we know the way?" Jesus' answer, so often quoted out of context, so often ontologized and made into a stumbling block unnecessarily, into exclusion rather than invitation, is that *Jesus himself is the way.* This should be a comfort to migrants in their homesickness: the way of Jesus is Jesus himself, and Jesus, too, can be understood as a migrant. Walking along the way of Jesus means walking along the way to God, and it is not a way for which migrants are untrained. It is a way of walking the walk as you talk the talk, taking it one step at a time, in hope, learning the language as you go. It is no coincidence that the *via theologica,* an expression we have used here to expand and dynamize the *locus theologicus,* is also a way of speaking of the spiritual life, of following Jesus by virtue of the Spirit of life. And this leads me to a further question: What might theologians as such learn from reflecting on the experience of migration—and from their own migrations, great and small?

MIGRATION AS EPISTEMOLOGICAL RUPTURE
FOR THE THEOLOGIAN

In theology our goal is to attempt a discourse born of God and about God that is both integrative and integral. And yet—though this may seem paradoxical at first sight—this integration is not achieved harmoniously, for significant God-talk requires *epistemological ruptures:* I was once blind, but now I see; or I was once deaf, but now I hear; or even I once could see only as those who have eyes, but now I can start to see as those who are blind can see; and I can start to hear as those who are called deaf can hear. The "integration" achieved is constantly submitted to a kind of wholesome "disintegration," as the idolatrous aspects of even our best theological attempts are brought to light. This disintegration can be called wholesome precisely because the shock of an *epistemological rupture* produced by experiencing "others" (and through "others," God) can lead us through the Spirit to start praying, together with our sisters and brothers, that God will transform us, so that we can be helpful in transforming habits and structures of injustice, both those that oppress others and those that oppress us personally.[55] The experience of migrants is precisely that of a series of epistemological ruptures; time and time again migrants are exposed to "others" in new ways. This opens up possibilities for discovering and rediscovering the gospel (and themselves) in new ways as well. When theologians think as migrants and migrants as theologians, epistemological rupture and renewal are almost unavoidable.

Let me offer one example of this process. Perhaps in part because the African heritage in Argentina tends to be overlooked (for reasons that would be worth investigating), as a theologian living and working in Argentina I never thought very much about the relevance of this heritage to my theology, even though it surrounded me and formed me in wonderful ways.[56] I regularly put James Cone on the syllabus but did not reflect much about my own white privilege as a structural reality independent of my own inclinations or opinions; certainly I had not meditated very much on its theological ramifications, nor—as a feminist—had I sat at the feet of womanist theologians. Racism seemed like somebody else's problem. I knew from experience that in the United States I was perceived as white and felt vaguely uncomfortable with what that might mean, but in my Argentine *locus theologicus* I felt no urgent need to pursue the question further. Our migration to the Chicago area ruptured my complacency. I began to realize that my theology had to undergo a deep learning process in order to repent and turn away from the sin of being what I began to call a colorless theology. A colorless theology is not a theology that has transcended racism but one that is in vital ways oblivious to the reality of racism, on the one hand, and drab and monochrome, on the other, because it does not allow structurally and systematically for the concerns and voices of people of color.[57] A theology marked by the experience of migration can and should not be colorless; at the same time, it should not accept and internalize the patterns of racialization and black/white binaries characteristic—for instance—of the United States.

My immersion in this tangibly racial society has opened my eyes to new aspects of sin and of the unfolding of grace in society and in my own life; as a result, my comparative obliviousness about the pervasiveness of racism has been shaken. As Peggy McIntosh writes, "Obliviousness about white advantage, like obliviousness about male advantage, is kept strongly inculturated in the United States, so as to maintain the myth of meritocracy, the myth that democratic choice is equally available to all."[58] Critical race theory, which started within the juridical sciences but has spread to other disciplines, can be helpful to theologians in getting a theoretical grip on racism. Two of its basic tenets are that racism (contrary to the "common sense" of many white people) is *not aberrational* in U.S. society, but rather the everyday experience of people of color; and that *white racism* serves both psychic and material purposes (that is to say, it promotes both the material interests of white elites and the psychic strength of working-class whites).[59] It stands to reason, then, that only white scholars, theologians, and ethicists could be in a position to be oblivious enough to the problems of racism to do theology without a continual reference to this sin, in the same way that male theologians have so often been oblivious to their own sexism. As soon as we become cognizant of this reality, it also becomes evident that we cannot remember Jesus faithfully without grappling with this problem, indeed, without it being constitutive of our biblical and theological hermeneutic. The way we read the Bible and tell its stories changes (or should change) when our personal and structural complicities in racism become evident to us, just as it changes when we become aware of sexism and classism. Some Latin American theologians, especially those among the *pueblos originarios* such as Aiban Wagua,[60] have been talking about these matters for a long time, but it was the experience of migration away from the River Plate area that allowed for an epistemological rupture deep enough for the applicability of their words *to me* to get through. I call the kind of epistemological rupture of which I have been speaking a *pneumatic* rupture, because in it the Holy Spirit is at work.

By walking in new places and learning to speak of God from more than one place, the migrant as theologian and theologian as migrant learn in new ways the truth of Luther's dictum in the Heidelberg Disputation: "A theologian of glory calls evil good and good evil. A theologian of the cross calls the thing what it actually is" (thesis 21). Because of the *pneumatic rupture* that the gospel can bring to our old (and often seemingly functional and useful) "common sense," it has the potential of unmasking many of our assumptions (and those of our societies) as destructive to life. This unmasking is, of course, not the end of the story. After the rupture comes the constructive attempt to make sense of what has been seen, to reformulate and regroup. Our reflection on such concepts as the *via theologica*, the possibility of a christological hermeneutic of cultural incommensurability, and the epistemological ruptures inherent to the process of migration are examples of such attempts. Perhaps migrants, weaving in and out of the old and the new, the here and the there, speaking of God from more than one place, nudging us to be transformed, remind us with particular poignancy that all theology is "on its way"; the *via theologica* requires a *theologia viae*. And yet, in God we are home.[61]

NOTES

[1] *Rumbo al Sur, deseando el Norte: Un romance en dos lenguas* (Buenos Aires: Planeta, 1998), 374. This is the author's own Spanish translation of his English original and refers to his (repeated) experiences of migration.

[2] Néstor Garcia Conclini, Carnahan Lectures, Instituto Universitario ISEDET, Buenos Aires, September 3–5, 2002; see idem, *Latinoamericanos buscando un lugar en este siglo* (Buenos Aires: Paidós, 2002).

[3] See, for instance, Franz Hinkelammert, *La deuda externa de América Latina: el automatismo de la deuda* (San José: DEI, 1989); idem, *Las armas ideológicas de la muerte: el discernimiento de los fetiches: capitalismo y cristianismo* (San José: EDUCA, 1977), English translation *The Ideological Weapons of Death* (Maryknoll, NY: Orbis Books, 1998); Hugo Assmann and Franz Hinkelammert, *A idolatria do mercado: ensaio sobre economia e teologia* (São Paulo: Vozes, 1989); Jung Mo Sung, *Desejo, mercado e religião* (São Paulo: Vozes, 1998); and idem, *Teologia e economia* (São Paulo: Vozes, 1995).

[4] The ideas of Latin American liberation theology continue to be of interest outside Latin America, as the publication of this book in English illustrates, but the phenomenon of circulation to which I refer is much wider than that. Two current examples are the circulation of Afro-Brazilian religions on the one hand, and of the Brazilian Igreja Universal do Reino de Deus, on the other, in Argentina and Uruguay. For a review of some of the relevant literature in anthropology and sociology of religion being produced in Brazil and the South Cone, see David Lehmann, "Religion in Contemporary Latin American Social Science," *Bulletin of Latin American Research* 21 (2002): 290–307.

[5] See P. Gammeltoft, "Remittances and Other Financial Flows to Developing Countries," *International Migration* 40 (2002): 181–21.

[6] For further details, see Robert Suro, "Remittance Senders and Receivers: Tracking the International Channels," a report of the findings of a two-year study by the Multilateral Investment Fund (MIF) and the Pew Hispanic Center (PHC), released on November 24, 2003. Available online.

[7] See A. Pellegrino, "Trends in Latin American Skilled Migration: 'Brain Drain' or 'Brain Exchange'?" *International Migration* 39 (2001): 111–32; and J.-B. Meyer, "Network Approach versus Brain Drain: Lessons from the Diaspora," *International Migration* 39 (2001): 92–110.

[8] I have argued elsewhere for a "perichoretic model" of theological education in Latin America flexible enough to utilize the talents of the Latin American diaspora (see "El futuro de la educación teológica," *Encuentro y Diálogo* 16 [2003]: 67–84).

[9] One of her best-known pieces, a distillation of her style and agenda, is the first chapter of her *Borderlands/La Frontera: The New Mestiza*, "La conciencia de la mestiza: Towards a new consciousness," which has been reprinted in many anthologies (e.g., C. McCann and S.-Y. Kim, eds, *Feminist Theory Reader: Local and Global Perspective* [New York: Routledge, 2003], 179–87).

[10] Ibid., 179.

[11] Sonia Saldívar-Hull, "Gloria Anzaldúa," online at http://college.hmco .com/english/lauter/heath/4e/students/author_pages/contemporary/ anzaldua_gl.html.

[12] See, for instance, the contributions in María Pilar Aquino, Daisy L. Machado, and Jeanette Rodríguez, eds., *A Reader in Latina Feminist Theology: Religion and Justice* (Austin, TX: University of Texas Press, 2002).

[13] Ofelia Schutte, "Cultural Alterity: Cross-Cultural Communication and Feminist Theory in North-South Contexts," in *Decentering the Center: Philosophy for a Multicultural, Postcolonial, and Feminist World*, ed. U. Narayan and S. Harding, 47–66 (Bloomington, IN: Indiana University Press, 2000).

[14] See Manuel Vásquez, "Toward a New Agenda for the Study of Religion in the Americas," *Journal of Interamerican Studies and World Affairs* 41 (1999): 1–21.

[15] See "Negotiating Political and Economic Crises: Peruvian and Salvadoran Christians in Latin America and the United States." The study was conducted in different congregations in Paterson, New Jersey, Washington, D.C., El Salvador, and Peru between May 1996 and August 1998. Manuel Vásquez was involved along with Ileana Gómez, Hortensia Muñoz, and Larissa Ruiz Baia. For a discussion of the study, see Vásquez, "Negotiating Political and Economic Crises."

[16] See Ana Margarita Cervantes-Rodríguez and Amy Lutz, "Coloniality of Power, Immigration, and the English-Spanish Asymmetry in the United States," *Nepantla* 4 (2003): 551; see also the studies referenced there, 523–60.

[17] There is something irritating to Spanish-speaking people about the noun *Americas* in the plural, since in Spanish we speak of *América* to mean North, Central, and South America; however, in English *America* in the singular has been coopted by U.S.-Americans to refer to the United States, a custom that reflects geopolitical aspects of the social-symbolic order.

[18] Forced migration in the guise of slavery is not just a phenomenon of the past. Each year, around two million girls between the ages of 5 and 15 are trafficked and sold into prostitution around the world. For example, 10–15 percent of the foreign prostitutes in Belgium were forcibly sold from abroad

(in this case, mainly from Central and Eastern Europe, Colombia, Nigeria and Peru). See *Not a Minute More: Ending Violence against Women* (UNIFEM, 2003). The booklet is available online.

[19] José Vasconcelos, *La raza cósmica: Misión de la raza ibero-americana* (Mexico: Aguilar, 1961).

[20] This group often does not identify particularly with the designation Latin Americans.

[21] Aquino, Machado, and Rodríguez, *A Reader in Latina Feminist Theology*, xv.

[22] For example, prior to 1998 few Ecuadorians lived in Europe, but they have now become the largest immigrant group in Madrid and one of the largest in Spain (see B. Jokish and B. Pribilsky, "The Panic to Leave: Economic Crisis and the 'New Emigration' from Ecuador," *International Migration* 40 [2003]: 75–102). As I learned in conversation with J. Eugenio Fernández Postigo, this has a direct impact on church life in the receiving country. For instance, when thirty or forty Latin Americans present themselves at once to join small evangelical churches in Spain, many cultural and theological challenges arise.

[23] See Cervantes-Rodríguez and Lutz, "Coloniality of Power, Immigration, and the English-Spanish Asymmetry in the United States."

[24] The latter is again, a question of considerable theological interest: What would it mean for our Hispanic *iglesias evangélicas* and *parroquias católicas* to understand Spanish as an instrument of empowerment for ourselves and for other people? What does it mean for the country with the fourth-largest Spanish-speaking population in the world to be a country in which Spanish is not the official language? What epistemological possibilities does this open up?

[25] For one cartography of this interventionism, see Philippe Rekacewicz, "Ingérences étatsuniennes," *Le Monde Diplomatique* (January 1995). Available online.

[26] The present U.S. states of Arizona, California, Nevada, and Utah, as well as parts of Colorado, New Mexico, and Wyoming, became part of the United States by this treaty; Texas was annexed in another fashion.

[27] Walter Mignolo, *Local Histories/Global Designs: Coloniality, Subaltern Knowledges, and Border Thinking* (Princeton, NJ: Princeton University Press, 2000), ix.

[28] See Ada María Isazi-Díaz, "By the Rivers of Babylon: Exile as a Way of Life," in *Mujerista Theology* (Maryknoll, NY: Orbis Books, 1996), 35–56. See also Fernando F. Segovia, "In the World But Not of It: Exile as Locus for a Theology of the Diaspora," in *Hispanic Latino Theology: Challenge and Promise*, ed. Ada María Isasi-Díaz and Fernando Segovia, 195–217 (Minneapolis: Fortress Press, 1996); Miguel A. de la Torre, "Constructing Our Cuban Ethnic Identity While in Babylon," in *A Dream Unfinished: Theological Reflections on America from the Margins*, ed. E. S. Fernández and F. Segovia, 185–202 (Maryknoll, NY: Orbis Books, 2001).

[29] See A. Lang, "Loci theologici," *Lexikon für Theologie und Kirche* (1961), 4:1110–12.

[30] Ignacio Ellacuría, "Los pobres, lugar teológico en América Latina," *Misión Abierta* 4–5 (1981), 224–40, here quoted from its reprint in *Teólogo mártir por la liberación del pueblo* (Madrid: Nueva Utopía, 1990), 48.

[31] Ibid., 50–52.

[32] Ignacio Ellacuría, "Hacer teología en América Latina," *Theologica Xaveriana* 91 (1989), 139–56; and idem, "Cristología Sistemática: Jesucristo, el Mediador Absoluto del Reino de Dios," in *Mysterium Liberationis*, ed. J. Sobrino and I. Ellacuría (Madrid: Trotta, 1990), 1:597. English translation *Mysterium Liberationis* (Maryknoll, NY: Orbis Books, 1993).

[33] Jon Sobrino, *Resurrección de la verdadera iglesia: Los pobres, lugar teológico de la eclesiología* (Santander: Sal Terrae, 1984), 110f. English translation *The True Church and the Poor*, trans. Matthew O'Connell (Maryknoll, NY: Orbis Books, 1984).

[34] Chandra Talpade Mohanty, *Feminism without Borders: Decolonizing Theory, Practicing Solidarity* (Durham, NC: Duke University Press, 2003), 4–5, 231.

[35] Gustavo Gutiérrez, *Beber en su propio pozo: el itinerario espiritual de un pueblo* (Salamanca: Sígueme, 1985). English translation *We Drink from Our Own Wells: The Spiritual Journey of a People*, trans. Matthew O'Connell (Maryknoll, NY: Orbis Books, 1984).

[36] I am not suggesting a move to replace the category of *locus theologicus* but rather to redefine it. Indeed, it is a prime example for understanding how the theological production of the next generation of Latin American theologians is unfolding; our theological production would be unthinkable without the influence of the liberation theologians who began to write in the 1960s and 1970s, yet it either responds to different problems or to the same problems in a slightly different guise (as in the case of poverty), using different socio-analytical mediations. It is, therefore, neither an apologetic of earlier liberation theology nor is it interested in the hardening of its categories; it simply presupposes the presence of that theology as one of the indispensable "wells" from which to drink as it continues to find its own way in a new time.

[37] Jon Sobrino, "El conocimiento teológico en la teología europea y latinoamericana," in Ellacuría and Sobrino, *Resurrección de la verdadera iglesia*, 39; *The True Church and the Poor*, chap. 1.

[38] Prosper's axiom, to be found in his anti-Pelagian treatise *Indiculus de gratia Dei* (long mistakenly attributed to Pope Celestine), was *ut legem credendi lex statuat supplicandi*, later popularized simply as *lex orandi, lex credendi*.

[39] "The Way of the Cross of a Migrant," in *El Peregrino, Boletín de Información de la Pastoral de Movilidad Humana* (Honduras), quoted in *Houston Catholic Worker* 17, no. 2 (March–April 1997). Available online.

[40] Hugo López, "El Divino Migrante," *Apuntes* 4 (1984): 14–18.

[41] Jung Young Lee, *Marginality: The Key to Multicultural Theology* (Minneapolis: Fortress Press, 1995), 83. Thanks to Hwa Young Chong Will for pointing out this text to me; in our conversations I have discovered suggestive commonalities between the Korean American experience and that of Latinos/as in the United States.

[42] Karl Barth, "Der Weg des Sohnes Gottes in die Fremde," in *KD IV/1* §59, 171ff.

[43] Rosi Braidotti, *Nomadic Subjects: Embodiment and Sexual Difference in Contemporary Feminist Theory* (New York: Columbia University Press, 1994), 22.

[44] For more on how this works, see Osvaldo Vena, "My Hermeneutical Journey and Daily Journey into Hermeneutics: Meaning-Making and Biblical Interpretation in the North American Diaspora," *Interpreting Beyond Borders,* ed. Fernando F. Segovia, 84–106 (Sheffield: Sheffield Academic Press, 2000).

[45] Karl Barth, *Erklärung des Johannes-Evangeliums (Kapital 1–8)* (Zurich: Theologischer Verlag Zürich, 1977), 361. Barth also points out the parallel between this passage and the pneumatological words in John 3:8: the Spirit is like a wind and neither its origin nor its goal are known.

[46] I'm assuming here that both the *Sitz-im-Leben* of the Gospel of John and our own are profoundly marked by the reality of empire; on this topic see Fernando Segovia, "Inclusion and Exclusion in John 17: An Intercultural Reading," in *What Is John?* vol. 2, *Literary and Social Readings of the Fourth Gospel,* ed. Fernando Segovia (Atlanta, GA: Scholars Press, 1998), 183–210, esp. 206ff.

[47] María Lugones explains this in the context of the dialogue (or lack thereof) between "white" feminists and feminists "of color" (María Lugones and Elizabeth Spelman, "Have We Got a Theory for You! Feminist Theory, Cultural Imperialism and the Demand for 'The Woman's Voice,'" in *Feminist Philosophies,* ed. J. Kourany, J. Sterba, and R. Tong (Upper Saddle River, NJ: Prentice Hall, 1999), 474–86.

[48] Ibid., 478.

[49] Bruce J. Malina and Richard L. Rohrbaugh, *Social-Science Commentary on the Gospel of John* (Minneapolis: Fortress Press, 1998), 157.

[50] To go back to Barth's metaphor, these two factors would allow a "flat," two-dimensional communication to acquire depth.

[51] Schutte, "Cultural Alterity," 56–57.

[52] James F. McGrath, *John's Apologetic Christology: Legitimation and Development in Johannine Christology* (Port Chester, NY: Cambridge University Press, 2001), 54.

[53] From the Definition of Chalcedon (451), in *Documents of the Christian Church,* ed. Henry Bettenson (New York: Oxford University Press, 1963), 51–52, slightly adapted.

[54] The language of *alteridad* and *afinidad* is used by Sobrino when he speaks of following Jesus as a practical way toward doxology. He points out that it is not irrelevant to our understanding of Chalcedon *how* we come to it: a theoretical approach alone, without the corresponding *seguimiento* or following of Jesus, will lead us to erroneous conclusions (see Jon Sobrino, *La fe en Jesucristo: Ensayo desde las víctimas* [Madrid: Trotta, 1999], 454–55). English translation *Christ the Liberator: A View from the Victims,* trans. Paul Burns (Maryknoll, NY: Orbis Books, 2001).

[55] I am somewhat following Sobrino's understanding of "epistemological rupture" (see Sobrino, "El conocimiento teológico en la teología europea y

latinoamericana"). For Sobrino, that rupture occurs primarily in the encounter with the poor and their sufferings, which point to the "truth of reality" that we too often overlook.

⁵⁶ I am thinking, for instance, of church music but also of the African roots of music that I love and think of as Argentine or Uruguayan: milonga, tango, candombe. On this and for a hymn with lyrics written by Charles Wesley set to milonga music by Pablo Sosa, see Pablo Sosa, "Wesley gaucho: Un poema olvidado de Charles Wesley," *Cuadernos de Teología* 22 (2003): 383–89.

⁵⁷ Through this designation I am indirectly paying my respects to Alice Walker's clever axiom to the effect that "womanism is to purple as feminism is to lavender."

⁵⁸ Peggy McIntosh, "White Privilege: Unpacking the Invisible Knapsack." Available online. I am indebted to Debbie Blades for this reference.

⁵⁹ Richard Delgado and Jean Stefancic, *Critical Race Theory: An Introduction* (New York: New York University Press: 2001), 7.

⁶⁰ See, for instance, Aiban Wagua, "Station VI: Jesus Is Scourged and Crowned with Thorns," in *Way of the Cross: The Passion of Christ in the Americas*, ed. Virgil Elizondo (Maryknoll, NY: Orbis Books, 1992), 47–56; see also Silvia Regina, "La teología negra latinoamericana como un espacio de descubrimiento y afirmación del sujeto," *Pasos* 89 (2000): 41–45.

⁶¹ "Quizás en apariencias/Te alejas o me alejo/El caso es que sufrimos de ausencia/Con un dolor ambiguo y parejo./Amor no significa querencia;/También se puede amar desde lejos" (Alberto Cortez, "Canción de amor para mi patria").

7.

Beyond the Postmodern Condition, or the Turn toward Psychoanalysis

Manuel J. Mejido

THE PROGRESSIVE THEOLOGIES of Western Europe and North America have for the most part understood themselves within the limits of the historical-hermeneutic sciences.[1] That is, they have established theological knowledge through the *interpretation* of the meaning of transcendence.[2] This theological knowledge has been possible only to the extent that transcendence has been grasped through the category of praxis (that is, intersubjectivity, interaction, communication). Insofar as modern theology has posited praxis as the very condition of possibility for interpreting the meaning of transcendence, we say it has labored under an interest in the maintenance of mutual understanding, that is, it has labored under a practical cognitive interest.

In the late 1960s theology for the first time understood itself as a critically oriented science. Indeed, the radicalness of the Latin American theologies of liberation stems from the fact that they were never satisfied with the practical cognitive interest of the historical-hermeneutic sciences; that is, they were never satisfied with the interpretation of the meaning of transcendence grasped through the restricted category of praxis. The theologies of liberation, rather, establish a theological knowledge that is interested in the *making* of transcendence. In other words, the theologies of liberation generate a theological knowledge that theoretically aims to grasp the invariance that exists

119

between the kingdom and the socio-historical conditions of misery and praxeologically aims to overcome this invariance through the making of transcendence understood as the making of "better" history. This theological knowledge has been possible only to the extent that transcendence has been grasped through the category of social labor (that is, the dialectic of praxis and poiesis, interaction and labor). Insofar as the theologies of liberation have posited social labor as the very conditions of possibility for the making of transcendence (the making of "better" history), we say they have labored under an interest in the making of liberation; that is, they have labored under an emancipatory cognitive interest.

Yet, from the beginning the radicalness of the theologies of liberation was dissimulated. Both detractors and advocates of the theologies of liberation contributed to this dissimulation: Detractors mistook the emancipatory interest of the theologies of liberation for vulgar materialism and put forth the "blackmail" that any radical emancipatory project that attempts to push beyond the coordinates of liberal-democratic capitalism would lead inevitably to totalitarianism. And, failing to understand fully their project as a critically oriented science, liberation theologians were never able to elucidate adequately the problem of a Marxian social theoretically oriented theory of knowledge as the implicit foundations of the theologies of liberation. And thus, as a consequence of this problem of "obscure foundations," liberation theologians were never able to formulate and implement a coherent and effective liberationist emancipatory project.

These two factors are today merging under the postmodern condition and generating the eclipse of the theologies of liberation. This eclipse has two dialectically related moments. On the one hand, this eclipse is manifesting itself as the *historical-hermeneutic reduction of the theologies of liberation*—a reduction that is taking form in and through the postmodern "turn" to language, alterity, and the plurality of particulars. And, on the other hand, this eclipse is manifesting itself as the *liberalization of the liberationist emancipatory project*—a liberalization that is taking form in and through the naturalization of global liberal-democratic capitalism. Indeed, today's postmodern condition represents what is arguably the most pernicious environment for the theologies of liberation. For while the postmodern turn seems to undercut the universality of the idea of socio-historical emancipation, the "triumph" of global liberal-democratic capitalism seems to reveal the futility of liberation theology's attempt to realize this emancipation to the extent that such a project has historically implied the implementation of real socialism. Only a reconstruction of the foundations of the theologies of liberation in light of—indeed against—the postmodern condition can overcome this eclipse.

These reflections thus have three parts that correspond to the three moments of the problematic we have just outlined: dissimulation, eclipse, and reconstruction. We will begin with a historically oriented analysis of the dissimulation of the radicalness of the theologies of liberation. We will then consider how this dissimulation has, under the present conditions of postmodernity, become an eclipse. And we will conclude by introducing the idea of psychoanalysis as a critically oriented science as the guiding principle for a reconstruction of the theologies of liberation.

THE DISSIMULATION OF THE RADICALNESS
OF THE THEOLOGIES OF LIBERATION

Detractors from the "outside" and advocates from the "inside" have contributed to the dissimulation of the radicalness of the theologies of liberation. With few exceptions, the external dissimulation of liberation theology by detractors has been a mix of ignorance and cynicism, an external "not taking seriously" that, over time, has become an external "silencing." But this type of dissimulation is transparent when one looks at things from within. And this is precisely why the internal dissimulation of liberation theology by the liberation theologians themselves has been much more pernicious. For the internal dissimulation has not been the unwillingness to engage this radicalness but rather a failure to fully come to terms with it. This internal dissimulation has led not to a silencing but rather to an enfeebling.

Detractors have misunderstood the theologies of liberation. This has been the case whether they have taken as their point of departure the epistemological critique of the "reduction" of faith by liberation theology, the theological system,[3] or the empirical critique of liberation theology, the social movement whose emancipatory project leads ineluctably to totalitarianism.[4] This dichotomization of the epistemological and empirical is, from the point of view of the theologies of liberation, a symptom of the limits of these critiques. If the epistemological critique of liberation theology is marshaled from within the limits of theology understood as a historical-hermeneutic science, the empirical critique is marshaled in and through the reification of liberal-democratic capitalism. But, more important, in their "onesidedness" each critique already presupposes the other. The practical (and not emancipatory) cognitive interest of theology understood as a historical-hermeneutic science implies the de facto acceptance of the status quo, namely liberal-democratic capitalism. And the reification of liberal-democratic capitalism implies theology as a historical-hermeneutic science, the way theology is "done" under these socio-historical conditions. The limits of these critiques can be shown from each side, although the unmasking of this one-sidedness is already the radical repudiation of both critiques.

Situated within the limits of theology understood as a historical-hermeneutic science, detractors have, on the one hand, mistaken the emancipatory cognitive interest of the theologies of liberation for a technical cognitive interest grounded in a vulgar materialism. That is, they have wrongly accused the theologies of liberation of reducing theology to an empirical-analytic science. This misunderstanding gravitates around the problem of the liberationist appropriation of the work of Karl Marx. The prevailing interpretation has been that the turn to Marx by the liberation theologians was an attempt to apply a Marxian analysis to theological reflection. This view, far from getting to the heart of the matter, reveals the limits of theology understood as a historical-hermeneutic science. For the idea of a Marxian analysis that exists "out there" beyond the boundaries of theology presupposes a dualism between the theological and the social sciences that the critically oriented theological sciences of liberation reject. The theologies of liberation, rather, occupy themselves with the more radical task of elucidating a certain social theoretical perspective that emerges from within the limits of theology, a perspective that is linked to the very problem of the foundations of theology. Detractors, however, have always lacked the epistemological leverage needed to generate a critique of the theologies of liberation at the level of their foundations. Indeed, the problem of the foundations of the theologies of liberation has always been beyond the reach of theology as a historical-hermeneutic science. Rather, it is liberation theology that, as a critically oriented theological science of liberation, has, since its inception, always possessed the leverage needed legitimately to repudiate the critiques of its detractors.

In and through the reification of liberal-democratic capitalism, that is, in and through the myth that liberal-democratic capitalism will generate the synthesis of Anglo- and Hispanic America—the synthesis of the Americas—detractors have attempted to "blackmail" the theologies of liberation with the idea that any radical attempt to push beyond the horizon of liberal-democratic capitalism necessarily will lead to totalitarianism.[5] This misunderstanding, which has historically manifested itself as the condemnation of the liberationist solidarity with

Marxist regimes and movements, stems from an avoidance of a fundamental social theoretical tension that separates the historical-hermeneutic and critically oriented sciences.

Only because they have silenced this tension in and through the mythical synthesis of the Americas have detractors been able to accuse the theologies of liberation of subordinating faith to the "instrumental" ends of "revolutionary praxis" and reducing religion to the Marxist paradigm of production. But, when the tension that separates the historical-hermeneutic and the critically oriented sciences is brought forth, when liberal-democratic capitalism is viewed, not as what will generate the mythical synthesis of the Americas, but rather as the latest movement of that dialectic of violence and domination that is the *dialectic of the Americas*, then it becomes evident that detractors too have "instrumentalized" faith and "reduced" religion. They have reduced religion to U.S. national and corporate interests—to "the American way of life"—and they have made faith subordinate to the instrumental ends of Manifest Destiny.

Liberation theologians have also internally contributed to the dissimulation of that crisis marked by the theologies of liberation to the extent that they have failed to understand their project reflectively as a critically oriented science. Although they have always recognized the rupture that was generated by the theologies of liberation,[6] liberation theologians have nevertheless failed to elucidate properly the root cause of this rupture, namely, that theology for the first time pushed beyond the limits of the historical-hermeneutic sciences. This failure can be understood, from one angle, as the epistemological problem of the *obscure foundations* of liberation theology, the system of thought, and, from another, as the empirical problem of the conceptualization and implementation of the *emancipatory project* of liberation theology, the social movement. Liberation theologians, however, have aimed to understand these two problems as dialectically interlocked to the extent that the critically oriented theological sciences of liberation (which the liberation theologians have always had in reach) push beyond the dichotomy between the theory of knowledge and the sociology of knowledge, between an epistemological subject and an empirical subject with epistemological interests.

Thus, for the theologies of liberation the epistemological problem of grounding liberation theology, the system of thought, is mediated by the empirical problem of conceptualizing and implementing the emancipatory project of liberation theology, the social movement. And the empirical problem of conceptualizing and implementing the emancipatory project of liberation theology, the social movement, is mediated by the epistemological problem of grounding liberation theology, the system of thought. This is the radical meaning of the back-and-forth between theory and practice under which the theologies of liberation have labored. The theoretical problem of grounding liberation theology, the system of thought—a problem that is generated by the liberationist rupture with the historical-hermeneutic theological sciences—is realized praxeologically by liberation theology, the social movement, as making a rupture with the basic coordinates of U.S.-style liberal-democratic capitalism, the latest moment of the dialectic of the Americas. Bringing forth and negotiating this dialectic, which has always been "there," is precisely the problem of a Marxian social theoretically oriented theory of knowledge as the implicit foundations of the critically oriented theological sciences of liberation.

That liberation theologians have tended to occupy themselves with the apologetic task of justifying their social scientific and not philosophical use of Marx or defending their use of a Marxian analysis, rather than with the more radical task of grounding the theologies of liberation on a social theoretically oriented theory of knowledge rooted in Marx, is perhaps the most acute manifestation of the epistemological problem of obscure foundations.[7] But, distinctions such as *social science, philosophy*, and *theology*, as well as the idea of a Marxian analysis as a theological instrument, are the way in which the historical-hermeneutic theological sciences negotiate the problem of the liberationist turn to Marx. From the point of view of the critically oriented theological sciences of liberation, however, it becomes evident that the liberationist turn to Marx is a "foundational" problem. Indeed, it becomes evident that the idea of a Marxian social theoretically oriented theory of knowledge has always been "there" as the implicit foundations of the theologies of liberation.

The inability of liberation theologians to elucidate adequately the problem of a Marxian social theoretically oriented theory of knowledge as the implicit foundations of the theologies of liberation has played itself out through two sets of tensions that have undergirded the history of the development of liberation theology: on the one hand, the tension between *poiesis* and *praxis*, and, on the other, the tension between *the universality of the idea of liberation* and *the plurality of particular liberationist perspectives*. Due to obscure foundations, rather than enhancing and radicalizing the liberationist point of view, the back-and-forth between these two tensions as the internal dialectic of the theologies of liberation would, with the demise of real socialism, end up actually enfeebling and even deradicalizing liberation theology to the point that, it could be argued, the theologies of liberation began to move "back" toward theology understood as a historical-hermeneutic science.

The tension between poiesis and praxis has manifested itself through what Juan Carlos Scannone has referred to as that "axial shift" *(desplazamiento de eje)* within the "paradigm" of liberation from a material-economic perspective to a symbolic-cultural one.[8] Although this shift, which has historically gravitated around the question of popular knowledge, culture, and religion, was already present in the Puebla (1979) idea of "integral liberation" as an attempt to push beyond Medellín (1968),[9] it would crystallize only after 1989 with the collapse of the Berlin Wall. Liberation theology's axial shift to liberation as praxeological transformation of symbolic-cultural conditions was not supposed to replace but rather to serve as a corrective for the reductionistic economism of the earlier idea of liberation as the poietic transformation of material-economic conditions. Yet, although they have always been aware that it is a matter of "both/and" and not "either/or," liberation theologians have still not been able to generate a theory that adequately integrates the two perspectives. The result has been, not the reduction of liberation as the poietic transformation of material-economic conditions to liberation as the praxeological transformation of symbolic-cultural conditions, but worse: the reduction of liberation as poietic and/or praxeological transformation to the *interpretation* of popular knowledge, culture, and religion as liberative. Scannone's work has exemplified this reduction.

Scannone argues that this axial shift toward a "cultural analysis" that does not neglect the "social" and "material" represents the "radicalization of the liberationist paradigm."[10] He is taking issue here with that nomological gaze that reduces liberation to the problem of the poor's objective position in the socioeconomic system. Scannone believes this reification can be overcome with a hermeneutical perspective that phenemenologically grasps those liberative elements that are always already there in the poor's life-world in the form of popular knowledge and culture. Toward this end he calls for a shift from the category of class to the category of the people *(pueblo)*; a shift from the tension between the bourgeoisie and the proletariat to the tension between *civilización* and *barbarie*; a shift from the problem of socioeconomic pauperization to the problem of cultural *mestizaje* (inculturation).[11] But, how exactly does this axial shift toward culture include a social analysis? For it seems that Scannone has simply replaced one reductionistic tendency with another. It seems that he has simply substituted a reductionistic economism with a reductionistic culturalism. Indeed, it seems that he has critiqued the poietic annihilation of praxis with the praxeological annihilation of poiesis. But one reduction does not justify the other. As we have suggested, the radicalness of the theologies of liberation stems from the fact that they grasp the problem of liberation—that is, the problem of a transformative-making—through the category of social labor understood as the dialectic of praxis *and* poiesis. Indeed, the dualism that Scannone posits between the cultural and the social, between the practical and the material drives a wedge through the category of social labor; it disintegrates the dialectic of praxis and poiesis.

Prima facie, it might appear that Scannone's axial shift is one-sided. It might appear that, by replacing the problem of material-economic liberation with the problem of symbolic-cultural liberation, Scannone has simply inverted things. But, to have inverted things Scannone would have had to have developed for the category of culture something analogous to Marx's theory of revolutionary praxis; that is, he would have had to have developed a theory of the transformative power of the symbolic cultural. This he does not do. Lurking behind the dualism between system and life-world is a *historical-hermeneutic conception of culture that forecloses the very possibility of formulating a theory of the transformative power of the symbolic cultural.* So, Scannone does not simply invert things. Situating himself within the limits of the historical-hermeneutic sciences, in addition to making the material-economic an external problem, Scannone also abandons the emancipatory cognitive interest of the critically oriented theological sciences of liberation.

Scannone does not see this dilemma for four interrelated reasons. First, he does not adequately distinguish between the practical cognitive interest of the historical-hermeneutic sciences and the emancipatory cognitive interest of the critically oriented sciences. Second, he fails to see that the theologies of liberation have always attempted to labor under the emancipatory cognitive interest of the critically oriented sciences. Third, Scannone fails to see that it is the Marxian horizon, and in particular, the idea of a Marxian social theoretically oriented theory of knowledge, that has provided the ground for the critically oriented sciences, and thus for the theologies of liberation. And fourth, he grossly underestimates the Marxian horizon. Scannone assumes that the Marxian horizon is unable to develop an adequate conception of culture. He believes that it is doomed to the totalitarian instrumentalization of the symbolic cultural "from above." This is why he turns to the historical-hermeneutic tradition, to the passive listening *(la escucha)* of the practical cognitive interest.[12] But by turning to hermeneutics Scannone abandons that emancipatory cognitive interest that sets liberation theology apart from other modern theologies. What Scannone overlooks is that the Marxian horizon has for quite some time now been struggling with a theory of symbolic-cultural liberation. This is precisely the idea of *psychoanalysis as a critically oriented science.* Psychoanalysis, unlike hermeneutics, is not satisfied with the understanding of intersubjective meaning structures. It attempts, rather, to transform symbolic-cultural distortions through the therapeutic power of language.[13] Having grounded his theology of inculturation in hermeneutics and not in psychoanalysis, Scannone forgoes the opportunity to bring forth the deeper logic of liberation.

The other tension that emerged as the theologies of liberation struggled to come to terms with the postmodern condition is the tension between the universality of the idea of liberation and the plurality of particular liberationist perspectives. This second tension is a radicalization of the first. The first tension, as we have just seen, emerged in the attempt to overcome a reductionistic Marxism through a shift from the material economic to the symbolic cultural. But in the end the category of culture is still grasped from within the horizon of the universal historical subject. The second tension takes issue with this universal historical (and cultured) subject, unmasking it as ethnocentric, logocentric, phallocentric, heterosexual, and the like. This is the space in which emerges, for example, the feminist, ethnic, indigenous, and gay theologies of liberation. But, although the turn to the particular is supposed to destabilize the pretension to universality of a liberationist project and thus the problem of internal domination, it also deradicalizes the theologies of liberation. For this turn to the particular is realized in and through a hermeneutic conception of praxis. Indeed, the turn to the particular is achieved in and through a postmodern conception of culture grounded in language that annihilates the category of social labor that, as the universal, is what sociohistorically mediates the particulars. In the end the second tension, like the first, falls captive to the historical-hermeneutic reduction of the emancipatory cognitive interest. The work of Ivone Gebara exemplifies this reduction.[14] We lack the space needed to elucidate this reduction here.

We suggested above that the internal dissimulation of the theologies of liberation can be understood now as the epistemological problem of the obscure foundations of liberation theology, the system of thought, and now, as the empirical problem of the conceptualization and implementation of the emancipatory project of liberation theology, the social movement. We saw how the epistemological problem of obscure foundations, which stems from the failure to properly elucidate the problem of a Marxian social theoretically oriented theory of knowledge, has manifested itself throughout the history of the theologies of liberation in the form of two tensions: the tension between poiesis and praxis, and the tension between the universality of the idea of liberation and the plurality of particular liberationist perspectives. We saw, moreover, how these two tensions, rather than generating a radicalization of the theologies of liberation, have in fact led to a recoil back toward the limits of the historical-hermeneutic sciences; that is, these two tensions have generated what we call the historical-hermeneutic reduction of the critically oriented theological sciences of liberation. Let us now briefly turn to the empirical problem of the liberationist emancipatory project.

We may recall that, as a social movement, the theologies of liberation aim to overcome praxeologically the invariance that exists between the present historical conditions and the kingdom through the making of transcendence understood as the making of "better" history, as the transformation of history into the kingdom. We may recall, moreover, that the theologies of liberation have socio-historically understood this making of "better" history specifically as making a break with the latest moment of the dialectic of the Americas, namely, U.S.-style liberal-democratic capitalism. Indeed, the problem of conceptualizing and implementing the liberationist emancipatory project is precisely the problem of overcoming the "ideological weapons of death" of U.S.-style liberal-democratic capitalism, which, by impeding the making of "better" history, have also impeded the transformation of the historical reality of the Americas into the kingdom.[15]

The theologies of liberation break with the traditional ways of reading the history of the Americas, and in particular the traditional interpretations of the conditions and causes of misery and suffering in this region of the world. This is one of the ways in which the radical theological crisis that is liberation theology has manifested itself. Whether as the early dependency theory or as the more sophisticated liberation philosophy, the theologies of liberation have historically grounded themselves in a Marxian-oriented philosophy of history and historiography that destabilize the historical idealism of those dominant approaches to the problem of history such as, for example, the Romantic, Neo-Kantian, evolutionary, phenomenological, positivist, and pragmatist approaches.

The theologies of liberation understand the causes and conditions of Latin American underdevelopment as part of, not the synthesis, but rather the dialectic of the Americas. Indeed, the theologies of liberation read the history of the Americas from the point of view of, not the teleological unfolding of Manifest Destiny, but rather that asymmetrical life-and-death struggle that has relegated this region of the world to the "periphery," to the "underside." This tension between mythical synthesis and dialectic has manifested itself as the tension between, for example, the evolutionary developmentalism of W. W. Rostow and the dependency theory of the early Fernando Henrique Cardoso,[16] the tension between the neoclassical economic theory of the Chicago School and the liberation philosophy of Enrique Dussel,[17] the tension between the North American Free Trade Agreement (NAFTA) and the EZLN's Declaración de la Selva Lacondana.[18]

Indeed, the empirical problem of conceptualizing and implementing the emancipatory project of liberation theology, the social movement, stems precisely from the failure to make a break with U.S.-style liberal-democratic capitalism. With the implosion of real socialism the theologians of liberation are increasingly accepting that liberal blackmail we alluded to above, namely, that any attempt to push beyond the basic coordinates of U.S.-style liberal-democratic capitalism will lead to totalitarianism. This blackmail, which is manifesting itself as the turn toward civil society, is generating the naturalization of this hegemonic system. But this failure is part of the very logic of the dialectic of the Americas.

THE POSTMODERN ECLIPSE OF THE THEOLOGIES OF LIBERATION

The external and internal dissimulations we just elucidated are today fusing under the postmodern condition and, as we have already suggested, are producing the eclipse of the theologies of liberation. But what exactly is the postmodern condition? We need to address this question if we are, on the one hand, to understand the two moments that constitute this eclipse—namely, the historical-hermeneutic reduction of the critically oriented theological sciences of liberation and the liberalization of the liberationist emancipatory project—and, on the other, to understand how these two moments are linked to the postmodern turn to language and the "triumph" of global liberal-democratic capitalism.

The postmodern condition is a historical condition. Postmodernism is not simply a style of thought that is skeptical of "grand narratives." It does not simply refer to the way of seeing the world that gravitates around the plurality of particulars, alterity, difference, fluidity, hybridity, playfulness, reflexivity. Postmodernism is first and foremost a cultural form that is related to the "rise of more flexible modes of capital accumulation, and a new round of 'time-space compression' in the organization of capitalism."[19] While postmodernism, the cultural form, can be traced to the passage from industrial to post-industrial societies, on the one hand, and the passage from colonial to postcolonial societies, on the other, postmodernism, the style of thought, can be traced to the linguistic turn in the human sciences.

Years ago Alain Touraine and Daniel Bell wrote definitive works on what at the time were the newly emerging post-industrial societies.[20] More recently, David Harvey has characterized the passage from industrial to post-industrial societies as a shift from "Fordist modernity" to "flexible postmodernism"; Fordist modernity is characterized by relative fixity and permanence—fixed capital in mass production, stable, standardized, and homogeneous markets; a fixed configuration of political—economic influence and power, easily identifiable authority and meta-theories, secure grounding in materiality and technical-scientific rationality, and the like. Post-industrial flexibility is "dominated by fiction, fantasy, the immaterial (particularly of money), fictitious capital, images, ephemerality, chance, and flexibility in production techniques, labour markets and consumption niches."[21] But it is Jean-François Lyotard who is of greatest interest to us here, for he, more than anyone else, has shown how the technological transformations that have undergirded the passage to post-industrial societies have influenced the nature of knowledge. Indeed, the leading sciences and technologies in post-industrial societies have to do with language. This state of affairs, Lyotard argues, has led to an increase in the quantity and intensity of language games, which in turn has eroded the legitimacy of meta-narratives.[22]

While the passage from industrial to post-industrial societies describes the emergence of the postmodern cultural form in the most advanced and industrialized societies of the center (for example, Western Europe, Japan, and the United States), in the periphery it is by contrast the passage from colonial to postcolonial societies that describes the emergence of this cultural form. The first studies of the problem of postcolonial societies were developed by the sociology of underdevelopment and dependency theory.[23] Over time, with the emergence of more nuanced postcolonial perspectives the problem of the Third World gave way to the problem of the subaltern,[24] and the problem of dependency gave way to the problem of orientalism.[25] Indeed, "postcolonial perspectives," Homi Bhabha writes, "emerge from the colonial testimony of Third World countries and the discourses of 'minorities' within the geopolitical divisions of East and West, North and South. They intervene in those ideological discourses of modernity that attempt to give a hegemonic 'normality' to the uneven development and the differential, often disadvantaged, histories of nations, races, communities, peoples."[26] Today, however, both post-industrial and postcolonial societies have fused in and through an international division of labor. This has given way to a new postmodern cultural form, namely, "deterritorialized" global liberal-democratic capitalism.[27]

The postmodern way of seeing the world, the other element that constitutes the postmodern condition, is rooted in the linguistic turn. By *linguistic turn* we mean a paradigm shift in the human sciences that grants language primordial ontological, epistemological, and methodological status. Indeed, the paradigm shift to language means that, whether we like it or not, we are all dependent on language, we are all constituted in and through language. Culture and the unconscious function like a language, society is grounded on communication (language), historical experience is linguistically transmitted, and the like.

The three basic epistemological coordinates of postmodern thought—the plurality of particulars, alterity, and difference—emerged in and through this turn to language. The first in the sense that it is always a plurality of particular beings that negotiate language. The second in the sense that the plurality of particular beings discover their finitude by coming to terms with one another as "alter."[28] And the third that the difference that exists between self and alter can either be overcome through conversation or simply be deconstructed. From the positive role of language as conversation and its negative role as deconstruction have emerged the two conceptions of language that have constituted the linguistic turn in the human sciences, namely, the hermeneutic and poststructuralist conceptions of language.

For post-Romantic hermeneutics the *logos* is no longer mediated by the Scholastic analogy of being, the Kantian transcendental consciousness, the Hegelian Absolute Spirit, or the early Heidegger's analytics of *Dasein*. It is, rather, mediated by language. Hermeneutics still has faith in the universality of the *logos*; it is language that discloses the *logos* and makes it present. Indeed, the universality of the *logos* manifests itself in the hermeneutic tradition through the presupposition that everything can be "linguistified," the presupposition that in the end language will set things right—a presupposition that is valid only if we accept the onto-theological claim that in the beginning was a meta-language, and that in the beginning this meta-language spoke, constituting the being of all beings. Indeed, language for hermeneutics functions positively as presence, disclosure, and understanding.

The hermeneutic conception of language emerged in and through Martin Heidegger's and Hans-Georg Gadamer's radicalization of that hermeneutic tradition inaugurated by Friedrich Schleiermacher and systematized by Wilhelm Dilthey.[29] With the delineation of his phenomenological method at the outset of *Being and Time*,[30] Heidegger laid the ground for his later turn to language: "Language is the house of being. . . . In thinking being comes to language."[31] But it was Gadamer who, in Part 3 of *Truth and Method*, "The Ontological Shift of Hermeneutics Guided by Language," secured the onto-theological status for language with the claims that "language is the universal medium in which understanding occurs" and "the linguisticality of understanding is the concretion of historically effected consciousness."[32]

Although Gadamer's *Truth and Method* would be one of the works behind the linguistic turn in the human and social sciences, it would immediately come under attack by Habermas. And Paul Ricoeur would attempt to tread a middle way between Gadamer and Habermas. Indeed, Gadamer's *philosophical hermeneutics*, Habermas's *depth hermeneutics*, and Ricoeur's *hermeneutics of suspicion* have constituted the debate over hermeneutics; from them stem the three chief variants of the hermeneutic conception of language.[33]

Poststructuralism breaks with that idealism which grants onto-theological status to language. It is a critique of the logocentric metaphysics of presence; a decentering of the knowing subject; an attempt to reinsert Western thought in the horizon of nihilism. Language for poststructuralism no longer functions positively as presence, disclosure, and understanding. It now functions negatively as lack, dissimulation, and alienation. Jacques Derrida and Jacques Lacan are the two most influential exponents of this tradition. Derrida takes issue with structuralism for laboring under the classic way of thinking the limit of a totality. It is not that there is a totality that is impossible to master, given the finitude of language. It is, rather, that the lack inherent to finite language excludes the possibility of positing a totality. Indeed, it is not that there is always too much that needs to be said. It is rather that one can never say enough.[34] Lacan uses this poststructuralist conception of language to rework that science inaugurated by Freud. Language for Lacan expresses the desire of the subject. Language is lack, dissimulation, and alienation—it is the torturer of being.[35] Indeed, the end of Lacanian psychoanalysis is to liberate the subject from language, or stated positively, to achieve the Real beyond language.

Thus, by the postmodern condition we mean the dialectic between the postmodern style of thought and the postmodern cultural form; while the turn to the plurality of particulars, alterity, and difference takes form in and through the conditions of late capitalism, the conditions of late capitalism are perpetuated in and through the turn to the plurality of particulars, alterity, and difference. Or, more precisely, the postmodern condition can be understood in terms of the elective affinity between the turn to language in the human sciences and the emergence of global liberal-democratic capitalism. And here we have the reason why this condition imposes itself as the "end of history."[36] For while the postmodern turn to the particular (through language) performs an *epoché* on the question of the totality (meta-narratives) and thus naturalizes global-liberal democratic capitalism, the new (compressed) way of experiencing space and time under the conditions of global liberal-democratic capitalism generates the illusion of unmediated particulars. Indeed, the postmodern condition imposes itself as inevitable due to the hegemonic fusion of postmodern thought, liberal-democratic multiculturalism ("identity politics"), and globalized, advanced capitalism.[37]

Having sketched the main contours of the postmodern condition, we are now in a better position to see why this condition is generating the eclipse of the theologies of liberation. First, the postmodern turn to the particular undercuts the validity of the meta-narrative of liberation. This is what we call the historical-hermeneutic reduction of the critically oriented theological sciences of liberation; the category of social labor is now reduced to the category of praxis understood specifically through the hermeneutic conception of language.

Second, the postmodern naturalization of global liberal-democratic capitalism reveals the futility of liberation theology's attempt to realize liberation to the extent that such a project has implied the implementation of real socialism. This is what we call the liberalization of the liberationist paradigm; the liberationist emancipatory project is now forced to accept the basic coordinates of global liberal-democratic capitalism. This eclipse is being generated from both the "inside" and the "outside."

On the one hand, liberation theologians are increasingly accepting the basic coordinates of postmodern thought and global liberal-democratic capitalism. This state of affairs is the natural extension of those two sets of tensions that have undergirded the history of the theologies of liberation. Indeed, the postmodern eclipse of the theologies of liberation can be understood as the radicalization of the tension between poiesis and praxis and the tension between the universality of the idea of liberation and the plurality of particular liberationist perspectives. That fundamental liberationist idea of making transcendence as the making a break with the dialectic of the Americas (and in particular U.S.-style liberal-democratic capitalism) has today become the talking about the meaning of transcendence as the making of conversation in a public sphere that naturalizes the idea of the Free Trade Area of the Americas. This is precisely the idea of the dialogue between liberation theology and the theology of religious pluralism *(teología del pluralismo religioso)*.[38]

On the other hand, yesterday's detractors have become today's "conversation partners." These days the theologies of liberation are no longer explicitly critiqued and pushed to the periphery. They are instead assimilated into the community of "particular" theologies. By understanding liberation theology as a "local," "contextual," or "public" theology, the liberal theologies of the center are reducing liberation theology to a historical-hermeneutic science. The work of David Tracy exemplifies this reduction. But more pernicious has been the reduction performed by the advocates of U.S. Hispanic theology. Let us unravel a bit these two reductions.

David Tracy has labored under the hermeneutic conception of language since his first publications. But it is in the third chapter of *Plurality and Ambiguity* that he has most clearly articulated this tendency with the claim that "we understand in and through language."[39] Indeed, Tracy not only situates himself in the linguistic turn but specifically labors under the hermeneutic conception of language. In like fashion Tracy not only attempts to grapple with the phenomenon of religious pluralism but grants pluralism a normative role. Pluralism for Tracy is a good thing; it generates a plurality of opinions that through reasoned, public discourse advances the state of a discipline.

Tracy posits a plurality but excludes the possibility of a radical incompatibility within this plurality. Tracy posits "otherness" but excludes the possibility of a radical otherness that undermines interreligious dialogue. It is the hermeneutic conception of language, and specifically the assumptions that all differences can be liquidated by a "meta-language" and that all particulars are driven by a "communicative interest" in reaching understanding, that grounds and legitimates this perspective. The claim that "all understanding is linguistic through and through" is not just an epistemological fact for Tracy; that is, it does not refer simply to the conditions of doing theology within the horizon of language. In addition, it carries the normative weight of the hermeneutic tradition.

The spurious universality of the hermeneutic tradition generates the spurious belief in a universal communicative interest that cuts across religious traditions. But not all religious traditions want to communicate. Some, for example, wish to transform. Indeed, this false universality of interreligious dialogue is today generating the historical-hermeneutic reduction of the critically oriented theological sciences of liberation.[40]

The other reduction of the theologies of liberation is being generated by U.S. Hispanic theology. U.S. Hispanic theology has systematically fallen captive to the hermeneutic reduction of the critically oriented theological sciences of liberation, failing to realize that such a reduction undercuts the very possibility of U.S. Hispanic theology to the extent that U.S. Hispanic theology understands itself as a theology that phenomenologically emerges from U.S. Hispanic reality and as a theology that grasps the theological *logos* in the interest of the liberation of U.S. Hispanics. This reduction is the result of the following fundamental obfuscation: *U.S. Hispanic theologians have methodically obfuscated the project of transplanting the critically oriented theological sciences of liberation in the U.S. context with the project of hermeneutically reinterpreting these theological sciences of liberation.*

This obfuscation has historically manifested itself through the restriction of the concept of *mestizaje* to symbolic-cultural conditions,[41] the aesthetic turn,[42] and the eclipse of the question of the relationship between popular religion and power.[43] Today, however, with the emergence of the postmodern linguistic turn, this tendency hermeneutically to reduce the critically oriented theological sciences of liberation is specifically taking the form of a bias in favor of the hermeneutic conception of language.

U.S. Hispanic theology has been driven by the attempt to transplant the Latin American theologies of liberation into the U.S. context. Today this specifically means taking the idea of liberation through the postmodern turn to language. But such a task is problematic to the extent that the postmodern condition is coercing U.S. Hispanic theologians to choose between either "liberation" or "language," that is, between either the socio-historical emancipatory project of making a break with the dialectic of the Americas, on the one hand, or the postmodern turn to language, alterity, and the plurality of particulars, on the other.[44]

U.S. Hispanic theologians are today choosing language over liberation; that is, they are choosing as their frame of reference the problem of conversation among a plurality of particular ethnic groups in the public sphere over the problem of the Free Trade Area of the Americas as the latest moment of the dialectic of Anglo and Hispanic America. An increasing number of U.S. Hispanic theologians understand U.S. Hispanic theology to be a *particular, local, contextual,* or *public* theology, not a liberation theology. What is at stake here is nothing more than the radical difference between the historical-hermeneutic theologies of interpretation and the critically oriented theological sciences of liberation.

This linguistic reduction of liberation, this confusion among U.S. Hispanic theologians between the project of transplanting the critically oriented theological sciences of liberation in the U.S. context and the project of hermeneutically reinterpreting these theological sciences of liberation finds its radical cause when it is grasped as the problem of intellectual assimilation, that is, when it is grasped as the problem of the absorption of the theologies of liberation of the periphery by the theologies of the center in and through the hegemonic fusion of postmodern thought and global liberal-democratic capitalism as the "end of history." This is the problem of U.S. Hispanic theology as the theological (intellectual) moment of the general social process of the assimilation of U.S. Hispanics into a multicultural society that ideologically functions as a buttress for Anglo-American hegemony. Today this dynamic is manifesting itself in and through the "inevitability" of the Free Trade Area of the Americas.[45]

But the alternative of either "liberation" or "language" is fallacious; this choice is a product of the postmodern style of thought, the hermeneutic conception of language in particular. Lurking behind this conception of language is that liberal blackmail we alluded to earlier, namely, that any radical attempt to push beyond the horizon of liberal-democratic capitalism (the Free Trade Area of the Americas) will lead inevitably to totalitarianism. Indeed, to the question of liberation or language, U.S. Hispanic theologians should answer, "Yes, please!"[46] This "Yes, please!"—this refusal of choice—implies a repudiation of the historical-hermeneutic tradition. Indeed, it implies rethinking the task of reconstructing the theologies of liberation.

RETHINKING THE TASK OF RECONSTRUCTION: THE TURN TOWARD PSYCHOANALYSIS

Only a reconstruction of the foundations of the theologies of liberation against the current situation—the postmodern condition—can overcome the eclipse and dissimulation of the crisis marked by the eruption of the Latin American theologies of liberation that is being generated, not only by the progressive theologies of North America, but also by U.S. Hispanic theologians in the name of liberation.

Returning to the foundations of the theologies of liberation can serve as a destabilization of the postmodern condition. But this, however, will not suffice. That the theologies of liberation are not reducible to the postmodern condition does not imply that they are exempt from the challenges generated by this condition. Indeed, a *return* to the foundations of the theologies of liberation must be completed by a *reconstruction* of these foundations in light of the postmodern condition. But what would such a project entail?

It is the coming to terms with liberation theology as a critically oriented science that generates the return to the foundations of the theologies of liberation. And the foundations of the theologies of liberation are brought forth only by a liberation theology that has understood itself as a critically oriented science. This is the dialectic of method and legitimation; rethinking theological method from the point of view of the critically oriented theological sciences of liberation provides the leverage that makes possible the project of legitimating the theologies of liberation. And the project of legitimating the theologies of liberation generates the method of the critically oriented theological sciences of liberation.[47]

We can better understand what is at stake in such a project by considering Leonardo and Clodovis Boff's image of the "tree" of liberation theology. The professional liberation theologians, the brothers Boff suggest, constitute the branches that are visible from afar. Religious specialists such as pastors, lay professionals, and the like constitute the trunk. And the thousands of Christian faith communities that concretely live and practice their faith according to a model of liberation constitute the roots.[48] Drawing on the Heideggerian metaphor we can thus say that our "return" aims to uncover that ground to which the roots of the tree of liberation theology are attached, and it seeks to make explicit that nourishment that flows up from the ground through the roots and trunk to the branches and back down.[49]

In a word, the project of reconstructing the foundations of the theologies of liberation in light of the postmodern condition requires that we take liberation theology's emancipatory cognitive interest through the linguistic turn, but *without reducing it to the hermeneutic conception of language*. We see the possibility of such a linguistified corrective to the theologies of liberation in that idea we alluded to during our critical exposition of Scannone, namely, the idea of psychoanalysis as a critically oriented science.

The idea of psychoanalysis as a critically oriented science is first and foremost the problem of the relationship between meta-psychology and social theory; though, ultimately, it is no other than the problem of grounding the human-social sciences.[50] As the most recent attempt to develop psychoanalysis as a critically oriented science, Slavoj Žižek's reworking of Jacques Lacan provides the possibility of theoretically overcoming the postmodern reduction of social reality to the hermeneutic conception of language and therapeutically going beyond the naturalization of global liberal-democratic capitalism.[51] In the hands of Žižek the Lacanian Real can serve as a linguistified corrective to liberation theology's emancipatory cognitive interest.

Psychoanalysis as a critically oriented science is a theory of reality, and from here it can function as a theory of religion and serve as the ground for a theological reflection that aims to push beyond the limits of the historical-hermeneutic sciences. Indeed, the idea of psychoanalysis as a critically oriented science can serve as a guide for the reconstruction of the foundations of the theologies of liberation.

This needs to be developed, for example, from the U.S. Hispanic point of view, not only because U.S. Hispanic reality is what mediates the tension between the historical-hermeneutic and critically oriented theological sciences, but also because under the conditions of postmodernity the problem of finitude, the problem of knowledge as crisis, must seek legitimation in and through the particular.

Let us now briefly sketch what the task of reconstructing the theologies of liberation from the U.S. Hispanic point of view involves. Because U.S. Hispanic theology is the intellectual moment of U.S. Hispanic religion, and because U.S. Hispanic religion is grounded in U.S. Hispanic reality, we will elucidate the turn to psychoanalysis in three moves: U.S. Hispanic reality, U.S. Hispanic religion, and U.S. Hispanic theology.

U.S. Hispanic reality needs to be understood in light of the history of the Americas. The history of the Americas, however, as we suggested above, is not a mythical synthesis, not a teleological unfolding of Manifest Destiny. The history of the Americas is rather that asymmetrical life-and-death struggle that has relegated one region of the continent to the "periphery," to the "underside." This history has taken form in and through four dialectics: (1) the dialectic of Cortés and La Malinche, of Spain and the Amerindian civilizations; (2) the dialectic of the *criollo* and the *peninsular*, of Hispanic America and Spain; (3) the dialectic of *civilización* and *barbarie*, of the urban elite and the rural peasant; and (4) the dialectic of Ariel and Calibán, of Hispanic and Anglo America.

U.S. Hispanic reality emerged in and through the fourth dialectic; that is, U.S. Hispanic reality is the mediation of Ariel and Calibán, the mediation of the dialectic between Anglo and Hispanic America. Indeed, U.S. Hispanic reality is that fragmented reality that has been generated by that perpetual tension, that logic of violence and domination that is the asymmetrical relationship between Anglo and Hispanic America. The heterogeneity of U.S. Hispanic reality—its racial, gender, national, religious, socioeconomic, political nuances—is subordinate to this movement of violence and domination. The dialectic of Anglo and Hispanic America is the transcendental condition for U.S. Hispanic reality. Indeed, U.S. Hispanic reality is U.S. Hispanic reality in and through the dialectic of Ariel and Calibán. This dialectic has had two movements, through which U.S. Hispanic reality has taken form: (1) Anglo-America moves south (first as territorial expansion and later as neo-imperialism and neocolonialism), and (2) Hispanic America moves north (as escaping its own fragmented reality). In and through these two movements emerge, for example, a Mexican American, a Puerto Rican, a Cuban American.

Mestizaje is the fundamental concept of U.S. Hispanic reality. This concept, however, as we suggested above, has been hermeneutically restricted. As a result, the fragmented character of U.S. Hispanic reality has been romanticized. Not only has U.S. Hispanic reality been reduced to culture, but U.S. Hispanic culture has been grasped through an integrationist perspective that does little justice to the fact that U.S. Hispanic culture exists at the margins of the dominant Anglo culture. Recasting *mestizaje* in light of the idea of psychoanalysis as a critically oriented science, we argue, can overcome this reduction. The idea of psychoanalysis as a critically oriented science grasps that fragmented reality that is U.S. Hispanic reality as this fragmentation has taken form through both the material economic *and* the symbolic cultural, through both poiesis *and* praxis, indeed, through both labor *and* interaction.

U.S. Hispanic reality is fragmented, on the one hand, to the extent that it is Anglo Americans that have historically controlled the means of production. On the other hand, U.S. Hispanic reality is fragmented to the extent that Anglo culture is the dominant culture of the United States. But ultimately the idea of psychoanalysis as a critically oriented science challenges us to understand *mestizaje* as it is generated in and through the dialectic of fragmented labor and fragmented interaction. Because they do not control capital, U.S. Hispanics lack the means to take their culture toward the center. And to the extent that the Hispanic culture is "ghettoized," a disproportionate amount of U.S. Hispanics have no choice but to sell their labor power to Anglo Americans. The only hope for the mestizo is thus assimilation. This is the paradox: mestizos are determined to adopt the American way of life. They must become pragmatic capitalists.

Rather than idealistically grasping the fragmented symbolic-cultural conditions of mestizo interaction hermeneutically as intentionally or consciously communicated meaning structures that constitute a life-world, we should grasp mestizo interaction psychoanalytically as corrupted and distorted, desires, memories, and dreams that have been repressed.[52] The history of the human being, argued Sigmund Freud, is the history of that individual's repression. This repression is what makes progress possible.[53] In like fashion we argue that the history of the mestizo is the history of the repression of the mestizo language. Indeed, this repression is what is making possible the Free Trade Area of the Americas.

The hermeneutic conception of language—as we suggested above—is grounded in the idealist idea of language as presence, disclosure, and understanding. Such a view of language does not do justice to the fragmented nature of U.S. Hispanic reality. On the contrary, the hermeneutic conception of language naturalizes the dialectic of Hispanic and Anglo America in and through the belief in communication, the public sphere, and multiculturalism. Indeed, to the extent that it deals with the problem of pathological states that need to be transformed in and through language, psychoanalysis is better suited to grapple with the problem of fragmented *mestizaje*. A psychoanalytic perspective—and in particular the Lacanian poststructuralist conception of language as lack, dissimulation, and alienation—unravels the problem of fragmented mestizo symbolic-cultural conditions as a problem of the loss of the Spanish language.

The mestizo is marginalized, "thrown" into the dialectic of Hispanic and Anglo America.[54] This "throwness" manifests itself in and through the anxiety of losing or having lost the Spanish language. Mestizo speech expresses this primordial loss.[55] Mestizos who speak English have lost the Spanish language and must confront the phantoms of their heritage. Mestizos who speak Spanish must face the fact that their children will lose the language. They must face the fact that in the United States the means of cultural production and reproduction (for example, the educational system) are controlled by the English language. And mestizos who speak in "Spanglish" are schizophrenic. Indeed, the mestizo language is the language of anxiety, fragmentation, and loss. This is so in and through the alienation of mestizo labor: Not controlling capital, U.S. Hispanics lack the means to construct and shape institutions for the production and reproduction of their language, of their culture.

Mestizaje is the primordial category of U.S. Hispanic reality, and popular religion is the primordial category of U.S. Hispanic religion. Popular religion is subordinate to *mestizaje* to the extent that religion is grounded in reality. U.S. Hispanic popular religion is that primordial religious moment of U.S. Hispanic reality that is always already phenomenologically "there," prior to any institutionalized manifestation of religion. U.S. Hispanic popular religion is the set of beliefs and practices that attempts to grapple with the radical finitude of the mestizo. This finitude, we have suggested, manifests itself as being "thrown" into the dialectic of Anglo and Hispanic America, as losing the Spanish language and labor. U.S. Hispanic popular religion posits the mestizo's "ultimate concern" in light of this existential-ontological state of fragmentation.[56] Indeed, a psychoanalytic approach to U.S. Hispanic religion explores the way popular religious beliefs and practices give U.S. Hispanics the "courage to be" in the face of the anxiety that is generated by that primordial loss of mestizo language and mestizo labor. Indeed, a psychoanalytic approach to U.S. Hispanic religion analyzes the way U.S. Hispanic popular religious beliefs and practices function both *ideologically* to assimilate U.S. Hispanics into the Anglo-American mainstream, and *liberatively* as resistance and forward-looking hope in the face of fragmentation.

U.S. Hispanic theology stands upon two pillars: U.S. Hispanic (mestizo) reality and (popular) religion. U.S. Hispanic theology needs not only to interpret but also to help rectify the pathological state of U.S. Hispanic reality that has been corrupted by the dialectic of Anglo and Hispanic America as this pathological state manifests itself in and through U.S. Hispanic religion. Toward this end, U.S. Hispanic theology needs to concern itself with the poietic transformation of U.S. Hispanic material-economic conditions in and through mestizo labor and the praxeological transformation of U.S. Hispanic symbolic-cultural conditions in and through mestizo language.

We conclude these reflections by positing two principles intended to guide U.S. Hispanic theology with this task. First, as a *system of thought* U.S. Hispanic theology needs to turn toward pastoral clinical psychology. That is, the traditional task of grounding a U.S. Hispanic systematic or constructive theology must be replaced with the task of grounding a U.S. Hispanic pastoral clinical psychology. Second, as a *social movement* U.S. Hispanic theology needs to turn toward Latin

America and Europe.[57] That is, U.S. Hispanic theologians need to realize that they will not be able to open a legitimate space for themselves in the U.S. academy (a task that they need to understand, first
of all, as an intellectual moment of the struggle against the general
social process of the assimilation of U.S. Hispanics into the American
way of life, and second of all, as the struggle against the Free Trade
Area of the Americas) so long as they remain at the mercy of Anglo-
American intellectual and economic capital.[58]

NOTES

[1] We are drawing here on Jürgen Habermas's early idea of knowledge-
constitutive interests (see *Knowledge and Human Interests* [London: Heinemann,
1972], 301–17). Habermas's idea of knowledge-constitutive interests provides
us with a scheme for categorizing theology that is more consistent with the
demands of the conditions of crisis. Indeed, the idea of knowledge-constitutive interests allows us to reconceive the theologies of liberation as the most
radical theological crisis of modern theology, perceived as a tension between
the practical interest of the historical-hermeneutical sciences and the
emancipatory interest of the critically oriented sciences (Manuel J. Mejido,
"Theology, Crisis, and Knowledge-Constitutive Interests, or Towards a Social Theoretical Interpretation of Theological Knowledge," *Social Compass* 51,
no. 4 (2004): 381–401.

[2] This has been the case whether these theologies have situated themselves
more specifically within the limits of the Kantian horizon of consciousness
(i.e., Friedrich Schleiermacher and Joseph Maréchal), the Heideggerian horizon of temporality (e.g., Karl Rahner and Paul Tillich), the Hegelian horizon
of becoming (e.g., J. B. Metz and Jürgen Moltmann), or the postmodern horizon of language (e.g., David Tracy and Jorg Rieger).

[3] Jürgen Moltmann, "An Open Letter to José Miguez Bonino," in *Mission
Trends* 4, ed. Gerald H. Anderson and Thomas F. Stransky (New York: Paulist
Press, 1970), 57–70; Thomas G. Sanders, "The Theology of Liberation: Chris-
tian Utopianism," *Christianity and Crisis* 33 (1973): 167–73; Roger Vekemans,
Teología de la liberación y cristianos por el socialismo (Bogotá: CEDIAL, 1976);
Dennis McCann, *Christian Realism and Liberation Theology: Practical Theolo-
gies in Creative Conflict* (Maryknoll, NY: Orbis Books, 1981); Joseph Cardinal
Ratzinger, "Instruction on Certain Aspects of the 'Theology of Liberation,'"
Sacred Congregation for the Doctrine of the Faith, Rome, August 6, 1984.

[4] Andrew Greeley, "Theological Table-Talk: Politics and Political Theolo-
gians," *Theology Today* 30, no. 4 (1974): 391–97; Michael Novak, *The Spirit of
Democratic Capitalism* (New York: Madison Books, 1982) and *Will It Liberate?*
(New York: Paulist Press, 1986); Arthur McGovern, *Liberation Theology and Its*

Critics: Toward an Assessment (Maryknoll, NY: Orbis Books; 1989), Richard John Neuhaus, *The Catholic Moment* (New York: Harper & Row, 1990), 186–89; Paul E. Sigmund, *Liberation Theology at the Crossroads: Democracy or Revolution?* (New York: Oxford University Press, 1990); and Humberto Belli and Ronald Nash, *Beyond Liberation Theology* (Grand Rapids, MI: Baker Book House, 1992).

[5] Slavoj Žižek, *Did Somebody Say Totalitarianism?* (New York: Verso, 2001).

[6] Juan José Tamayo, "Recepción en Europa de la teología de la liberación," in *Mysterium Liberationis: Conceptos fundamentales de la teología de la liberación,* vol. 1, ed. Ignacio Ellacuría and Jon Sobrino (Madrid: Trotta, 1990), 54–58; English translation *Mysterium Liberationis: Fundamental Concepts of Liberation Theology* (Maryknoll, NY: Orbis Books, 1993); Enrique Dussel, "Teología de la liberación y Marxismo," in ibid., 123–24; and Julio Lois, "Cristología en la teología de la liberación," in ibid., 228–29; Juan Carlos Scannone, *Teología de la liberación y praxis popular: Aportes críticos para una teología de la liberación* (Salamanca: Ediciones Sígueme, 1976), 21–23, 241.

[7] Dussel, "Teología de la liberación y Marxismo," 121–31; Ricardo Antoncich, "Teología de la liberación y doctrina social de la iglesia," in Ellacuría and Sobrino, *Mysterium Liberationis,* 156–61; Pablo Richard, "Teología en la teología de la liberación, in ibid., 210–12.

[8] Juan Carlos Scannone, "'Axial Shift' instead of 'Paradigm Shift,'" in *Liberation Theologies on Shifting Ground: A Clash of Socio-economic and Cultural Paradigms* (Leuven: Leuven University Press, 1998), 87–103.

[9] III Conferencia General del Episcopado Latinoamericano, *Documento de Puebla* in *Puebla: Comunión y participación* (Madrid: Biblioteca de autores cristianos, 1982), "De Medellín a Puebla," 608–9.

[10] Scannone, "'Axial Shift' instead of 'Paradigm Shift,'" 95.

[11] Scannone, *Teología de la liberación y praxis popular,* 63–80.

[12] Juan Carlos Scannone, *Teología de la liberación y doctrina social de la iglesia* (Buenos Aires: Guadalupe, 1987), 246–51.

[13] Habermas, *Knowledge and Human Interests,* 214–45.

[14] Ivone Gebara, *La mal au féminin: Réflexions théologiques à partir du féminisme* (Paris: Harmattan, 1999).

[15] Franz J. Hinkelammert, *The Ideological Weapons of Death: A Theological Critique of Capitalism* (Maryknoll, NY: Orbis Books, 1986).

[16] W.W. Rostow, *The Stages of Economic Growth: A Non-Communist Manifesto* (Cambridge: Cambridge University: Press, 1962); Fernando Henrique Cardoso and Enzo Faletto, *Dependencia y desarrollo en América Latina: ensayo de interpretación sociológica* (Mexico: Siglo Veintiuno editores, 1969).

[17] Milton Friedman, *Capitalism and Freedom* (Chicago: University of Chicago Press, 1962); Enrique Dussel, *Método para una filosofía de la liberación: Superación analéctica de la dialéctica hegeliana* (Salamanca: Ediciones Sígueme, 1974).

[18] Subcomandante Marcos, *Detrás de nosotros estamos ustedes* (Mexico: Plaza y Janés, 2000).

[19] David Harvey, *The Condition of Postmodernity* (Cambridge, MA: Basil Blackwell, 1989), vii; see also Fredric Jameson, *Postmodernism, or the Cultural Logic of Late Capitalism* (London: Verso, 1991); and Terry Eagleton, *The Illusion of Postmodernism* (Cambridge, MA: Blackwell, 1996).

[20] Alain Touraine, *La société postindustrielle* (Paris: Denoël, 1969); English translation *The Post-Industrial Society*, trans. L. F. X. Mayhew (New York: Random House, 1971); and Daniel Bell, *The Coming of the Post-Industrial Society* (New York: Basic Books, 1973).

[21] Harvey, *The Condition of Postmodernity*, 338–39.

[22] Jean-François Lyotard, *La condition postmoderne* (Paris: Les Editions de Minuit, 1979).

[23] Cardoso and Faletto, *Dependencia y desarrollo en América Latina*.

[24] Gayatri Chakravorty Spivak, "Can the Subaltern Speak?" in *Marxism and the Interpretation of Culture*, ed. Cary Nelson and Lawrence Grossberg (Chicago: University of Illinois Press, 1988), 271–313.

[25] Edward Said, *Orientalism* (New York: Pantheon Books, 1978).

[26] Homi K. Bhabha, "The Postcolonial and the Postmodern," in *The Location of Culture* (New York: Routledge, 1994), 171.

[27] Michael Hardt and Antonio Negri, *Empire* (Cambridge, MA: Harvard University Press, 2000).

[28] Emmanuel Lévinas, *Totalité et infini: Essai sur l'extériorité* (Paris: Brodard et Taupin, 2001), 59–80.

[29] Friedrich Schleiermacher, *Hermeneutics* (Missoula, MT: Scholars Press for the American Academy of Religion, 1977); Wilhelm Dilthey, *Introduction to the Human Sciences* (Princeton, NJ: Princeton University Press, 1989).

[30] Martin Heidegger, *Being and Time* (New York: Harper & Row, 1962), 49–63.

[31] Martin Heidegger, "Letter on Humanism" in *Basic Writings,* ed. David Farrell Krell (New York: Harper & Row, 1977), 217.

[32] Hans-Georg Gadamer, *Truth and Method,* 2nd rev. ed. (London: Sheed & Ward, 1975), 389.

[33] Paul Ricoeur, "Herméneutique et critique des idéologie," in *Du texte à l'action*: *Essais d'herméneutique* (Paris: Seuil, 1986), 2:333–76.

[34] Jacques Derrida, "La structure, le signe et le jeu dans le discours des sciences humaines," *L'Écriture et la Différence* (Paris: Éditions Du Seuil, 1967), 409–28. Derrida would further develop this perspective with the idea of *différance* as that which creates an empty place for meaning, as that trace of absence ("La différance," in *Marges de la philosophie* [Paris: Les Éditions de Minuit, 1972], 1–29).

[35] Jacques Lacan, *Le séminaire* (Paris: Éditions du Seuil, 1981), 3:276.

[36] Francis Fukuyama, *The End of History and the Last Man* (New York: Free Press, 1992).

[37] Slavoj Žižek, "Class Struggle or Postmodernism? Yes, Please!" in *Contingency, Hegemony, Universality*, ed. Judith Butler, Ernesto Laclau, and Slavoj Žižek (London: Verso, 2000), 90–135.

[38] Joaquín Garay, "Teología del pluralismo religioso y teología de la liberación." Available online.

[39] David Tracy, *Plurality and Ambiguity* (Chicago: University of Chicago Press, 1987).

[40] Manuel J. Mejido, "The Real beyond Language: A Response to David R. Brockman," *Koinonia* 15, no. 1 (2003): 34–37. Available online.

[41] Manuel J. Mejido, "Rethinking Liberation," *Rethinking Latino/a Religion and Identity*, ed. Miguel Angel de la Torre and Gastón Espinosa (Cleveland: The Pilgrim Press, 2005).

[42] Manuel J. Mejido, "A Critique of the 'Aesthetic Turn' in U.S. Hispanic Theology: A Conversation with Roberto Goizueta and the Positing of a New Paradigm," *Journal of Hispanic/Latino Theology* 8, no. 3 (February 2001): 18–48.

[43] Manuel J. Mejido, "The Illusion of Neutrality: Reflections on the Term 'Popular Religion,'" *Social Compass* 49, no. 2 (2002): 295–311; idem, "Theoretical Prolegomenon to the Sociology of U.S. Hispanic Popular Religion," *Journal of Hispanic/Latino Theology* 7, no. 1 (August 1999): 27–55.

[44] Manuel J. Mejido, "The Postmodern: Liberation or Language?" *Handbook of Latino/a Theologies*, ed. Edwin Aponte and Miguel Angel de la Torre (St. Louis: Chalice Press, 2005).

[45] Manuel J. Mejido, "The Fundamental Problematic of U.S. Hispanic Theology," in *New Horizons in U.S. Hispanic/Latino(a) Theology,* ed. Benjamin Valentin, 163–78 (Cleveland: The Pilgrim Press, 2003); and idem, "Propaedeutic to the Critique of the Study US Hispanic Religion: A Polemic Against Intellectual Assimilation," *Journal of Hispanic/Latino Theology* 10, no. 4 (May 2003).

[46] Žižek, "Class Struggle or Postmodernism? Yes, Please!," 90.

[47] The idea of a critically oriented theological science of liberation refers to a logical-methodological framework, that is, to the way theology is to be done. This framework is not imposed to theology from the "outside"; rather, theology achieves it from "within," through the process of coming to terms with its own trajectory (Clodovis Boff, "Epistemología y método de la teología de la liberación," in Ellacuría and Sobrino, *Mysterium Liberationis*, 1:82). The idea of the foundations of the theologies of liberation refers to a legitimating project, that is, it refers to that process by which the theologies of liberation gain validity for themselves in light of the movement of the problem of knowledge (Dussel, "Teología de la liberación y Marxismo," 121–22).

[48] Leonardo and Clodovis Boff, *Qu'est-ce que la théologie de la libération?* (Paris: CERF, 1987), 26–28; English translation *Introducing Liberation Theology*, trans. Paul Burns (Maryknoll, NY: Orbis Books, 1987).

[49] Martin Heidegger, *Qu'est-ce que la métaphysique?* in *Questions* (Paris: Gallimard, 1968), 1:23–24.

[50] See, for example, Herbert Marcuse, *Eros and Civilization: A Philosophical Inquiry into Freud* (Boston: Beacon Press, 1966); Habermas, *Knowledge and Human Interests*, 214–45; and Gilles Deleuze and Félix Guatari, *Capitalisme et schizophrénie*, 2 vols. (Paris: Minuit, 1975–80).

[51] Slavoj Žižek, *The Sublime Object of Ideology* (London: Verso, 1989); idem, *The Ticklish Subject: The Absent Centre of Political Ontology* (London: Verso, 1999); idem, *The Fragile Absolute—or, Why Is the Christian Legacy Worth Fighting for?* (London: Verso, 2000).

[52] Habermas, *Knowledge and Human Interests*, chap. 10.

[53] Marcuse, *Eros and Civilization*.

[54] Heidegger, *Being and Time*, 232.

[55] Jacques Lacan, "Le stade du mirroir comme formateur de la fonction du Je," *Écrits* (Paris: Éditions du Seuil, 1966), 1:92–99.

[56] Paul Tillich, *Systematic Theology*, vol. 1, *Reason and Revelation, Being and God* (New York: University of Chicago Press/Harper & Row, 1967).

[57] Carlos Fuentes, "L'Amérique latine en mal d'Europe," *Le Monde diplomatique* (November 2003): 36.

[58] Pierre Bourdieu, *Méditations pascaliennes* (Paris: Seuil, 1997).

8.

Liberation Theology— A Programmatic Statement

Ivan Petrella

WORKS ON LIBERATION THEOLOGY PRODUCED since the fall of the Berlin Wall typically fall within four broad categories. First, there are books and essays heralding liberation theology's demise. Works in this category give up on the project, sometimes gleefully.[1] Second, there are works by mainstream liberation theologians arguing that their central intuitions—the preferential option for the poor, the reign of God, liberation—remain unscathed. These works, unfortunately, shed little light onto how the original liberationist project might be reformulated for a new time.[2] Third, there are assessments that often include calls for revision that are usually little more than statements of desire. Ultimately, they remain unsatisfactory.[3] Fourth, there are works from the North Atlantic academy that succeed in revising liberation theology so well that none of the foundational liberation theologians would recognize the final product. These works betray the central theological categories liberationists have worked with since the inception of liberation theology.[4]

This essay outlines the way I think liberation theology should be reformulated—others avenues of revision are both possible and necessary.[5] It is, however, an attempt that goes beyond merely calling for revision while at the same time remaining faithful to liberation theology's original understanding of itself as theology, as a theology different from those produced in affluent Western Europe and the United States. The argument develops in the following fashion: First, I claim that the recovery and development of the notion of a historical project (as José Míguez Bonino defined it, a halfway term between a utopia and a developed model for the organization of society) is the central task ahead. Second, I argue that liberation theology must reassess the role of the social sciences and the placement of theology in its methodological statements. Third, I argue that new historical projects can draw from liberation theology's insight that the definition of democracy cannot be separated from the analysis of the economic foundation of society. Fourth, I argue that liberation theology's imagination of historical projects is hindered by its current theoretical approach to capitalism. Fifth, I draw from Roberto Unger's social theory to present an alternative approach that can open a space for political and economic possibility. While many liberation theologians today call for the incorporation of new social-scientific mediations to understand the political, economic, and social context within which they work, few have been attempted. This essay is one such attempt.[6]

INTRODUCTION: THE SITUATION

At its best, in its pursuit of a *material* and *social* liberation for the nonperson—human beings not considered human by the dominant social order[7]—liberation theology had two interrelated parts, one directed toward the Christian tradition, the other directed toward society. The former included a rereading of Christianity from history's underside. This had three elements: first, the notion of God as a God of concrete bodily life; second, a unified anthropology that made the body the locus of salvation and thus food, drink, and shelter part of God's plan for all people; and third, a unified understanding of history in which the history of salvation is the very heart of human history. These elements formed the theological background for concepts such as the preferential option for the poor and liberation. The latter part included the use of the social sciences; liberation theologians incorporated economics, political science, and sociology as intrinsic elements in the theological enterprise. They did so for one critical reason and one constructive reason. In the first place, liberation theologians sought to better understand the causes of oppression. If the goal is liberation, then there is a need to discover the underlying causes of oppression. In second place, they did so in order to develop historical projects to achieve liberation. If the goal is liberation, then there is a need to develop models of political and economic organization that can effectively contribute to that cause. These elements—the rereading of Christianity, the critical and constructive use of the social sciences—worked together in the pursuit of liberation.

Today, liberation theology has abandoned the construction of historical projects. This central element of early liberation theology—indeed, the element that according to liberation theologians themselves made their theology distinctive and different from North Atlantic theology—lies forgotten, a mere historical curiosity.[8] Yet the development of historical projects must remain central to liberation theology for at least two reasons. First and most important, historical projects are needed because it is through them that liberation is most truly pursued. Liberation for liberation theology was never abstract; it was, and remains, social and material. As such, pursuing the goal of liberation requires historical projects that can confront a new global order marked by increasing inequality and exclusion—a growing division between those who are able to participate within its boundaries and those who are excluded from those boundaries. The current order is marked by "an accelerated withdrawing, a *shrinking* of the global map, rather than an *expanding* phenomenon, and one which expels ever more people from the interactive circle of global capitalism."[9] Look at the data: share of developing country participation in world trade has increased by a mere 3.6 percent from 1953 to 1996. That increase, however, includes Hong Kong, Korea, Taiwan, and Singapore—the Asian Tigers—which account for 33 percent of the developing world's share of trade while representing only 1.5 percent of its population. In 1995, once you exclude the Asian Tigers, the developing world's share of global trade was only 18.3 percent, down from the 1950 share of 25.9 percent, calculated again excluding the Asian Tigers. Latin America's share of world trade in 1995 was 4.8 percent, down from 10 percent in 1950. Recorded growth in world trade, therefore, has bypassed rather than integrated the developing world into the world economy. Similarly, the developing world's share of foreign direct investment (FDI) has dwindled. Up to 1960, the developing nations received half the world's total direct investment flows. By 1988–89 that percentage was down to 16.5 percent, with over half going to different parts of Asia. The 1990s saw a turnaround, with the developing world receiving 38 percent of FDI by 1997, yet fully one-third of this investment was concentrated in China's eight coastal provinces and in Beijing. In fact, in the first half of the 1990s, 86 percent of all FDI went to 30 percent of the world's population. In addition, the distance in income between the rich and the poor countries continues to grow at a dramatic pace—from 35:1 in 1950, to 44:1

in 1973, to 72:1 in 1992. All this in a context in which the rich industrial nations consume 70 percent of the world's energy, 75 percent of
its metals, 85 percent of its wood, and 60 percent of its food, while
becoming proportionally a smaller part of the world's population.
So, while the population of the developing world increases, its participation in the global economy and its consumption of the world's
resources decreases. Exclusion and irrelevance are the hallmark of
the new global order.

The second main reason why historical projects are still necessary
is that without them liberation theology's terminology is empty. It is
through the development of such projects that liberation theology
gave, and must give, specific content to its theological terminology.
Simply put, it is not clear what "liberation" and the "preferential option for the poor" mean in the absence of historical projects. Take
Franz Hinkelammert's analysis of a speech delivered by Michael
Camdessus, then head of the International Monetary Fund (IMF), at
a Congress for French Christian businessmen in 1992. In this speech
Camdessus echoes a number of themes from liberation theology. He
states (referring to the IMF and businessmen everywhere):

> Our mandate? . . . It is a text of Isaiah which Jesus explained; it
> says (Luke 4, 16–23): "The spirit of the Lord is upon me. He has
> anointed me in order to announce the good news to the Poor, to
> proclaim liberation to captives and the return of sight to the blind,
> to free the oppressed and proclaim the year of grace granted by
> the Lord." And Jesus only had one short response: "Today this
> message is fulfilled for you that you should listen." This today is
> our today and we are part of this grace of God, we who are in
> charge of the economy (the administrators of a part of it in any
> case): the alleviation of suffering for our brothers and the pro-
> curers of the expansion of their liberty. It is we who have re-
> ceived the Word. This Word can change everything. We know
> that God is with us in the work of spreading brotherhood.[10]

In his speech Camdessus makes the IMF God's vehicle on earth.
He takes central tenets of liberation theology—the preferential option for the poor, the reign of God, liberation—to develop a theology
whose practical political outcome is godly support for the very same
structural adjustment policies denounced by liberation theologians.
Hinkelammert draws two crucial consequences: First, "the fact that
these two contrary theologies (the theology of the IMF and liberation
theology) cannot be distinguished on the level of a clearly theological

discussion stands out. At this level liberation theology does not visibly distinguish itself from the anti-theology presented by the IMF. The conflict seems to be over the application of a theology shared by both sides."[11] Second, "imperial theology is in agreement with the preferential option for the poor and with the economic and social incarnation of God's Kingdom. It presents itself as the only realistic path for fulfilling those demands. . . . The option for the poor can no longer identify any specification and natural affinity for liberation theology. Now, the question is over the realism of the concretization."[12]

In the face of the dramatic inequality at the heart of the new global order and such attempts at cooption, the key issue becomes what practical political, social, and economic content liberation theology gives to its theological terms. Gustavo Gutiérrez, for example, has argued that the preferential option for the poor is the most important legacy bequeathed by liberation theology.[13] This may be true, but it leaves us empty-handed when confronted with other, conflicting, interpretations of the term. What exactly is meant by the preferential option for the poor? What exactly is meant by liberation? Leonardo Boff once warned:

> What sort of liberation are we talking about? Here we must be careful not to fall into the semantic trap of endowing the same word with several very different meanings. The liberation involved here has to do with economic, social, political and ideological structures. It seeks to operate on structures, not simply on persons. It proposes to change the power relationships existing between social groups by helping to create new structures that will allow for greater participation on the part of those now excluded.[14]

While Boff alludes to the danger inherent in not specifying the concrete meaning of liberation, he also remains too vague. At this level of generality there is nothing in his statement that the IMF could not also espouse. Back in the early 1970s, Hugo Assmann tried to avoid this danger by arguing that liberation theology had to confront three levels of specification: the level of socioeconomic and political analysis, the option for a specific set of political theses, and the strategic-tactical level or the implementation of the political theses. He saw that the main difference between liberation theology and other Catholic groups lay not in the abstract terminology they used but in what that terminology meant in practice.[15]

Liberation theology needs to recover the intimate link between thinking about ideals and thinking about institutions embodied in the notion of a historical project. That the loss of a historical project means, most important, the loss of a particular way of thinking combining an attention to both the religious ideal and the concretization that might approach that ideal, remains unacknowledged. Generic concepts such as the preferential option for the poor and liberation, democracy and capitalism, hide more than they reveal about the way life chances and social resources may be theoretically approached and institutionally realized. The focus needs to be on the practical political and economic mediations of these ideals and concepts; the lack of such mediations opens up the space for the cooption of the language of liberation theology that is taking place. In liberation theology, while the critique of current society is presented in concrete political, economic, and sociological terms, liberation, and thus the constructive part of the liberationist agenda, is vaguely posited as the overcoming of slavery, a new person, or a new culture of solidarity.[16] The upshot is a theology powerless to define and pursue its own ideals, a domesticated theology that talks about liberation rather than concretely pursuing liberation where it matters most to most people—in the economic and political structures of society.

The future of liberation theology is thus tied to recovering a central notion from its past. The current situation takes us back to an original assumption of liberation theology, that historical projects are needed to make real a material and social liberation as well as truly to understand what is at stake in ideals such as the preferential option for the poor and liberation.[17] This is the way that the marginalization at the heart of the global order may be countered; this is the way that the emptying and cooption of the language of liberation can be avoided. The notion of a historical project, however, has fallen far into the backdrop of current liberation theology. The rest of this essay shows how it might be placed at the forefront again.

HISTORICAL PROJECT: METHODOLOGY

To develop historical projects, liberation theology needs to reassess the role of the social sciences and the placement of theology in its methodological statements. The best summary statement of liberation theology's dominant methodological position remains Clodovis Boff's "Epistemology and Method of the Theology of Liberation."[18] According to Boff, liberation theology is composed of four steps: a living commitment to the cause of the poor, a socio-analytical mediation, a hermeneutical mediation, and a practical mediation. The first step, therefore, requires participating in the liberative process. The second step, the socio-analytical mediation, involves using the social sciences to understand the root causes of oppression. The hermeneutical stage, the third stage, is where the theologian develops the implications of God's word for the oppression revealed through the socio-analytical mediation. To do so, the theologian in alliance with the poor rereads the Bible and Christian tradition through a hermeneutic of liberation. These two mediations—the socio-analytical and hermeneutic—are the tools the theologian uses to construct a new theology. Finally, the practical mediation involves the development of plans of action that seek to help the oppressed better their situation. The actual shape and definition of these plans will vary according to whether one is a professional, pastoral, or popular theologian. According to Boff, professional theologians can only point to broad lines of change; pastoral theologians can be somewhat more determinate; and popular theologians can be quite specific because of their own location closer to the everyday struggles of the oppressed. For the dominant view, these stages make up liberation theology.

The problem with this position is that it sets up a divide between theology and the social sciences that disables liberation theology from moving from a discourse *about* liberation to the pursuit of liberation as social reality. For Boff, it is only by virtue of the hermeneutical stage that liberation theology is theology.[19] Even though the social sciences are a necessary part of doing theology as liberation theology, they are, as Gutiérrez puts it, "simply a means to better understand reality."[20] Relegated to the socio-analytical stage, the social sciences are thus of little intrinsic theological worth. This strict non-theological delimitation of the social sciences' role in the socio-analytical stage, however, ends up negating liberation theology's supposed focus on liberation. In the same essay, when distinguishing liberation theology's and Vatican theology's respective emphases, Boff writes that "Rome takes 'ethical-social' liberation for granted, while Latin American liberation theology does the same for soteriological salvation."[21] So a central difference between liberation theology and Vatican theology is that the former seeks to make liberation become social, that is, concretely incarnated in society. The goal, therefore, is not, as Boff writes, "the construction of genuinely new syntheses of faith."[22] Boff himself recognizes that for liberation theology *liberation*, in contradistinction to a document such as *Libertatis conscientiae*, should be understood as "specifically social and historical. . . . It was precisely toward this socioliberative aspect that liberation theology, without question, looked."[23] Yet again: "There is only one goal—the liberation of the oppressed."[24] In this case, however, the focus of liberation theology as theology should fall on the practical rather than the hermeneutical stage, for it is in the former that the goal is formally pursued. At this point, though, the relegation of the social sciences into the socio-analytical stage and the divide between social science and theology come back to haunt the dominant position by leaving the practical stage without the possibility of devising historical projects. There is no possibility of constructing historical projects if the social sciences do not return into the practical mediation and detail the vision of society for which the call to action is heralded. Boff's insistence that the professional theologian can only point to "broad lines of change" reveals this separation's fatal flaw, for the broadness, and really the vagueness, of liberation theology's practical mediation stems from relegating the social sciences to a mere tool for understanding the causes of oppression. The "broadness" is the product of a particular way of assigning priority and theological weight to the different stages. The result is that the dominant position comes dangerously close to taking *both* soteriological and social liberation for granted.

This delimitation of theology to the rereading of scripture and tradition functions to push the construction of historical projects out of the realm of what is considered "proper" theology; it becomes an afterthought to the orthodox theological enterprise. Indeed, what is not part of theology cannot be asked of the theologian. This delimitation thus enshrines liberation theology's inability to construct historical projects as good theology. It masks a vice as a virtue; as such, it must be overcome. To construct historical projects, a more expansive view of "theology" is required. Liberation theology must deny the theology/sociopolitical analysis in two ways: First, by collapsing the distinction between the theological and the political, by insisting on the development of what could be called the material component of liberation theology's categories. The "preferential option for the poor" and "liberation" are not just values by which the theologian judges society. They are to be developed as alternative social forms; that is, political, economic, and social institutions that can be enacted at society's many levels: at the level of the church as well as grass-roots organizations, at the level of civil society as well as the state, at the level of local economies as well as the national and eventually global economies as a whole. The role of the social sciences in liberation theology needs to be more than the uncovering of the causes of oppression. Besides this critical role, there is also a central constructive role in the development of historical projects that help define liberation theology's own terminology. Second, the split is refuted by remembering that liberation theology's goal is not to talk about liberation but to effect concrete social liberation: "The most progressive theology in Latin America is more interested in being liberative than in talking about liberation."[25] I have already suggested that it was by relating ideals and institutions through the development of historical projects that liberation was truly pursued. Thus, in its current denial of a role for the social sciences in the construction of historical projects, liberation theology fails fully to take the goal of liberation to heart.

HISTORICAL PROJECT: DEMOCRACY

Today the search for historical projects should take the shape of an alternative to the Latin American formal democracies legitimized by influential modes of thinking in the U.S. academy. The dominant social-science approach to democracy in Latin America subscribes to a minimalist procedural definition of democracy—a form of government in which citizens choose candidates frequently and fairly—whose roots trace back to Joseph Schumpeter.[26] In this tradition criteria of efficiency, stability, and even merely electoral mandate are the sole prerequisites that confer legitimacy to a democratic regime. This hegemonic definition of democracy serves the apologetic function of separating the understanding of democracy from the foundation of poverty, marginalization, and exclusion upon which it rests.[27] It forgets that the right to vote allows for a change in masters while a nation remains in slavery. The increasing influence of a minimalist definition of democracy owes its ascendancy, moreover, to a momentous shift in the historical context within which thinking about democracy takes place. The demise of socialism and the lowering of people's expectations about the role of government in alleviating inequality has led to a situation in which a minimalist definition smacks of realism. Such a democracy no longer needs legitimization through material improvement or social inclusion; its very definition can dispense with these elements. Its legitimization lies, in fact, in the negative claim that there is no alternative.[28] No wonder that in Latin America the triumph of democracy runs beside the increasing political apathy and/or cynicism of the population.[29]

Since its inception, liberation theology has consistently opposed such a reduction of the meaning of democracy. There are at least three distinct but related phases in liberation theology's understanding of democracy: democracy through revolutionary socialism, participatory democracy through the base communities, and the current analysis of stagnant democracy. Central to all three phases is the refusal to separate democracy as a political mechanism from the social, political-participatory, and economic basis upon which it rests.

First, contrary to what some interpreters believe, early liberation theology's espousal of socialism is best read as an attempt to deepen democratic forms of political and economic organization.[30] When Bonino called for the exposure of "the hoax of democracy" and allied himself with a "socialist project of liberation,"[31] and when Gutiérrez claimed that "the movement toward modern liberties, democracy and rational thought in Europe and the United States, meant for Latin America a new oppression and the more virulent exploitation of the underclass,"[32] they were not rejecting democracy itself but the actual practice of democracy in Latin America. Thus Gutiérrez could also write, while referring to the Bonino-Moltmann debate around the notion of a historical project, that "our historical experience is different, and this difference makes us aware of bourgeois society's lies and the paths that the popular classes must take to conquer an *authentic democracy* and real freedom. This process is a part of what we call liberation."[33] These statements must be read within the local sociopolitical context of the time. Between the mid 1960s and early 1970s Brazil, Chile, Peru, and Bolivia suffered military coups to keep democratically elected leftist alliances from assuming power.[34] It is not surprising, therefore, that liberation theologians saw democracy in Latin America as a sham, valid insofar as its operation did not threaten society's underlying structure of privilege. For them, democracy could not be separated from a process of incorporation for excluded segments of the population (the great majority of Latin Americans). This, in turn, required attacking structural inequality at both the political and economic levels to give people the tools to exercise citizenship. Finally, revolutionary socialism was seen as the only way to break the alliance among military, local, and foreign elites, and inaugurate a truly democratic order. Even in its earliest phase, therefore, Latin American liberation theology should not be read as opposed to democracy but rather as geared toward deepening democratic forms of political and economic organization.

While the first approach to democracy—through revolutionary socialism—is contextualized through the quashing of leftist movements by the military, the second approach—the attempt to make of the base communities a stepping stone for the creation of a new participatory democracy—is contextualized through the heady days of democratization in Latin America.[35] For Leonardo Boff, participatory democracy should

> transcend the limits of bourgeois representative democracy which in Latin America functions in an elitist and anti-popular way, frequently introducing a military dictatorship in order to prevent the advancement of the people and to safeguard the interests of capital. Participatory democracy is based on the organized people; it can and must have representation, but this is continually controlled by the popular organizations themselves, the true subjects of social power. This participatory democracy is not just a project. The seed of it is alive in the popular movements, in the Christian communities on the ground and other movements. . . . Participatory democracy represents the new and the alternative to the capitalist social mould which up to now has not succeeded, in any country in the world, in resolving the basic problems of the people in terms of work, shelter, health and education.[36]

Here the base communities are the tool to work toward a parliamentary democracy and, at a later stage, popular or participatory democracy. This would then lead to economic democracy or socialism, this time reached by an open political process rather than revolution, socialism built from the ground up rather than imposed top down.[37]

The first two approaches to democracy contain elements critical of their context and constructive in relation to the future; the third approach—the analysis of stagnant democracy—is emblematic of our time in remaining purely critical in its inability to envision a more positive future. Liberation theologians display a general sense of unease with Latin American democracies.[38] These regimes are described as "low-intensity democracies" and "restricted democracies," which require limiting the scope for economic and participatory demands to avoid chaos; "facade democracies," in which democratic rights embodied in the constitution are incapable of being met; and "democracies under tutelage," in which an outside agent such as the United States or the IMF is needed to ensure a regime's stability.[39] Not only have participatory democracies not emerged, but existing democratic regimes have presided over increasing conditions of misery for the vast majority of Latin Americans.

HISTORICAL PROJECT: CAPITALISM[40]

Liberation theology's theoretical approach to the concept of capitalism is a hindrance to the development of new historical projects. While liberation theology's approach is useful as a resistance strategy highlighting the economic woes of a continent, it remains devoid of constructive power. It is, in fact, this particular understanding of capitalism that is also responsible for liberation theology's Achilles' heel—its inability to construct historical projects. Capitalism is theorized as an abstractly defined, hegemonic, unified, and indivisible totality. Thus, either there is no escape outside a radical revolutionary overcoming of existing society, or, given the present impossibility of revolution, only a willful and defiant resistance is possible from within hegemonic capitalism. In either case the imagination of alternative historical projects remains paralyzed. The image of capitalism that liberation theologians work with actively participates in creating an intellectual image in which a deepening of political and economic democracy seems an impossibility.

In the first phase of liberation theology's approach to democracy its understanding of capitalism as a total system was taken from the dependency theory espoused by Theodonio dos Santos and Andre Gunder Frank.[41] In the words of Frank:

> Underdevelopment is the *necessary product* of four centuries of capitalist development and of the internal contradictions of capitalism itself. These contradictions are the expropriation of economic surplus from the many and its appropriation by the few, the polarization of the capitalist system into metropolitan center and peripheral satellites, and the continuity of the fundamental structure of the capitalist system throughout the history of its expansion and transformation, due to the *persistence or re-creation* of these contradictions *everywhere and at all times.*[42]

Note that, for Frank, capitalism necessarily will produce underdevelopment in the Third World; there is no escaping this system, which encompasses the whole globe. Capitalism's contradictions, as well as their tendency to persist and re-create themselves, are spatially omnipresent and untouched by time or history; capitalism is a totality encompassing the whole globe, and a unity that stands or falls in one piece. Its essence is understood as a hegemonic totality that is necessarily exploitative. Such a capitalism is a beast immune to step-by-step reform. Small wonder that, for Frank and liberation theologians, only a radical revolutionary upheaval would overcome such a system.

While liberation theologians have, to an extent, distanced themselves from dependency theory, they have not abandoned a notion of capitalism as a monolithic totality. Such an understanding of capitalism, for example, is the implicit presupposition and explicit result of liberation theology's "undertheorizing" of capitalism. To undertheorize capitalism is to use the concept without developing the social theoretical background that specifies its meaning and implications. Undertheorizing capitalism thus occurs when capitalism is critiqued from a perspective that lacks grounding in a developed social theory. The end result is a capitalism that is rarely defined concretely but that nonetheless retains the systemic and all-encompassing quality of early dependency theory. In this undertheorizing capitalism is often, for example, invoked as an inescapable radical evil. Maclean gives a colorful example from liberation theology's first phase. Leonardo Boff, in a short commentary on the Lord's Prayer, declared that the petition to deliver us from evil should be translated as "deliver us from the evil one." Boff then went on to state: "He has a name; he is the capitalism of private property and the capitalism of the state."[43] A more recent example is Hinkelammert's claim that "today we are before a system of domination which includes even our souls, and which tries to suffocate even the very capacity for critical thinking."[44] Here capitalism becomes the devil itself; nothing, not even our souls, lies beyond its scope. The terms *market* or *globalization* are also catch phrases—capitalism's alter egos—depicting entities marching toward world domination or as already triumphant. So Pablo Richard can write that "it is not possible to live *outside* the system, since globalization integrates everything, but it is possible to live *against* the spirit of the system."[45] Once again, the main trait of this opponent is that it remains vaguely defined as a system that is impossible to escape. Given the failure of revolution the only possible resistance becomes a vague shift in attitude that leaves the actual structures of oppression untouched.

Another version of this legacy, taken from Wallerstein and Frank's world-systems theory, is the theoretical construction of capitalism as part of a bankrupt Western civilization. Here capitalism is given more content and thus is less of a throwaway phrase, but this content, instead of portraying capitalism as a "set of concrete specificities" or a "category in self-contradiction,"[46] only strengthens and makes more daunting the entity to be combated. According to Hinkelammert:

> We face not only a crisis of capitalism but a crisis of the foundational basis of modernity. . . . The crisis of capitalism has been transformed into a crisis of Western civilization itself. . . . Now, instead of the polarization capitalism/socialism, there emerges another, which is capitalism/life, capitalism/survival of humankind. Only that now capitalism has a wider meaning. . . . It means Western civilization, modernity and the belief in universal institutional systems that can homogenize all human relations. For this reason, the crisis includes socialism as well, as it emerged in the socialist societies of the Soviet tradition.[47]

For Hinkelammert, therefore, liberation theology must overcome not just an economic system but Western civilization as a whole. For Boff,

> the dominant system today, which is the capitalist system . . . has developed its own ways of collectively designing and constructing human subjectivity. . . . The capitalist and mercantile systems have succeeded in penetrating into every part of the personal and collective human mind. They have managed to decide the individual's way of life, the development of the emotions, the way in which an individual relates to his or her neighbors or strangers, a particular mode of love or friendship, and, indeed, the whole gamut of life and death.[48]

This is the final straw. Capitalism is everywhere and is responsible for everything. Within this conception it is practically impossible to find a place to anchor the construction of new historical projects; even envisioning a means of negative resistance is a close-to-impossible task. There is no escape.

HISTORICAL PROJECT: ALTERNATIVE PLURALISMS

An alternative strategy, one that could clear a space for historical projects, would be for liberation theology to approach capitalism and democracy as partial and contradictory creatures amenable to change and recombination. Currently, however, liberation theology's understanding of capitalism exhibits the paralyzing assumptions of what Roberto Unger calls "deep structure" social theory: the closed-list idea, the indivisibility idea, and the determinist idea. According to the closed-list idea there is a small list of possible institutional systems such as feudalism, capitalism, and socialism with predefined conditions of actualization. This assumption lies behind the belief that the death of socialism posits a crisis of alternatives.[49] But this is true only if institutional systems follow this closed list pattern, in which case the death of socialism leaves us only with a monolithic capitalism that must be rejected as a whole. Thus the indivisibility idea, according to which the systems that compose the closed-list idea (feudalism, capitalism, and socialism) form indivisible wholes that stand and fall as a single piece. Finally, the determinist idea assumes that law-like forces (the imperative of profit or technological advance) govern the evolution of institutional systems.[50] These three assumptions—the closed list idea, the indivisibility idea, and the determinist idea—are at the root of liberation theology's inability to imagine historical projects. I have argued, however, that the indivisibility idea is the central assumption that must be rejected. If capitalism is theorized as the scene of specific, incomplete, and partial practices, different in different contexts, then both the closed-list and determinist assumptions no longer hold. The idea of capitalism as an all-pervasive indivisible totality, encompassing the nation, the globe, and even the inner recesses of the human heart, suffocates the constructive imagination.

So remember the consequences of thinking about capitalism as a unified all-encompassing totality: either there is no escape outside a radical revolutionary overcoming of existing society (as in early liberation theology), or given the present impossibility of revolution, only a willful and defiant resistance is possible from within hegemonic capitalism (as in present-day liberation theology). Instead of thinking of the demise of socialism as the triumph of an increasingly hegemonic all-encompassing capitalism, liberation theologians should see this event as the opportunity to revise their understanding of capitalism itself. Without socialism as its opposing unified totality (thus making possible the imaginative leap from capitalism to socialism) capitalism too is deprived of its abstract unity and self-resemblance. Central to this contention is the notion of contingency in social life: the artificial, contextual, and haphazard nature of our economic and political institutions. Numerous arguments show that modern society can be theorized as partial, fragmentary, and incomplete, thus allowing for greater leeway in imagining alternatives than the picture of a unified system would allow. Michael Piore and Charles Sabel, for example, have shown that the emergence of the signature institution of industrial capitalism, mass-production Fordist industry, was not the product of the imperatives of functional specialization but the result of political struggle among different social groups.[51] Critical legal studies has demonstrated that the law does not possess a single and coherent view of human relations; rather, a number of different and competing views can be found on key issues with different consequences for the distribution of resources in society.[52] Ernesto Laclau and Chantal Mouffe have demystified the idea of historical laws in socialism and made evident the accidental and partial nature of social forms.[53] There is a whole school of political economy literature that emphasizes the diversity of forms the supposedly generic category of capitalism takes in different contemporary contexts.[54] And empirical studies have put the belief in the inevitability of neoliberal globalization under increasing pressure.[55]

A form of thinking about society that focused on the piecemeal traits hiding behind concepts such a capitalism and democracy would avoid dualisms such as capitalism/socialism, capitalism/life, and even market/state. Such thinking would instead focus on what Roberto Unger calls "alternative pluralisms," the idea that representative democracies, market economies, and civil societies can take different institutional forms. In this case the task is not to counterpose different systems against each other but to find the gradual steps that will democratize access to political and economic opportunity. Such a form of thinking, first, sees the political and economic institutions that compose society as "frozen politics," the result of contained political and ideological strife. These institutions do not fit into a neat system that must be overthrown all at once, but rather remain always partial, fragmented, and incomplete. Second, it is contextual, finding its starting point in existing debates about economic and political reconstruction (such as those that became so widespread with the fall of the Eastern bloc). Since the starting point is concrete, change can be envisioned in a step-by-step process rather than the empty imaginative leap from a monolithic capitalism to an equally monolithic socialism or abstractly defined participatory democracy. Liberation theology would pay the same attention to the literature on comparative political economy—raiding it for ideas for political and economic diversity and possibility—as it does to the critique of Hayek and Friedman. Third, this thinking envisions a type of change that is neither revolution (the wholesale change of one structure for another) nor reform (the humanization of the existing structure) but revolutionary reform: the step-by-step change of the formative context of society. This formative context includes, for example, the relations among branches of government, the relation between the state and private enterprise, rules of inheritance; in short, what could be called the rules of the game.

Let me give two examples of this type of thinking. The first focuses on the organization of the economy, and the second on the organization of the state. The debate around the impact of property rights on the nature of society usually juxtaposes private property as the "natural" form of capitalism to collective or state or social property as the socialist mode of ownership. A change of regime (from, say, a socialist to a capitalist society) would then also require the replacement of one type of property with another. Notice here that this debate counterposes two systems against each other—capitalism and private property, on the one hand; socialism and state or social property, on the other. They are seen as whole and mutually exclusive. With the demise of socialism in the Eastern bloc and statism in Latin America, private ownership becomes the ruling paradigm for the organization of the economy. Unger, however, rejects this false dichotomy by developing ideas found in the literature that analyzes economic vanguardism or flexible specialization regimes. These regimes have begun to disaggregate the property right—rejecting the dominant view of property as an exclusionary power of the owner over the things that he or she possesses—seeing property as a bundle of rights, and vesting those rights in governments, intermediate organizations, communities, and firms. Such a property system distributes the benefits of property ownership more democratically by restricting the absolute claim any person can make on its productive base. The end result is neither capitalism nor socialism but a democratized market economy.[56]

Another example focuses on the organization of the state. Recall liberation theology's discussion of democracy, especially the dichotomy between Boff's high hopes for participatory democracy and the current analysis of stagnant democracy. Liberation theologians are right to express skepticism for the emancipatory potential of current Latin American democratic regimes. They are wrong, however, insofar as their analysis tacitly equates the institutional shape of democracy with its U.S. and Western European forms. In the same way that the straitjacket of a monolithic capitalism must be escaped, so too must an imaginary of democracy constrained by the imitation of received forms. Once again, though, the task is to envision a series of reforms that would lead, step by step, to a more radical democracy. Unger, for example, argues that the dominant constitutional tradition today draws from two main sets of ideas. The first set prioritizes constitutional forms that fragment power, favors deadlock among branches of government, and places legal and practical obstacles to the transformative aspirations of a political program. Both the U.S. system of checks and balances and the need for broad consensus among a parliamentary political class are examples of this tradition. The second set of ideas is the adoption of rules that keep society at a low level of political mobilization. Instead of such a system one could imagine a democratic regime with rules of mandatory voting, proportional representation, free access to the media for political parties at stipulated periods before elections, and public financing of campaigns. This could be coupled with a system that resolves impasse among branches of government by appealing, through plebiscites or referendums, to the general populace. The system would work in the following way: First, reform programs would be given priority over episodic legislation. Second, when the president and parliament disagree over a certain issue, the situation would be resolved by plebiscites or referendums. Third, if they disagree on the terms of popular consultation either branch could call for anticipated elections faced by both branches at the same time. Impasse is thus resolved by appealing to the people at large.[57] While such a democratic regime offers a much wider scope for popular participation—and thus gives institutional content to Boff's participatory democracy as well as liberation theology's focus on the poor as subjects rather than objects of political power—it may have another advantage as well; that is, such a democracy would be less easily preyed upon by parasitic moneyed elites and thus would be better equipped to enact policy for the nation as a whole.[58]

Once again, this democratic experimentalist type of thinking prefers to avoid generalized conceptions of capitalism and democracy to focus on their concrete expressions. Because the starting point is concrete—in the institutional here and now of society—the imaginative leap from an empty capitalism to an empty alternative is avoided. In the same way, however, one can envision step-by-step historical projects that go far beyond the denunciation of capitalism and the mere call for greater state intervention to alleviate poverty. The dual traps of resistance within a monolithic and ultimately unchangeable system (unless it collapses of its own accord) and millenarian revolutionary fervor are overcome. Part of what produces liberation theology's difficulty in devising new historical projects is the image of what liberation theology is fighting against. To recognize that there is no capitalism but only capitalisms, to recognize that "the market, which has existed throughout time and over vast geographies, can hardly be invoked in any but the most general economic character-ization,"[59] is to grasp the lesson of thinking in terms of alternative pluralisms. In the same fashion, to understand that the institutional form of democracy is not set in stone but that more radical versions can be devised piecemeal with materials already at hand is to expand the imaginative space available for the construction of historical projects.

HISTORICAL PROJECT: CONCLUSION

Born with the promise of making theology itself liberative, libera-tion theology remains today unable to move beyond a mere discourse about liberation. The reconstruction of liberation theology developed in this essay seeks to break through this impasse by placing the de-velopment of historical projects at the heart of liberation theology as theology. Such a placement, however, requires accepting, first, that liberation theology's incapacity to develop historical projects stems primarily from internal deficiencies rather than the shift in context within which liberation theologians work, a shift that includes the fall of the Berlin Wall, the "end of history," the emergence of the United States as the only global superpower, and the Vatican's condemna-tion of liberation theology's Marxist analysis and silencing of major theologians. These are important contributing, but not decisive, fac-tors. Second is the claim that the first internal deficiency lies in the way liberation theology has come to understand its status as theol-ogy. Liberation theology's dominant methodological statement blesses the incapacity to construct historical projects with the status of good theology. This inability must instead be seen as a failure to be over-come. Indeed, liberation theology needs to recover the role historical projects had in its inception; that is, historical projects were the means by which liberation as a goal was truly pursued as well as the means by which concepts such as liberation and the preferential option for the poor were given a degree of analytical rigor, clarified, and under-stood. The development of historical projects thus lies at the heart of working within liberation theology as theology. The third element is the claim that the second internal deficiency lies in liberation theology's approaches to capitalism. These approaches fail to pay at-tention to the "performativity of social representations—in other words, the ways in which they are implicated in the worlds they osten-sibly represent."[60] They fail to realize that our descriptions add to the world; they block rather than facilitate the development of historical projects. Instead, an approach to capitalism and society that opens rather than closes political and economic possibility is required. The fourth element lies in the presentation of one such approach. While here I base my understanding of political and economic systems on Roberto Unger's social theory, the shape of this element may vary. The element itself, however, is urgently needed.

Allow me to conclude by mentioning two aspects of the general relation between liberation theology and historical projects that I do not deal with but which nonetheless need to be acknowledged and developed as future areas of research. In the first place, any attempt to open a space in which to develop localized alternatives to the reigning economic order must also be tied to a transformation of the world-system as a whole.[61] This requires paying attention to the cultural, economic, political, and ecological linkages between the rich and the poor nations, and how those linkages hinder, block, and deny attempts by the latter to become masters of their own fate.[62] Second, throughout this chapter I have stressed the indissoluble link between the theological and the political in liberation theology. While I focus on the implications of this link for recovering the notion of a historical project in an attempt to reconstruct liberation theology for the twenty-first century, I also believe that liberation theology is a spiritual exercise, a call to both social *and* personal conversion, as well as a hope for ultimate redemption.

Let us not forget that, to paraphrase Georges Friedmann, in order to prepare for the revolution, we must seek, in addition, to become worthy of it.[63]

NOTES

[1] Works of this type are often connected to the Vatican. See, for example, Cardinal Joseph Ratzinger, "The fall of the European governmental systems based on Marxism turned out to be a kind of twilight of the gods for that theology" (Joseph Ratzinger, "Relación Sobre la Situación Actual de la Fe y la Teología," *Fe y Teología en América Latina* [Santa Fe de Bogota, Colombia: CELAM, 1997], 14). See also works by "new liberationists," such as Humberto Belli and Ronald Nash, *Beyond Liberation Theology* (Grand Rapids, MI: Baker Book House, 1992).

[2] See, for example, Gustavo Gutiérrez, "Una Teología de la Liberación en el Contexto del Tercer Milenio," in *El Futuro de la Reflexion Teologica en América Latina* (Bogota, Colombia: CELAM, 1996), 102–3; idem, "La Teología: Una Función Eclesial," *Paginas* 19, no. 130 (December 1994): 15; idem, "Renovar 'la Opción por los Pobres,'" *Revista Latinoamericana de Teología* 36

(September-December 1995): 269–90. See also Jon Sobrino, "Que Queda de la Teología de la Liberación," *Exodo* 38 (April 1997): 48–53; idem, "La Teología y el 'Principio Liberación,'" *Revista Latinoamericana de Teología* 35 (May-August 1995): 115–40; José Maria Vigil, "Cambio de Paradigma en la Teología de la Liberación?" *Alternativas* 8 (1997): 27–46; José Ignacio Gonzalez Faus, "Veinticinco Años de la Teología de la Liberación: Teología y Opción por los Pobres," *Revista Latinoamericana de Teología* 42 (September-December 1997): 223–42; idem, in *Exodo* 38 (March-April 1997), an issue dedicated to the future of liberation theology.

³ For the most complete attempt to revise liberation theology's presuppositions—from a mainstream liberationist—see Pedro Trigo, "El Futuro de la Teología de la Liberación," in *Cambio Social y Pensamiento Cristiano en América Latina*, ed. José Comblin, José I. Gonzalez Faus, and Jon Sobrino (Madrid: Editorial Trotta, 1993), 297–317. For other assessments and/or calls for revision, see Joerg Rieger, ed., *Opting for the Margins: Postmodernity and Liberation in Christian Theology* (Oxford: Oxford University Press, 2003); Rolando Alvarado, "Teología de la Liberación en el Post-Socialismo," *Revista Latinoamericana de Teología* 47 (May-August 1999): 173–87; José Comblin, *Called for Freedom: The Changing Context of Liberation Theology*, trans. Phillip Berryman (Maryknoll, NY: Orbis Books, 1998); Rui Manuel Gracio das Neves, "Neoliberalismo, Teología de la Liberación y Nuevos Paradigmas," *Alternativas* 9 (1998): 57–96; G. De Schrijver, ed., *Liberation Theologies on Shifting Grounds: A Clash of Socio-Economic and Cultural Paradigms* (Leuven: Leuven University Press, 1998); Joerg Rieger, ed., *Liberating the Future: God, Mammon and Theology* (Minneapolis: Augsburg Press, 1998); Joerg Rieger, *Remember the Poor: The Challenge to Theology in the Twenty-First Century* (Harrisburg, PA: Trinity Press International, 1998); J. Amando Robles Robles, "Postmodernidad y Teología de la Liberación," *Cristianismo y Sociedad* 137 (1998): 49–66; Adolfo Galeano, "Desafios de la Postmodernidad a la Teología en América Latina," *Cristianismo y Sociedad* 137 (1998): 67–85; David Batstone, Eduardo Mendieta, Lois Ann Lorentzen, and Dwight Hopkins, eds., *Liberation Theologies, Postmodernity, and the Americas* (New York: Routledge, 1997); Enrique Dussel, "Transformaciones de los Supuestos Epistemológicos de la Teología de la Liberación," *Cuaderno de Teología* 16, no. 1–2 (1997): 129–37; Vigil, "Cambio de Paradigma en la Teología de la Liberación?"; Gonzalez Faus, "Veinticinco Años de la Teología de la Liberación"; Gustavo Gutiérrez, "Una Teología de la Liberación en el Contexto del Tercer Milenio," in *El Futuro de la Reflexión Teologica en América Latina* (Bogota, Colombia: CELAM, 1996), 97–166; Diego Irarrázaval, "Nuevas Rutas de la Teología Latinoamericana," *Revista Latinoamericana de Teología* 38 (May-August 1996): 183–97; Sobrino, "La Teología y el 'Principio Liberación'"; Hugo Assmann, "Teología de la Liberación: Mirando Hacia el Frente," *Pasos* 55 (September-October 1994): 1–9; Edward A. Lynch, "Beyond Liberation Theology?" *Journal of Interdisciplinary Studies* 6, no. 1–2 (1994): 147–64; Duncan B. Forrester, "Can Liberation Theology Survive 1989?" *Scottish Journal of Theology* 47, no. 2 (1994): 245–53; José Comblin, José I. Gonzalez Faus, and Jon

Sobrino, eds., *Cambio Social y Pensamiento Cristiano en América Latina* (Madrid: Editorial Trotta, 1993); Max Stackhouse, "Now That the Revolution Is Over," *The Reformed Journal* 40, no. 7 (September 1990): 16–20.

⁴ See radical orthodoxy revisions of liberation theology, such as Daniel M. Bell Jr., *Liberation Theology after the End of History: The Refusal to Cease Suffering* (London: Routledge, 2001); Stephen D. Long, *Divine Economy: Theology and the Market* (New York: Routledge, 2000); William Cavanaugh, *Torture and Eucharist* (Oxford: Blackwell Publishers Ltd., 1998).

⁵ This essay is the bare bones of an argument extensively developed in Ivan Petrella, *The Future of Liberation Theology: An Argument and Manifesto* (Aldershot, England: Ashgate, 2004). You should turn to this book if interested or unclear about any part of the essay. The initial idea was published as "Liberation Theology and Democracy: Toward a New Historical Project," in *Journal of Hispanic/Latino Theology* 7, no. 4 (May 2000). I thank both Ashgate and the *JHLT* for allowing me to use passages and ideas from those works. See also Ivan Petrella, "Latin American Liberation Theology, Globalization, and Historical Projects: From Critique to Construction," in *Latin American Perspectives on Globalization: Ethics, Politics, and Alternative Visions*, ed. Mario Saenz (Lanham, MD: Rowman and Littlefield Publishers, 2002).

⁶ The two works that have most influenced my thinking about liberation theology's future are Jung Mo Sung, *Economía: Tema Ausente en la Teología de la Liberación* (San José, Costa Rica: DEI, 1994), and Franz Hinkelammert, "Liberation Theology in the Economic and Social Context of Latin America: Economy and Theology, or the Irrationality of the Rationalized," in *Liberation Theologies, Postmodernity, and the Americas*, ed. David Batstone, Eduardo Mendieta, Lois Ann Lorenzten, and Dwight N. Hopkins (New York: Routledge, 1997), 25–52. Sung's other books are also worthwhile: *Deseo, Mercado y Religión* (Santander: Editorial Sal Terrae, 1999); *Neoliberalismo y Pobreza* (San José, Costa Rica: DEI, 1993); and *La Idolatría del Capital y la Muerte de los Pobres* (San José, Costa Rica: DEI, 1991).

⁷ See Gustavo Gutiérrez, "Two Theological Perspectives: Liberation Theology and Progressivist Theology," in *The Emergent Gospel: Theology from the Underside of History*, ed. Sergio Torres and Virginia Fabella (Maryknoll, NY: Orbis Books, 1978), 241.

⁸ See, for example, Bonino's critique of Moltmann in José Míguez Bonino, *Doing Theology in a Revolutionary Situation*, ed. William H. Lazareth (Philadelphia: Fortress Press, 1975), as well as Moltmann's open letter in reply, Jürgen Moltmann, "An Open Letter to José Míguez Bonino," in *Liberation Theology: A Documentary History*, ed. Alfred Hennelly (Maryknoll, NY: Orbis Books, 1990), 195–204.

⁹ See Ankie Hoogvelt, *Globalization and the Postcolonial World: The New Political Economy of Development* (Baltimore: The Johns Hopkins University Press, 1997), 70. The following discussion draws from her excellent discussion of global economic trends on pages 67–93.

¹⁰ Cited in Hinkelammert, "Liberation Theology in the Economic and Social Context of Latin America," 40.

[11] Ibid., 44.

[12] Ibid., 44–45.

[13] See Gustavo Gutiérrez, "La Teología: Una función eclesial," *Paginas* 19, no. 130 (December 1994): 15; and Gutiérrez, "Una Teología de la Liberación en el Contexto del Tercer Milenio," 109.

[14] Leonardo Boff, *Jesus Christ Liberator: A Critical Christology for Our Time* (Maryknoll, NY: Orbis Books, 1981), 275.

[15] See Hugo Assmann, *Teología Desde la Praxis de la Liberación* (Salamanca: Ediciones Sigueme, 1973).

[16] Sung, *Economía*, 96.

[17] Thus Gutiérrez's claim that "the lyrical and vague calls for the defense of human dignity that do not take into account the real causes of the present social order and the concrete conditions for the construction of a just society are totally useless, and in the long run subtle ways to delude and be deluded" (see Gustavo Gutiérrez, *Praxis de Liberación y Fe Cristiana* [Madrid: Zero, 1974]).

[18] Clodovis Boff, "Epistemology and Method of the Theology of Liberation," in *Mysterium Liberationis: Fundamental Concepts of Liberation Theology*, ed. Ignacio Ellacuria and Jon Sobrino (Maryknoll, NY: Orbis Books, 1993), 57–84. In reality, there are two main methodological statements within liberation theology: the "dominant" (analyzed here) and the "marginal," defined in accordance with their current influence within liberation theology as well as their degree of visibility within the North Atlantic academy. For reasons of space, in this essay I can only deal with what I have called the dominant position. I deal with both in chapter 2 of *The Future of Liberation Theology: An Argument and Manifesto*. Explicating the marginal position, however, would further develop, but not alter, the focus of my critique.

[19] Clodovis Boff, "Epistemology and Method of the Theology of Liberation," 79.

[20] Gustavo Gutiérrez, "Teología y Ciencias Sociales," in *La Verdad los Hara Libres* (Lima: CEP, 1986), 87.

[21] Clodovis Boff, "Epistemología y Metodo de la Teología de la Liberación," in *Mysterium Liberationis: Conceptos Fundamentales de la Teología de la Liberación*, ed. Ignacio Ellacuría and Jon Sobrino (Madrid: Editorial Trotta, 1990), 86. I cite from the Spanish—with my own translation—because the English version mistranslates *descontada* (takes for granted) for "arrives at." See Clodovis Boff, "Epistemology and Method of the Theology of Liberation," 62.

[22] Clodovis Boff, "Epistemology and Method of the Theology of Liberation," 83.

[23] Clodovis Boff, "Como Veo Yo la Teología Latinoamericana Treinta Años Despues," in *El Mar Se Abrio: Treinta Años de Teología en América Latina*, ed. Luis Carlos Susin (Santander: Sal Terrae, 2000), 85.

[24] Clodovis Boff and Leonardo Boff, *Salvation and Liberation: In Search of a Balance between Faith and Politics* (Maryknoll, NY: Orbis Books, 1984), 24.

[25] Juan Luis Segundo, *The Liberation of Theology* (Maryknoll, NY: Orbis Books, 1985), 9.

[26] For democracy defined as a political method for electing capable leaders, see Joseph Schumpeter, *Capitalism, Socialism and Democracy* (New York: Harper & Row, 1950); for a programmatic statement of this position, see Samuel Huntington, "The Modest Meaning of Democracy," in *Democracy in the Americas: Stopping the Pendulum*, ed. Robert A. Pastor (New York: Holmes & Meier, 1989), 11–28.

[27] See Philip Oxhorn and Pamela Starr, eds., *Markets and Democracy in Latin America: Conflict or Convergence?* (Boulder, CO: Lynne Rienner, 1999); and Graciela Ducatenzeiler and Philip Oxhorn, eds., *What Kind of Democracy? What Kind of Market? Latin America in the Age of Neoliberalism* (University Park, PA: The Pennsylvania State University Press, 1998).

[28] I owe this argument to Paul Cammack, *Capitalism and Democracy in the Third World: The Doctrine for Political Development* (London: Leicester University Press, 1997). This book has heavily influenced my understanding of democracy and democratic theory in relation to Latin America.

[29] Patricio Silva, "The New Political Order in Latin America: Towards Technocratic Democracies?" in *Latin America Transformed: Globalization and Modernity*, ed. Robert N. Gwynne and Cristobal Kay (London: Arnold, 1999), 62.

[30] For the view that liberation theology opposed democracy, see Paul Sigmund, *Liberation Theology at the Crossroads: Democracy or Revolution?* (New York: Oxford University Press, 1990); Michael Novak, *Will It Liberate? Questions about Liberation Theology* (Lanham, MD: Madison Books, 1991).

[31] Bonino, *Doing Theology in a Revolutionary Situation*, 15, 39.

[32] Gustavo Gutiérrez, *La Fuerza Historica de los Pobres* (Lima: Centro de Estudios y Publicaciones, 1979), 341.

[33] Ibid.

[34] Paz Estenssoro in Bolivia (1951), Haya de la Torre in Peru (1962), Goulart in Brazil (1964), and Allende in Chile (1973), to give some examples.

[35] For the best analysis of this period and approach, see Iain Maclean, *Opting for Democracy: Liberation Theology and the Struggle for Democracy in Brazil* (New York: Peter Lang, 1999); see also Iain Maclean, "Participatory Democracy—The Case of the Brazilian Ecclesial Base Communities: 1981–1991," *Religion and Theology* 5, no. 1 (1998).

[36] Leonardo Boff, "Liberation Theology: A Political Expression of Biblical Faith," *Christian Jewish Relations* 21, no. 1 (Spring 1988): 20–21.

[37] For an analysis by a liberation theologian of "participatory democracy" in relation to the base communities, see Maclean, *Opting for Democracy*.

[38] See, for example, José Comblin, "La Iglesia Latinoamericana Desde Puebla a Santo Domingo," in Comblin, Gonzalez Faus, and Sobrino, *Cambio Social y Pensamiento Cristiano en América Latina*, 36; and Enrique Dussel, *Teología de la Liberación: Un Panorama de su Desarrollo* (Mexico City: Potrerillos Editores, 1995), 187–88.

[39] Xavier Gorostiaga, "La Mediación de las Ciencias Sociales," in Comblin, Gonzalez Faus, and Sobrino, *Cambio Social y Pensamiento Cristiano en América Latina*, 132.

[40] For this section I am indebted to J. K. Gibson-Graham, *The End of Capitalism (As We Knew It): A Feminist Critique of Political Economy* (Cambridge: Blackwell Publishers, 1996).

[41] For a discussion of liberation theology's incorporation of dependency theory, see Sung, *Economía,* 34–48.

[42] Andre Gunder Frank, *Capitalism and Underdevelopment in Latin America: Historical Studies of Chile and Brazil* (New York: Monthly Review Press, 1967), 3, emphasis added.

[43] Leonardo Boff, quoted in Maclean, *Opting for Democracy,* 142.

[44] Franz Hinkelammert, "Determinación y Autoconstitución del Sujeto: Las Leyes Que Se Imponen a Espaldas de los Actores y el Orden por el Desorden," *Pasos* 64 (March-April 1993): 18.

[45] Pablo Richard, "El Futuro de la Iglesia de los Pobres: Identidad y Resistencia en el Sistema de Globalización Neo-Liberal," *Pasos* 65 (May–June 1996): 31.

[46] Gibson-Graham, *The End of Capitalism,* 15.

[47] Franz Hinkelammert, "Capitalismo y Socialismo: La Posibilidad de Alternativas," *Pasos* 48 (July-August 1993): 14.

[48] Leonardo Boff, *Ecology and Liberation: A New Paradigm* (Maryknoll, NY: Orbis Books, 1995), 33–34.

[49] For a statement on the significance of the fall of the Eastern bloc emerging from an important congress see José Gomez Caffarena, "Dialogos y Debates," in Comblin, Gonzales Faus, and Sobrino, *Cambio Social y Pensamiento Cristiano en América Latina,* 330.

[50] See Roberto Mangabeira Unger, "Social Theory: Its Situation and Its Task," in *Politics: A Work in Constructive Social Theory* (Cambridge: Cambridge University Press, 1987), 87–93; idem, *Democracy Realized: The Progressive Alternative* (New York: Verso, 1998), 22–23.

[51] See Charles Sabel and Jonathan Zeitlin, "Stories, Strategies, Structures: Rethinking Historical Alternatives to Mass Production," in *World of Possibilities: Flexibility and Mass Production in Western Industrialization,* ed. Charles Sabel and Jonathan Zeitlin (Cambridge: Cambridge University Press, 1997); Michael Piore and Charles Sabel, *The Second Industrial Divide: Possibilities for Prosperity* (New York: Basic Books, 1984).

[52] As examples, see Duncan Kennedy, *A Critique of Adjudication* (Cambridge, MA: Harvard University Press, 1997); Duncan Kennedy, *Sexy Dressing Etc.: Essays on the Power and Politics of Cultural Identity* (Cambridge, MA: Harvard University Press, 1993).

[53] Ernesto Laclau and Chantal Mouffe, *Hegemony and Socialist Strategy: Towards a Radical Democratic Politics* (New York: Verso, 1985).

[54] See, most recently, Herbert Kitschelt, Peter Lange, Gary Marks, and John D. Stephens, eds., *Continuity and Change in Contemporary Capitalism* (Cambridge: Cambridge University Press, 1999).

[55] See Suzanne Berger and Ronald Dore, eds., *National Diversity and Global Capitalism* (Ithaca, NY: Cornell University Press, 1996), esp. Robert Wade,

"Globalization and Its Limits: Reports of the Death of the National Economy Are Greatly Exaggerated," 60–89; see also Robert Boyer and Daniel Drache, eds., *States against Markets: The Limits of Globalization* (New York: Routledge, 1996).

[56] See Unger, *Democracy Realized*, 95–105; Roberto Mangabeira Unger, *What Should Legal Analysis Become?* (New York: Verso, 1996), 12–13; idem, *False Necessity: Anti-Necessitarian Social Theory in the Service of Radical Democracy*, in *Politics: A Work in Constructive Social Theory* (Cambridge: Cambridge University Press, 1987), 480–506; see also a work influenced by Unger, Fred Block, *PostIndustrial Possibilities: A Critique of Economic Discourse* (Berkeley and Los Angeles: University of California Press, 1990), 191–94.

[57] For a summary, see Unger, *Democracy Realized*, 264–66; see also, Unger, *What Should Legal Analysis Become?* 15–17, 163–69; and Unger, *False Necessity*, 444–76.

[58] A large body of political-economy literature stresses the importance of a "hard state" for economic progress. See, most recently, Alice Amsden, *The Rise of the "Rest": Challenges to the West from Late-Industrializing Economies* (Oxford: Oxford University Press, 2001). In addition, see Stephen Haggard, *Pathways from the Periphery: The Politics of Growth in the Newly Industrializing Economies* (Ithaca, NY: Cornell University Press, 1990); Robert Wade, *Governing the Market: Economic Theory and the Role of Government in East Asian Industrialization* (Princeton, NJ: Princeton University Press, 1990); Alice Amsden, *Asia's Next Giant: South Korea and Late Industrialization* (New York: Oxford University Press, 1989).

[59] Gibson-Graham, *The End of Capitalism*, 261.

[60] Ibid., ix.

[61] Note my use of world-system over world system. I agree with Dussel's analysis of the origin and dating of the contemporary world-system, which sees 1492 as its inaugural event, over Andre Gunder Frank's. Dussel's position is closest to James Blaut's. For Blaut, see *1492: The Debate on Colonialism, Eurocentrism and History* (Trenton, NJ: Africa World Press, 1992). For the argument over "world system" versus "world-system," and thus the dating of the world-system, among Frank, Immanuel Wallerstein, and others, see Andre Gunder Frank and Barry Gills, eds., *The World System: Five Hundred Years or Five Thousand?* (New York: Routledge, 1993).

[62] This must be done, however, without theorizing capitalism as a monolithic entity encompassing the whole globe. This is a flaw in current versions of world system and world-system theory.

[63] Georges Friedmann, cited in Pierre Hadot, *Philosophy as a Way of Life* (Cambridge, MA: Blackwell, 1995), 81.

Index